NOBODY
SEES THESE
ENEMIES

HOW TO DISCERN AND
DISARM UNSEEN TEMPTERS

PAUL RENFROE

PARADIGM LIGHTHOUSE

Destin, Florida, United States of America

Published by Paradigm Lighthouse

P.O.Box 48, Freeport, FL 32439

ParadigmLighthouse.com

ISBN: 979-8-9853944-6-7 paperback; 979-89-853944-7-4 ebook.

Library of Congress Control Number: 2024900695

Published in the United States of America.

IN THE *UNSEEN* SERIES:

OTHER BOOKS BY THE AUTHOR:

available through ParadigmLighthouse.com

CONTENTS

FOREWORD BY
APOSTLE TOM HAMON

We don't see the wind—but we see its effect, and what it carries. Though we have eyes, we can still not see—because we are not properly discerning our world. We easily perceive the seen—but it's the unseen that affects us more.

In both world events and our daily lives, unseen forces are at a fever pitch. More than ever, we must perceive the unseen.

This book remedies our deficiencies for this battle of the ages. In these pages, Paul Renfroe clarifies revelation from God's Word that unmasks the enemy and his accomplices today.

All my life, my father Bishop Bill Hamon has said, 'in the last days, heaven and hell will come face to face in the human race'. As the latter days unfold, the unseen world is going to be pressed more and more in mankind. Each person will be either Holy Spirit possessed or demonically possessed.

> The devil needs human accomplices, and you don't want to be one.

The enemy operates in the dark, behind the scenes, to accomplish his purposes in the earth. However, he needs human accomplices, and you don't want to be one. For our own protection, and to counteract his intents in the earth, we must understand his schemes.

Paul helps us understand the devil's schemes and their biblical origins. His book will empower a generation for warfare against darkness! God has decreed victory in this season. Our part is to recognize and oppose the work of the devil.

> Be sober, be vigilant, because your adversary the devil walks about like a roaring lion, seek whom he may devour. Resist him, steadfast in the faith, knowing that the same sufferings are experienced by your brotherhood in the world. (1 Peter 5-9)

God instructed us to be aware of the unseen enemies, or they would take advantage of our ignorance. We are exhorted to submit to God, be diligent and resist the devil.

The scriptures in this book teach you how to exercise your authority and weaponry. God designed us to walk with authority as living spirits. Only that way can we advance the kingdom of God in the earth as we are called.

However, too often, we prefer to resist the devil by ignoring him, or even denying his existence. Such refusal of God's clear biblical revelation about the unseen enemies deprives us of the opportunity to be God's victors.

To some, these principles may be only theological or theoretical. But to me, as a Pastor over the last 40 years, these truths are practical and indispensable. Discerning our unseen enemies and exercising our authority to disarm them gives us victory in our lives and our world!

> For your own protection, you must understand the enemy schemes.

Paul's book reveals the ancient strategies of darkness—and how they are still at work today. The problem: we have forgotten them. The enemy wants to blind us, confuse us, and distract us. That's how he deceives and destroys. Our charge is to stay awake, be alert and recognize how the enemy works.

Our Lord told us He would build His Church, from the Greek word Ekklesia, meaning ruling body. God has given us the capacity to prevail against the gates of hell. We turn the battle at the gate by shifting the atmosphere, in both the heavens and the earth, by our anointed proclamations.

> "...on this rock I will build My church, and the gates of Hades shall not prevail against it. And I will give you the keys of the kingdom of heaven, and whatever you bind on earth will be bound in heaven, and whatever you loose on earth will be loosed in heaven." (Matthew 16:18-19)

Our Lord delegated authority to every believer so they could also destroy the works of the devil. We His people hold a unique position, authority and opportunity in the earth.

Our weapons are not of this world, but are effectual, spiritual and powerful. In the seen world, these weapons can be discounted and disdained. However, in the spiritual realm, they are mighty and devastating against the devil's kingdom.

This is no time to shrink back! The Army of the Lord has been activated and commissioned and you are called to fight! We must know how our enemy operates and how to negate his plans. Apostle Paul, like Apostle Peter above, taught us to understand these truths.

...lest Satan should take advantage of us; for we are not ignorant of his devices. (2 Corinthians 2:8)

Paul Renfroe's nine-book Unseen Series, and this fourth book in particular, releases an impartation of truth to you—and with it, a charge to run to the front lines of this battle. Don't be found on the sidelines in the historic war. Instead, ready yourself for the front lines. Volunteer for the army of the Lord in this pivotal time.

> Our God is a man of war. We must know how our enemy operates, and negate his schemes.

Our God is a man of war! Those who follow Him into battle get to free the captives, stop the destroyer, and restore what was stolen!

The Lord shall go forth like a mighty man; He shall stir up His zeal like a man of war. He shall cry out, yes, shout aloud; He shall prevail against His enemies. (Isaiah 42:13)

Lift up your heads, O you gates! And be lifted up, you everlasting doors! And the King of glory shall come in. Who is this King of glory? The Lord strong and mighty, The Lord mighty in battle. Lift up your heads, O you gates! Lift up, you everlasting doors! And the King of glory shall come in. Who is this King of glory? The Lord of hosts, He is the King of glory. Selah. (Psalms 24:7-10)

The battle of the ages is upon us. God is looking for loyal soldiers to enter the fray. Psalms 149 decrees this privilege has all his saints, that includes you, to execute the judgments written upon the enemy. Every saint and believer is needed! Let us rise up as informed, effective partners with Lord Sabbaoth, the King of Glory, Jesus Christ, our Warrior King!

Let the high praises of God be in their mouth, and a two-edged sword in their hand, to execute vengeance on the nations, and punishments on the peoples; to bind their kings with chains, and their nobles with fetters of iron; to execute on them the written judgment— this honor have all His saints. Praise the Lord! (Psalms 149:6-9)

Apostle Tom Hamon
Vision Church @ Christian International
Author of 7 Anointings for Kingdom Transformation
Author of The Apostolic Mantle

PREFACE

The nine-book *Unseen* Series exposes the unseen tempters and their identifiable strategies habitually used against humanity. This fourth installment identifies the first four strategies of the kingdom of darkness against people.

I subtitled Book Two in the *Unseen* Series, *How to Unlock Bible Mysteries.* The Bible study techniques used throughout the *Unseen* Series impart a new grid of perception to you. By applying the Standard of Explanatory Power, you will gain a new paradigm of reality in the following pages. That's why my wife and I named our ministry Paradigm Lighthouse.

SPIRIT

From experience, everyone believes unseen spirits of darkness exist; too much is unexplainable otherwise. Even people who don't follow Jesus talk about the devil and use the word *tempt*.

But if we can't discern these unseen tempters, how can we defend ourselves? How can we identify them?

Book One in the *Unseen* Series explored Jesus' teaching about spirit poverty and spirit birth. We are mortal, but our enemies are spirits, immune to scientific testing. These evil spirits can damage human beings for life. Only a spirit from the unseen realm can reveal how we defend ourselves. But who?

Our invisible enemies reveal the unseen realm, but only in ways that seduce people deeper into their kingdom of darkness. We can't depend on them to tell us the truth. In the section titled "SATAN," we'll investigate his truthful distortions in the first strategy against our first parents.

God, the original spirit, is dependable for truth. Jesus revealed God and ascended into heaven. God's Bible is the authority given for us.

THE BIBLE

The Bible is words because our God is verbal and wants to communicate. But its words are not all that it says. Much of its revelation is *between* the lines. Book Two in the *Unseen* Series prioritizes explanatory power by using inductive study, reverse engineering, and understanding of spiritual war.

As we learn about God's ambush plan against the unseen rebels, we realize the Bible is wartime cryptography. In it, He placed His secrets for us who love Him and hid them from darkness. Right in His plain words is a kingdom communiqué which only those with the code key can decipher. That code key is meekness, a key that satan can never mimic.

MEEKNESS

In Romans, Apostle Paul contested the capital-city attitude that results prove truth. Instead, truth comes by revelation. The Bible reveals; we must receive. If you combine meek receptivity with a hungry curiosity, you are primed to hear from God in its pages. Without that combination, the Bible becomes your judge as Jesus warned His opponents.

> You search the Scriptures, for in them you think you have eternal life; and these are they which testify of Me. (John 5:39)

If you are born again, the Holy Spirit lives within you—the same Spirit who inspired the Bible. When Jesus' followers read God's Word, deep calls to deep. He reads its meaning to us, from within us. In the Bible, God's Holy Spirit reveals our invisible enemies and how to be saved from them.

But He is not cheap, so we prove our meek hunger to Him over a lifetime of studying it.

> Man shall not live by bread alone, but by every word that proceeds from the mouth of God. (Matthew 4:4)

SYNOPSIS OF BOOK FOUR

The devil used four distinct strategies against early humanity: 1) ruin human multiplication; 2) release Sin; 3) mix impurity into the human bloodline; and 4) claim nations and their leaders as bottlenecks. We will explore the biblical revelation about these strategies. Genesis chapters one through eleven form the skeleton of our study. The original four strategies then put the race of man on the victim track.

But each destructive attempt fails to extinguish God's plan for our race. That's why there is a sequence of strategies.

Isaiah 14 reveals that satan has a prison, and resists releasing his partners from it—a discovery from the Bible's origin passages. Each successive strategy of darkness requires more partners to be released. How humbling that must be for the former archangel.

The leaders of the kingdom of darkness are angelic in their nature. They learn from each incomplete success. With cunning inventiveness, these unseen tempters constantly adapt their strategies.

They want to make us odious to God.

NEW PARADIGM

The above conclusions enable a new paradigm for understanding existence itself. These ancient mysteries are in the Bible and have foundational influence over all of human life.

These realizations are new to many, so I apply them frequently in these pages. Each application shows the explanatory power of this paradigm. Its practicality for your daily life will be evident on virtually every page.

Book Three in the nine-book *Unseen* Series took a deep dive into Ezekiel 28, Isaiah 14, Revelation 12, Luke 11, and Genesis 1–2. Its title is *Nobody Sees This Creation: The Origin of the Devil and His Replacements.* Those five passages provide the biblical foundation for this new paradigm.

OLD PARADIGM

As Jesus warned above, the Bible will also support our old paradigm. Thanks in part to the persistent effect of Sin, you and I make ourselves the reference point for interpreting reality. We can't replace God on *His* throne, but we easily replace Him on the throne of our lives, and use the Bible to excuse it.

His letter to the Ephesian church warns us. They were committed to defending their gospel beliefs and protecting the flock. They thought they were doing right, as all churches and pastors desire to do. Yet they were in danger, because their grid of beliefs replaced loving Him as first in their priorities. They were so committed, they unwittingly shifted the Lord Jesus into second place.

> Nevertheless, I have this against you, that you have left your first love. (Revelation 2:4)

He knows when we are using Him for something that matters more to us. When the needs I feel are my starting point, I see everything else from behind my own eyeballs. All my relationships—even God Almighty—are demoted into a resource to meet my needs, whether felt and unfelt. Apostle Paul illustrated it in Romans 7 simply with his subject/object sentence structure: everything starts with *I, I, I, I.*

Our spiritual needs are no different. In fact, we easily fit them into this old paradigm which excuses our focus on them. Consider how many religious sentences begin with *I* and *we.*

I subtitled this book *How to Discern and Disarm Unseen Tempters.* Resisting temptation is worthy but it must result from, rather than justify, our love for the Lord Jesus. Otherwise we are using Him. Even if it's defeating unseen enemies, it is still *using* God rather than *loving* Him for who He is.

USING GOD

We all know that using people debases true love; it manipulates them to get something we love more greatly. If your relationship with Him ebbs and flows in sync with the spiritual needs you feel, you are using Him. If your church's priorities shoehorn its leadership into preaching to needs, they may be using Him as well. For this, He removes lampstands in His seven church letters of Revelation 2–3.

Our religious desires are long-indulged and habitual, so we easily make Him their servant. The old paradigm rightly begins with our inadequacy and vulnerability, but our long-accustomed charade of compliance and bargaining corrupts this into false meekness.

In the coming pages, the danger of this worn-out approach to God will become clear. We'll see that Cain was the first recorded worshiper; look where it got him. You will learn how our enemies use the old manipulative paradigm to pollute our relationship with Him. This book will help you discern that old paradigm in your life, so you can disarm your unseen enemies.

AN ENTIRE KINGDOM OF ANIMOSITY

These evil spirits hate the entire human race. Despite their origin in rebellion against God, the spirits of evil retain their angelic power to contest His favor upon us. Humanity remains under the thumbs of these unseen enemies.

They are enemies, plural, because the devil is not everywhere. He has a physical body which limits him to time and place. Jesus spoke of satan's throne in a city (Revelation 2:13). The devil only interacts with four people in the Bible: Eve, David, Jesus, and Peter.

To impose his tyranny and advance his kingdom, satan delegates to a vast array of henchmen. The unseen tempters are many. In his fourth strategy, satan deploys them as chokepoints for controlling the largest number of people with the least effort. These unseen enemies insinuate themselves into our lives, families, governments, cultures, and ethnic groups.

To understand them, we will frequently consult Apostle Paul's list in his letter to the Ephesians.

> For we do not wrestle against flesh and blood, but against principalities, against powers, against the rulers of the darkness of this age, against spiritual hosts of wickedness in the heavenly places. (Ephesians 6:12)

AN ENTIRE KINGDOM OF LOVE

But the Bible reveals they never achieve full success. Instead, God uses darkness for His purposes. In fact, Almighty God set up this conflict. It was He who created us on the same Earth where He had previously exiled the fallen Lucifer and his partners. We will explore His strategy behind this.

The Bible reveals that people alone are created in God's image. It describes no angelic being that way, as mighty or as human as they may appear. By God's design, we—the poorest of the created races in spirit—are far exalted over our unseen enemies.

Before our creation, the kingdom of darkness previously ruled everything and devolved it into the conditions of Genesis 1:2. God then reversed their destructive malformations in six twenty-four-hour days, crowned with the race of men.

He created mortal man to demonstrate His character of love to all the other beings He created in Genesis 1:1. In the Scripture, those angelic races relate to God with honor, but only His relationship with the human race is characterized by covenant and love. And when we offend Him, only we people can repent and be restored to God. Living human spirits populate His kingdom of love. He welcomes us as His royal family.

MATURING

But we must mature. After we are reborn as living human spirits, a process of repentance and transformation ensues. God tutors us to discern and disarm the schemes of unseen tempters. This book is one tool for God to tutor you, as He did Adam and his firstborn, Cain. Hopefully, you will respond better than they did. The choice is yours.

God authorized humanity alone to dominate Earth. He welcomes people alone into His governing family. The devil and his fallen angels know we are their replacements—both on the Earth they considered theirs, and in Heaven where they forfeited their places.

> Woe to the inhabitants of the earth and the sea! For the devil has come down to you, having great wrath, because he knows he has a short time. (Revelation 12:12)

Where the angelic duty of honor to God was betrayed, the human choice of love for Him will be exalted.

OUR CHOICE

You may be a lifelong Christian, or you may not think of yourself as a Christian. Neither is necessary to benefit from this book.

In between are many stages of spiritual hunger and maturity. I want every Christian to mature for their own benefit, but that includes change and discomfort. Jesus' leadership requires these, as He repeatedly said.

> If anyone desires to come after Me, let him deny himself, and take up his cross daily, and follow Me.... Foxes have holes and birds of the air have nests, but the Son of Man has nowhere to lay His head.... Let the dead bury their own dead, but you go and preach the kingdom of God.... No one, having put his hand to the plow, and looking back, is fit for the kingdom of God. (Luke 9:23, 58, 60, 62)

Knowing this, our enemies in the spirit seduce us with comfort. They score victories easily. Sadly, the kingdom of darkness receives extensive cooperation from our sinful nature. We can know about God without relating to Him personally. We unwittingly accept and support lifelong agreements with these enemies.

But by discerning these sneaky unseen tempters, we can disarm them.

...lest Satan should take advantage of us; for we are not ignorant of his devices. (2 Corinthians 2:11)

In the coming pages, I presume you are unwilling to settle, and desire advancement. Let's escape the deception of these invisible oppressors and be closer to our Father every day. Unwilling to become stagnant, we want to love Him more—higher up and further in.

He must increase, but I must decrease. (John 3:30)

PRODUCTION NOTES

ABOUT CAPITALIZATION

To disarm religious awkwardness, and to identify personal participants in the unseen world, each book in the *Unseen* Series follows these guidelines.

Referring to God or a person of the Trinity, we capitalize the first letter of those pronouns. Current style guidelines regard this as archaic; I regard it as respectful. It also helps us keep the characters straight as we talk about the many spirits in the unseen world.

Because capitalization suggests honor, I've chosen not to use an uppercase first letter for the devil and the kingdom of darkness, even though it may irritate your traditional expectations. The word satan means "accuser" in the Bible; that is a functional description and therefore not capitalized. His original name is Lucifer (Isaiah 14). It has a first letter cap as his given name prior to falling.

You'll learn that the Bible reveals active but unseeable personal entities—but the revelation of them is shaded, not direct; implied, rather than stated. When I refer to them, it is with an uppercase first letter. Examples are Creation, Sin, and Earth. When lowercase first letter, those words indicate the acts of creating and sinning, or refer to land, dirt, or acreage.

ALPHABETS

In the *Unseen* Series, some phrases and words of the New Testament appear in the Greek alphabet—the language and alphabet of the New Testament authors. The purpose is to enable you to test my interpretation. If these Greek words and phrases do not interest you, proceed without hesitation; those words will also be transliterated into the English alphabet.

SYNONYMS

Only three parties dominate the following pages: God, darkness, and mankind. To prevent monotony, I use a wide variety of synonymous phrases.

For example, the phrase *"our first parents"* denotes Adam and Eve. *"The archangel"* in passages about Lucifer obviously refers to him.

People, human beings, humankind, mankind, and *mortal race* are all customary names for humanity. *Ethnos, nation,* and *people group* describe tribes and families of people.

I've coined two additional phrases for us that may be new to readers. *Image-creatures* refers to the only creatures ever made in God's image. *Spirit-creatures* indicates the only race that can have living spirits in mortal bodies. I explain these in greater depth in Book One, titled *Nobody Sees This You: How to Live as a Spirit in the Unseen Realm.*

BETA READERS

Each chapter has been tested by beta readers. They help sharpen each book of the *Unseen* Series.

My loyal beta readers represent many age groups and walks of life. Unknown to you, each reviewed this Book Four in manuscript form. Such servants earned all our gratitude; they catch many potential misunderstandings and add much clarity to my writing. If you would like to volunteer as a beta reader for future installments of the *Unseen* Series, please sign up at the Paradigm Lighthouse website (described below).

SPREAD THE WORD

Please tell your bookstore what you think of this book. If no bookstore is near, visit online booksellers to purchase and then review *Nobody Sees These Enemies: How to Discern and Disarm Unseen Tempters.* Examples include traditional booksellers such as BarnesAndNoble.com, social media for readers such as Goodreads.com, and online-only stores such as Amazon.com.

Every reader review helps someone else feel safe to purchase and benefit from this Book Four of the *Unseen* Series. Your review can help release others from spiritual victimization. As you know from your own online shopping, the number of reviews for a book matters—whether or not the reviewer agrees. Short or long, general or specific, your review will make a positive impact.

SOCIAL MEDIA

On Facebook, please friend Paradigm Paul Renfroe and join the podcast group, also named *The Unseen Realm with Paul Renfroe and Friends*. If the book imparts understanding to you, please help publicize it for others to gain in the same way. Post your picture with the book, and/or include the purchase link to ParadigmLighthouse.com/books-and-products. Our ranking among booksellers benefits when people search for the book by name.

HELP YOURSELF GROW

A fellowship is growing around the *Unseen* Series, a place we can discuss and test our Bible discoveries about life as spirits, among evil spirits. Each reader can request log-in credentials at ParadigmLighthouse.com.

HELP OTHERS GROW

Churches often have study groups for books like this one that help us know and apply the Bible. The appendix of this book includes discussion questions for each chapter and other Reader Engagement Resources.

Please help me publicize this *Unseen* Series for the benefit of many.

PODCAST

I lead Bible studies on Zoom with some friends, which are recorded and released as podcasts to help a larger audience engage with Scripture about the unseen realm. Please help the ranking by subscribing to the podcast, titled *The Unseen Realm with Paul Renfroe and Friends*. Posting it in your social media will also help.

GOD

The unseen realm revolves entirely around God.

A.W. Tozer began his book, *Knowledge of the Holy*, with this truth. What comes into our mind when we think about God is the most important thing about us.

The average person—Christian or not—doesn't think deeply about God. We might call upon Him for help, or blame Him for trouble. People try to make exchanges with Him, often disguised as religion using old, outdated paradigms.

Sensing danger from the unseen world, or allured by it, many seek safety without going through God. Satanists rely on the powers of darkness. All world religions offer spiritual safety in their way. Christians can be enamored of theology, angels, demons, power, or prayer. People's conforming behaviors and religious rituals can consume their attention.

The unifying motive of mankind is to keep God at a safe distance. We all know: He is the biggest unseen threat.

"Then he isn't safe?" said Lucy.
"Safe?" said Mr. Beaver. "Don't you hear what Mrs. Beaver tells you? Who said anything about safe? 'Course he isn't safe. But he's good. He's the King, I tell you." (*The Lion, The Witch and the Wardrobe*, C.S. Lewis)[1]

THE PLOT OF ALL EXISTENCE

God alone existed before the foundation of the world, and He made three eternal decrees. Everything that exists supports their fulfillment. A four-step creation sequence produced the reality for all humanity, beginning with our first parents.

- God created the original heavens and earth. This included the populace of the unseen realm: cherubim, seraphim, archangels, and angels.
- The rebellion of Lucifer caused his exile to original Earth.
- The ruination of original Earth by the kingdom of darkness made it formless and void, with darkness everywhere.
- God reclaimed Earth in six staccato twenty-four-hour days and placed us on Earth to reclaim it from darkness.

The kingdom of darkness is led by satan, the former Lucifer, a.k.a. the devil. His rebellion initiated the war of the present age. But God further provoked their hostility by creating our race on the planet of Lucifer's exile.

The devil craves domination over the visible Earth, and we are God's obstacle to that conquest. The current war between the two unseen kingdoms centers on us. God's original blessing on our race threw down the gauntlet and escalated the conflict.

Be fruitful and multiply; fill the earth and subdue it. (Genesis 1:28)

CHAPTER 1

GOD IS OUR WORST ENEMY

Jesus said, *"Blessed are those who mourn, for they shall be comforted"* (Matthew 5:4). Why is it appropriate for us to mourn? Because in the Bible, God reveals His enemy status to us. Mourning it signifies that we are acknowledging our agreements with His enemies, and maturing beyond them.

If we are to enjoy the blessings Jesus extends to us, a sorrowful awakening is required. Apostle Paul said this about repentance to the Corinthian Christians.

> For godly sorrow produces repentance leading to salvation, not to be regretted; but the sorrow of the world produces death. (2 Corinthians 7:10)

STUPID, STUPID, STUPID

Using the old paradigm, it seems contrary to list God in a book about unseen enemies. The old approach presumes that we can offer God something He can't get otherwise, and we can have territorial limits in our relationship with Him. The obvious stupidity of negotiating with the Almighty does not stop us from getting on that treadmill. Our flesh powers that old paradigm, as if we can make trades with God.

The prophetic diagnosis by Isaiah in 720 BC is as accurate now as it was then. We enter agreements with God's enemies. Lying to ourselves becomes a necessity, to fool ourselves into such self-destructive covenants.

We have made a covenant with death,
And with Sheol we are in agreement.
When the overflowing scourge passes through,
It will not come to us,
For we have made lies our refuge,
And under falsehood we have hidden ourselves. (Isaiah 28:15)

WE TRADE WITH DARKNESS

Each book in the *Unseen* Series offers additional depth about the trading system of the unseen realm. Trading, covenant, love, and agreement are different faces on one diamond, originating in the triune nature of God. All reality bears its imprint.

God likes trading, in both the visible and invisible; Revelation 22 reveals that trading will characterize all eternity. In His kingdom, love and honor powers trade, using abundance. But not all unseen trading is good.

Contrast the trades of love and honor with the kingdom of darkness. They fuel their trades with self-seeking and survival, using scarcity to amass security and domination.

If we trade with God's enemies, there are dire and eternal consequences. His own holiness requires Him to judge enemy agreements—especially if the creature in His own image is making them.

> Our periodic descriptions of trading by Lucifer will be new for almost all readers. Its revelation is inbetween the lines of the Bible. For the *directly* stated things to be true, these required realities must also be true. Thus, they are revealed *indirectly*. If desired, in-depth study of the passages comprises Book Three, *Nobody Sees This Creation: The Origin of the Devil.*

Discerning and disarming our unseen antagonists requires us to recognize, confess, and shred every agreement we may have with darkness. This is a lifetime process which requires momentum for maturing—one deliverance after another.

That's one reason Jesus said the meek are blessed. With humble candor, a meek person increasingly recognizes their vulnerability to the unseen liars, and utilizes every resource He ordains against them.

TRADING IN THE UNSEEN

How do we get suckered into agreeing with satan? Five Bible passages yield revelation about Lucifer's trades in heaven and how they led to his pride.

Ezekiel 28 directly reveals that Lucifer was the only one of his kind, created with majesty and splendor. He walked the fiery stones around the throne on the mountain of God.

Ezekiel's prophecy explicitly pinpointed trading activity as the source of Lucifer's iniquity.

> By the abundance of your trading
> You became filled with violence within,
> And you sinned. (Ezekiel 28:16)

These truths indirectly reveal that Lucifer had a responsibility far beyond all other angelic beings: Lucifer was gatekeeper for God. Angels needed Lucifer's permission, who wanted something for letting them pass and see the Almighty.

It's no surprise that angels might make trades in order to interact with God or gain His favor. We do it all the time, in our old paradigm of bargaining and negotiating.

UNSEEN IOUs

We must understand Lucifer's brand of trading if we are to discern his henchmen. Reverse engineering from God's plain statements, we surmise that the future rebel needed nothing, being second to God alone. What could any angel offer him? And how did he leverage this trading into the rebellion he attempted?

To grant the angelic petitioners' requests, Lucifer exacted IOUs from a third of the angels; payment would be determined later. Such an IOU trade then subjected an angel to an obligatory covenant with Lucifer.

- Angel: "May I interact with God, please?"
- Lucifer: "What can you give me, to let you pass?"
- Angel: "What could I offer that you don't already have?"
- Lucifer: "Tell you what—I'll decide later. You may go in."

SATAN THE REPLACER

The archangel became proud of himself. Isaiah 14:13–14 directly reveals that he rebelled to replace God. Lucifer concocted a replacement plan to replace God on the mountain of God. His many IOUs from angels were a key element, using his gatekeeper status as leverage.

To mount his replacement war, he must have called in the IOUs: "Your payment shall be joining my effort to replace God." A full third of heaven's angels were thus manipulated to join his rebellion against God, who has revealed this to us in Revelation 12, Ezekiel 28, and Isaiah 14. The profundity of explanatory power lends further credence to this interpretation, as the nine-book *Unseen* Series shows.

From that point forward, Lucifer has been a replacement strategist. He and his kingdom remain so today. Knowing their replacement ambition gives you a powerful alert system to discern their emissaries.

WE HAVE IOUs TO SATAN

Likewise, the IOU system is also a powerful discernment we can use, because such trading still governs the entire kingdom of darkness. Even our fiction portrays deals with the devil and his hidden IOUs. God's kingdom trading of love is a stark contrast, and great relief for all who enter it.

First angels and now people are the victims of Lucifer's system. Unlike angels, we are far more vulnerable and don't even know it. His IOUs could manipulate only a third of angels. In contrast, all people are suckered in.

We accept these agreements with God's enemies into our lives as if they are normal. Some we know are wrong, but excuse; others we actually believe will work for us. IOU trading becomes a habit in everything.

Not even our miracles and spiritual gifts are immune to agreements with darkness. When Jesus fingered people who used His gifts without knowing Him, they replied as if He owed them, because they had done things for Him (Matthew 7:21–23, 16:22–23, and Luke 4:23). They demonstrated IOU thinking toward God.

People do this without knowing, because we are poor in spirit. Owning up to our vulnerability against these evil spirits is the first in the nine Beatitude blessings.

Blessed are the poor in spirit, for theirs is the kingdom of heaven. (Matthew 5:3)

Our spiritual poverty pervasively affects all our lives, but our unseen enemies expose its most acute vulnerability. Don't expect to discern spirits unless you discern your own poverty of spirit. As frightening as it is, Jesus calls it blessed. And why? Because the kingdom of heaven belongs to us when we own up to our inadequacy for living in this spirit world.

Our covenants with darkness and death reveal themselves in our lives; we'll see them throughout this book. The cycle of belief, expectation, and fulfillment reinforces our trust in these unwitting agreements with satan. Mistakenly or willfully, the result is the same:

We have covenants with the enemies of God, and He becomes our worst enemy.

FEAR GOD

That's one reason Scripture teaches us to fear God. Ninety percent of the Bible's revelation about hell is from Jesus' lips. That makes sense; otherwise, why would He die to save us? Jesus said that it's one thing to fear a person who abuses you unjustly, but quite another to fear the Person who can justly cast you into Hell.

> Do not fear those who kill the body but cannot kill the soul. But rather fear Him who is able to destroy both soul and body in hell. (Matthew 10:28)

Consider our precarious situation. God hasn't destroyed the unseen enemies because they test our loyalty to Him (Deuteronomy 8:2; 2 Corinthians 12:7–10). These invisible opponents are not all-powerful; God limits their ability to harm us (Job 1:12, 2:6). They can't take us to hell; only He can send a person there.

And that is the God we offend by having secret covenants with His enemies, agreements we don't even see. Even after we are born again as living human spirits, our flesh inclines us to our own way. The Spirit of God dwells in us yet we tolerate limits on Him. The test of our loyalty reveals our immaturity. It's like a law with us, as Apostle Paul exclaimed with sorrow.

> For I delight in the law of God according to the inward man. But I see another law in my members, warring against the law of my mind, and bringing me into captivity to the law of sin which is in my members.

O wretched man that I am! Who will deliver me from this body of death? (Romans 7:22–24)

Judgment Day awaits each person, and it won't be a pretty sight.

Vengeance is Mine, and recompense;
Their foot shall slip in due time;
For the day of their calamity is at hand,
And the things to come hasten upon them. (Deuteronomy 32:35)

WILLFUL BLINDNESS

Of all the races God made, only human beings can repent. Yet sadly, the vast majority of us avoid it. God directly challenged our first parents, yet not even Adam and Eve said, "I'm sorry. I was wrong. Will You please forgive me?"

Instead, we prefer the hope of outracing evil by our own devices. Our optimism is unwarranted. These coping strategies began with the ridiculous fig leaves—like children who think you can't see them when they cover their own eyes.

God sees the futility of our cloaking efforts, and waits for us to admit it sorrowfully. Through Jesus Christ, God offers a full pardon to the penitent person. Yet the world refuses to yield to Him and His terms. Every person can be released from captivity and oppression with simple repentance. As the saying goes, simple—but not easy.

Avoiding the blessed Beatitudes makes people into the cannon fodder for darkness in its replacement war against God. Without mourning our poverty of spirit, we cannot disarm these tempters. These experienced enemies easily trick us with their centuries of experience in deception. Each of us has only one lifetime to wake up to them, let alone defend ourselves or fight back.

GOD'S JUSTICE

In the Bible and in Jesus Christ, God has revealed that He is just.

God is a just judge,
And God is angry with the wicked every day. (Psalm 7:11)

People have reduced justice to a moral concept, and misused it. Using leaders' voices, our expert enemies manipulate large numbers of people in the name of justice. The destructive results of such unseen puppetry do not change the fact of who God is. Our Creator is just. We owe justice to Him—an immensely large and outstanding debt.

People are His image on Earth, to demonstrate who He is and how He acts. He made us to multiply so His image can fill Earth. He rightfully expects each of us to exhibit His qualities.

Instead, each person tolerates individual and group agreements with the satan who is trying to replace Him. Most often, these covenants with darkness are unknown to us. The unseen deceivers are exceptionally well-practiced. Yet we cooperate with willful blindness.

Blind or seeing, we remain accountable to our just Creator. We betray His purpose for creating us, a violation of all justice.

OUR DEBASEMENT

We know the good but cannot do it. Paul described our universal experience autobiographically.

> For what I am doing, I do not understand. For what I will to do, that I do not practice; but what I hate, that I do. (Romans 7:15)

Yes, humanity is a victim of enemies that nobody sees. The apostle identified Sin as the active personal enemy within him (Romans 7:20). But through enduring human choice, the iniquity of the generations passes down. Rebellion is baked into our nature, a constant vexation to the rightful wrath of God.

To make matters worse, we adopt a vested interest in debasing ourselves. Toward God, we act like pretend injury plaintiffs, like sick people who thrive on medical attention. This is functional agreement with God's enemies, and by it we invite our own destruction.

> Although they knew God, they did not glorify Him as God, nor were thankful, but became futile in their thoughts, and their foolish hearts were darkened.... Therefore God also gave them up to uncleanness … to vile passions … to a debased mind. (Romans 1:21, 24, 26, 28)

GOD'S WRATH

> The wrath of God is revealed from heaven against all ungodliness and unrighteousness of men, who suppress the truth in unrighteousness. (Romans 1:18)

He is justifiably wrathful and angry—and we are the focus. The wicked are not only death row criminals, abusers, or thieves. The wicked "R" us. We each sin; we each tolerate dark agreements.

In 1098, Anselm was the archbishop of Canterbury and wrote a book. In Latin, its title is *Cur Deus Homo*, which means *Why God Became Man*. Using an interlocutory style, Boso the questioner dialogs with Anselm's character and poses the question, "Since God can do anything, why can't He simply forgive sin by fiat declaration?" The famous answer: "You have not yet considered the gravity of sin."

OUR ROBBERY

Imagine the future we could have had! God made Adam and Eve for an exalted relationship with Him and dominion on Earth. We, their children, could have been born holy, sustained for eternity by the tree of life. Instead, our Creator inherited an entire history of death and destruction. Our first parents did it, and we continue it. The devil's kingdom gloats against God, claiming His Earth while they imprison us—their replacements—in hell.

All this is our robbery from God. Wherever our outside agreements supersede His will for goodness, we worsen the theft. James lambasted his Christian recipients for making light of what we owe the holy God.

> Cleanse your hands, you sinners; and purify your hearts, you double-minded. Lament and mourn and weep! Let your laughter be turned to mourning and your joy to gloom. Humble yourselves in the sight of the Lord, and He will lift you up. (James 4:8–10)

CRIMINAL CONDITIONING

The agreements become unseeable to us. Generationally transmitted as normative, they are individually tolerated with our willful blindness. Generation after generation, our race is conditioned as sinners. Our systemic expectations excuse our culpability and reinforce our covenants with the thieving kingdom of darkness.

MINIMUM PAYMENTS

With defiant arrogance, people believe we even up our score with God whenever we do something good. We owe the holy God of love each good we do, but proudly believe a minute's restitution could outweigh our lifetimes of burglary. Our goodness is not our merit, but rather His just desserts. When we do what He asks, we are only doing our duty.

NO WAY TO REPAY

Even if we could act justly toward Him for the entire remainder of human history, it represents only His due. Restitution for what was lost remains owed, over and above our obligation to Him today. Fair compensation for the injuries to His greatest desires is an outstanding debt that we can never satisfy.

For this, He judges mankind, and exacts what He is due.

JESUS JUDGES OUR DEEDS

The Bible reveals that Jesus is Judge of all evil spirits and all deeds of men. Imagine yourself being judged by a man who never sinned.

For the Father judges no one, but has committed all judgment to the Son, that all should honor the Son just as they honor the Father. He who does not honor the Son does not honor the Father who sent Him. (John 5:22–23)

Truly, these times of ignorance God overlooked, but now commands all men everywhere to repent, because He has appointed a day on which He will judge the world in righteousness by the Man whom He has ordained. He has given assurance of this to all by raising Him from the dead. (Acts 17:30–31)

We can wish for our misdeeds to remain hidden: it is a false hope.

And I saw the dead, small and great, standing before God, and books were opened. And another book was opened, which is the Book of

Life. And the dead were judged according to their works, by the things which were written in the books. (Revelation 20:12)

For there is nothing covered that will not be revealed, and hidden that will not be known. (Matthew 10:26)

Jesus the Judge personally executes the judgment each person deserves. It is personal between Him and you. He responds to each person's choices, and each of us will hear His judgment directly. No wonder Jesus advised us to fear God rather than men.

For the Father judges no one, but has committed all judgment to the Son. (John 5:22)

Come, you blessed of My Father, inherit the kingdom prepared for you from the foundation of the world. (Matthew 25:34)

Depart from Me, you cursed, into the everlasting fire prepared for the devil and his angels. (Matthew 25:41)

THE ABUSE OF LOVE

Despite the terror of being judged for our every deed and word, despite the doom of disdaining our eternal Judge, we defy all sense by the arrogance we actually show. With our great powers of mind and heart, we delusively rationalize: "That doesn't apply to me."

With the flimsiest of rationale, we excuse ourselves from the wrath of God. Christian practitioners are not immune; in fact, we are subject to greater judgment for it.

Therefore, since we are receiving a kingdom which cannot be shaken, let us have grace, by which we may serve God acceptably with reverence and godly fear. For our God is a consuming fire. (Hebrews 12:28–29)

Despite God's justifiable anger at us, people actually try to have His qualities without Him. We not only demote justice into a human standard; we also counterfeit His love. Think how loving it is to do miracles and liberate people from demonic oppression, yet we can mimic even that love.

Many will say to Me in that day, "Lord, Lord, have we not prophesied in Your name, cast out demons in Your name, and done many wonders in Your name?" And then I will declare to them, "I never knew you; depart from Me, you who practice lawlessness!" (Matthew 7:22–23)

The origin of true love is a love relationship with Him. By saying, *"I never knew you,"* Jesus condemns even our loving and effective actions from any other origin, motive, or influence. How many ministers run afoul of this? The Beatitude attitudes open our eyes to the only antidote: repent.

Christians, like everyone, can use our commendable acts of kindness like a ticket, as if God will owe us admission into His holy courts—*owe* as in *IOU*. Kindness is good; the community of humanity does many good deeds. But by severing our good actions from love for Him, we poison those efforts with the trade habits of God's enemies.

Such counterfeit practices are rampant throughout humanity, in every religion, and among Christians ourselves.

WILLFUL STAGNATION

We readily limit our religious observances and Bible study. With resolute rebellion, we only reinforce what we already believe, and how we like to live. God sees through such willful blindness. The gospel record shows that Jesus Himself drove away such halfhearted people; He was not willing to be used by them.

Apostle John records one such lengthy conversation in John 8:31, when Jesus was talking with people who believed in Him. Seeing through their pretenses to their stubborn willful stagnation, He spoke with harsh love: *"You are of your father the devil, and the desires of your father you want to do"* (John 8:44). It is His love that persistently tries to waken us to the brutal truth about our enemy status. We can repent, until we hear it from the Judge of all the Earth.

God sees when we are loving our comfort more than Him. The unseen enemies can't claim people for Hell, and can't prevent someone's salvation. The next best thing is to promote stagnation in us, a perpetual babyish immaturity.

For though by this time you ought to be teachers, you need someone to teach you again the first principles of the oracles of God; and you have come to need milk and not solid food. For everyone who partakes only of milk is unskilled in the word of righteousness, for he is a babe. (Hebrews 5:12–13)

The usual ministries of your church or fellowship are all worthy in their place: preaching, small groups, counseling. Human restoration requires self-esteem, comfort, physical needs, emotional repair, and certainty.

Yet even these can unwittingly promote the objectives of God's unseen enemies, because Christians can hide behind these subordinate priorities. We people so easily excuse ourselves from the highest call: a maturing relationship with our Father. When ministry outweighs the passion to know Christ, a negative cycle ensues. Willfully immature Christians and churches hurt other people, one of many reasons for declining church attendance.

THE SUCCESS OF THE TEMPTERS

We did this to ourselves. With a flimsy protest (*"The devil made me do it!"*), we rationalize behind our fig leaves and futile coverups. People opened the door—made in God's image, yet yielding to the spiritual interlopers.

That's why you and I are so vulnerable to these enemy spirits who tempt us. With eons of practice, they skillfully turn each of us into their victim. With our cooperation, the enemies drug us. We become a Sleeping Beauty, completely inactive and unaware of our royal authority against the unseen tempters.

God is holy in His character and makes judgments consistent with that holiness. Our race has agreed with the rebel kingdom. The situation is dire, and as Christians, we receive the first, most exacting judgment. Is there any hope? Yes.

CHAPTER 2

GOD IS OUR BEST LOVER

If God is angry with our wickedness, why isn't the race of man wiped out and replaced with a more obedient race? The wrath He expresses daily does not extinguish us, as we deserve. Why not?

God is love. (1 John 4:8)

When God created us, He blessed our race. No other creatures or beings in the Bible received this blessing. Never has He retracted it. His blessing is the original force of nature.

Then God blessed them, and God said to them, "Be fruitful and multiply; fill the earth and subdue it; have dominion…." (Genesis 1:28)

Included in it was a directive: multiply, fill, and subdue Earth. Because His words contain His power, the blessing also imparted the ability to fulfill the directive. We have indeed multiplied from the two He made in Eden. Now we fill the earth; the population count recently passed eight billion.

God intended for the multiplied image-creatures to replace the dominion of darkness. So, despite all our evil, our race still is under His unique blessing.

HE ACCEPTS THE PENITENT

In the movie *Indiana Jones and the Last Crusade,* the protagonist entered a terrifying tunnel with doom around every corner, and survived only by understanding his father's collected clues. The phrase, *"Only the penitent man will pass,"* told him to kneel, right before a pendulum swung where his neck would have been otherwise.[2]

Only human beings can repent. Only we can be restored to our Creator. He granted no other created race this opportunity. This is God's true love, this receptivity to all who repent.

> For godly sorrow produces repentance leading to salvation, not to be regretted; but the sorrow of the world produces death. (2 Corinthians 7:20)

If we consider John 3:16–17 overused, it shows our impoverished perception of God's love character.

> For God so loved the world that He gave His only begotten Son, that whoever believes in Him should not perish but have everlasting life. For God did not send His Son into the world to condemn the world, but that the world through Him might be saved.

JESUS' MISSION

Our imprisonment by the haters of humanity is so profound, people are unaware of its depth. Yet, as deep and dark as our dungeon is, Jesus' mission was to free you and me from it.

> The Spirit of the LORD is upon Me,
> Because He has anointed Me
> To preach the gospel to the poor;
> He has sent Me to heal the brokenhearted,
> To proclaim liberty to the captives
> And recovery of sight to the blind,
> To set at liberty those who are oppressed;
> To proclaim the acceptable year of the LORD. (Luke 4:18–19)

One way Jesus described His purpose included the restoration of all that God originally intended for mankind. Despite our theft of what might have been, Jesus came to reclaim the potential and activate our original mandate once again.

> The Son of Man has come to seek and to save that which was lost. (Luke 19:10)

> I bestow upon you a kingdom, just as My Father bestowed one upon Me. (Luke 22:29)

How can such things be possible, for a race so greatly deserving of a just God's wrath? A holy God doesn't excuse sin; His holiness must be satisfied like His love must be. Considering the greatness of His love for us, it would be as close to a dilemma as God Almighty could possibly experience.

PROPITIATION

In *Cur Deus Homo,* Anselm famously captured the dilemma which elicited God's incarnation into human flesh: *"Only Man should pay for sin, but only God can."*

As the Son of Man, Jesus was the ideal representative of what God intended us to be. Without sin, He deserved the full inheritance intended for Adam and Eve. Instead, He chose instead to pay our penalty, which He did not deserve.

> For even the Son of Man did not come to be served, but to serve, and to give His life a ransom for many. (Mark 10:45)

> In this the love of God was manifested toward us, that God has sent His only begotten Son into the world, that we might live through Him. In this is love, not that we loved God, but that He loved us and sent His Son to be the propitiation for our sins. (1 John 4:9–10)

As the Son of God, He could pay what only God could pay. His death for the debt we owe was the full *propitiation*, which means His payment had the infinite merit to fully satisfy the justifiable and infinite wrath of God.

Propitiation is performed by a substitute, who absorbs the divine wrath that is justly due to someone else. A parent will push a child out of a speeding car's path at cost to their own life. Likewise, Jesus pushed us out from God's speeding wrath, and stood in the place we deserve. By Jesus' death, God's wrath is satisfied.

LOVED BY THE PROPITIATOR

You and I each owed our Creator a debt we couldn't pay. Our entire race owes the same debt. The self-sacrifice of God Incarnate paid the debt. He was the only possible propitiator, and He bravely bore all the divine wrath against our betrayal. Jesus' voluntary death achieved what only He could, because only Man should pay for our sins, and a Man did. Only God could pay for sins, and God did. Both occurred in the person of God Incarnate, Jesus of Nazareth.

Greater love has no one than this, than to lay down one's life for his friends. (John 15:13)

For even the Son of Man did not come to be served, but to serve, and to give His life a ransom for many. (Mark 10:45)

ALWAYS THE PLAN

Before making the heavenly host, God's decisive decrees included the *"Lamb slain before the foundation of the world"* (Revelation 13:8). Once filled with the Holy Spirit, the first Christians recognized immediately: Jesus' crucifixion as our substitute had been the plan all along.

But those things which God foretold by the mouth of all His prophets, that the Christ would suffer, He has thus fulfilled. Repent therefore and be converted, that your sins may be blotted out. (Acts 3:18–19)

Seven centuries before Jesus was even born, God revealed through the prophet Isaiah His intent for Jesus to die and its explanation.

Surely He has borne our griefs
And carried our sorrows;
Yet we esteemed Him stricken,
Smitten by God, and afflicted.
But He was wounded for our transgressions,
He was bruised for our iniquities;
The chastisement for our peace was upon Him,

And by His stripes we are healed.
All we like sheep have gone astray;
We have turned, every one, to his own way;
And the Lᴏʀᴅ has laid on Him the iniquity of us all. (Isaiah 53:4–6)

KISS THE SON

That is why faith in Jesus is the only way to be reconciled and have peace with God, who is otherwise our worst enemy. Yielding yourself to Him brings you under the effectiveness of His propitiation, and the wrath you deserve is satisfied. An old saying uses the italicized homonyms to express our new status: "When I am *justified*, it is *just as if I'd* never sinned."

The faith is no mere lip service. Psalm 2 prophesied Jesus' crowning, as the early church recognized in Acts 4:25–26. It concludes by expressing the choice of love that this King deserves.

Kiss the Son, lest He be angry,
And you perish in the way,
When His wrath is kindled but a little.
Blessed are all those who put their trust in Him. (Psalm 2:12)

JUSTICE DEMONSTRATED IN LOVE

God's love did not suspend His character of justice. Using the word *propitiation* as Apostle John did above, Apostle Paul gave two reasons that the crucifixion of Jesus demonstrated God's deep justice, in Romans 3:25–26.

God set [Jesus] forth as a propitiation by His blood, through faith, to demonstrate His righteousness, because in His forbearance God had passed over the sins that were previously committed, to demonstrate at the present time His righteousness, that He might be just and the justifier of the one who has faith in Jesus.

God had not exacted the penalty for the many sins and costs of human history. In the unseen realm, this was an outstanding, long-overdue justice that was always increasing. The heavenly host never saw a moment that God stopped being righteous. He had every right to exterminate the entire race of offenders, yet did not. Why didn't He wipe out Adam and Eve and start over?

He demonstrated His justice for all previous sins when the Son of *Man* died—because only *man* should pay for sin. The debt of the past was satisfied.

Second, God's righteousness was demonstrated because He created a new standard of justice going forward. The Son of *God* died on the cross in order to trade places with us. Because all must give the Son of God what He earned; even God Himself justly owes Jesus the fruit of His labors.

Jesus is due the full functionality of His substitution for us—because only *God* could pay for sin. Every human being, no matter their offensiveness, can accept Jesus' substitution. His offer to trade places with you must be honored throughout heaven, when you accept it. That's what it means to repent and trust in Jesus.

> If you confess with your mouth the Lord Jesus and believe in your heart that God has raised Him from the dead, you will be saved. For with the heart one believes unto righteousness, and with the mouth confession is made unto salvation. For the Scripture says, "Whoever believes on Him will not be put to shame." For there is no distinction between Jew and Greek, for the same Lord over all is rich to all who call upon Him. For "whoever calls on the name of the Lord shall be saved." (Romans 10:9–13)

NEVER A REAL DILEMMA

Because the Scripture reported the decree of the Lamb's death prior to any creation in Revelation 13:8, we know the conflict of His justice and love was a dilemma only for us. He created all reality to conform to that eternal decree and the others reported in the Word of God.

It was always His intention to show His justice and love through Jesus. God's love always wanted to offer full forgiveness and restoration to everyone who calls on Jesus. This is not because of our merit. The forgiveness of His followers is the justice that Jesus merits from the Father.

That is love. That is our Divine Lover at work.

LOVE'S MOMENTUM

Maturing momentum is the opposite of the willful stagnation discussed earlier. The latter signals secret agreements with disobedience and rebellion. The former causes our secret agreements to come to light and be severed.

Growth as living spirits is not a matter of knowledge or behaviors, but pursuing God's companionship ever more fervently so He can have free rein in us.

> We all, with unveiled face, beholding as in a mirror the glory of the Lord, are being transformed into the same image from glory to glory, just as by the Spirit of the Lord. (2 Corinthians 3:18)

Earlier, we admitted our lingering covenants with darkness. Consider how graciously our Father customizes our timetable for freedom; He does not suddenly expose and strip us of all the agreements that we don't see.

His imperative to mature is why stagnation signals a willful tolerance for His enemies. Our refusal to mature reveals we are protecting those dark covenants from God's holy hand. In contrast, momentum telegraphs that we are shedding these substandard, destructive covenants. In their place, the maturing Christian enters new agreements—with Him.

LESSER FOR GREATER

If we are moving forward and pursuing Him, God favors our desire. Likewise, He knows when we are settling in. Stagnation reveals a preference for our comfort zone over the love He deserves from us. During Jesus' three-year ministry, thousands of His admirers peeled away as His leadership become more challenging; John 6:66 is one such instance.

Only a few people accepted His implant of momentum and followed Him wholeheartedly, relinquishing all expectations. It is true today as well. The choice belongs to each one of us.

To pursue God is a life of trading lesser for greater. We release our grip on what *partially* satisfies, in order to grasp the One who *fully* satisfies.

> But what things were gain to me, these I have counted loss for Christ. Yet indeed I also count all things loss for the excellence of the knowledge of Christ Jesus my Lord, for whom I have suffered the loss of all things, and count them as rubbish, that I may gain Christ.... (Philippians 3:7–8)

> ...always carrying about in the body the dying of the Lord Jesus, that the life of Jesus also may be manifested in our body. (2 Corinthians 4:10)

LOVE'S JUSTICE TO JESUS

In the Beatitudes, Jesus laid out His terms for us to be blessed. They are His first teaching recorded in the New Testament sequence. He progressively tells us what He wants from us, and explains why each one is blessed.

Blessed are the poor in spirit,
For theirs is the kingdom of heaven.
Blessed are those who mourn,
For they shall be comforted.
Blessed are the meek,
For they shall inherit the earth.
Blessed are those who hunger and thirst for righteousness,
For they shall be filled.
Blessed are the merciful,
For they shall obtain mercy.
Blessed are the pure in heart,
For they shall see God.
Blessed are the peacemakers,
For they shall be called sons of God.
Blessed are those who are persecuted for righteousness' sake,
For theirs is the kingdom of heaven.
Blessed are you when they revile and persecute you, and say all kinds of evil against you falsely for My sake. Rejoice and be exceedingly glad, for great is your reward in heaven, for so they persecuted the prophets who were before you. (Matthew 5:3–12)

Note the culmination: *"for My sake,"* that is, out of loyalty to Him. Jesus was not a softie. He expects us to yield our lives for Him, as He did for us. The same love He showed dying for us, He requires us to show for Him. Jesus' disciples were quite agitated when He put it this way in Luke 9:23–24.

I thoroughly considered the sequential progression of the Beatitudes in Book One of the Unseen Series. Their impact reverberates throughout the entire nine books.

If anyone desires to come after Me, let him deny himself, and take up his cross daily, and follow Me. For whoever desires to save his life will lose it, but whoever loses his life for My sake will save it.

Apostle Paul described our debt to Jesus in terms of slavery, in Romans 6:22–23.

But now having been set free from sin, and having become slaves of God, you have your fruit to holiness, and the end, everlasting life. For the wages of sin is death, but the gift of God is eternal life in Christ Jesus our Lord.

LOVE'S HOLINESS

Earlier we cited Apostle Paul's autobiographical testimony about inward pressure to sin (Romans 7). He next wrote how the outpouring of God's Spirit upon us gets us off that treadmill.

There is therefore now no condemnation to those who are in Christ Jesus, who do not walk according to the flesh, but according to the Spirit. For the law of the Spirit of life in Christ Jesus has made me free from the law of sin and death. (Romans 8:1–2)

Apostle John also described the process in which our love for Jesus makes us increasingly holy. In His love for us, He acts as our Advocate in the courts of heaven.

If we confess our sins, He is faithful and just to forgive us our sins and to cleanse us from all unrighteousness. If we say that we have not sinned, we make Him a liar, and His word is not in us. And if anyone sins, we have an Advocate with the Father, Jesus Christ the righteous. (1 John 1:9–2:1)

CHOOSE LOYALTY

These provisions give us no excuse for indulging our sins. When we choose sin, we telegraph disloyalty and ingratitude. It shows we love something more than Him. We flirt with Judas' betrayal.

Excusing our sin choices also exposes us to the unseen tempters who obscure themselves. These deceivers promote presumptive tolerance of sin whether big or small, so we treat disobeying God as a light matter.

His love for us deserves a loyal love from us, and we are blessed for it.

We love Him because He first loved us. (1 John 4:19)

CHAPTER 3

GOD'S PREFERRED WAY

God has one preferred way to relate to Him: meekness. It is the humble faith that honors and yields to what He says about Himself, about us, and about everything. This meek trust makes us depend on the truth revealed by God the Spirit.

God has offered one way to be reconciled to Him (John 14:6). Coming any other way is *not* coming to God. The measure is not sincerity, but submission to what He has revealed. True meekness doesn't set the terms for Him. Instead, we yield to His terms.

Most people come to Him without the meekness that yields, because we want to do things our way. Desiring His benefits, yet at a safe distance, we simultaneously press the accelerator and brake. This leaves the door wide open for the evil deceivers and destroyers.

> The upcoming study of downtown Eden's two trees will show the insistent curiosity which evidences the hunger of the meek.

When we awaken to our vicious blindness, we realize how we have tolerated God's opponents. Being born anew as a living spirit introduces us to a new world. We poor in spirit are unqualified for it; the inadequacy is glaring. The shock of our spiritual poverty produces mourning and humility. It makes us crave righteousness and immunizes us from judging others without mercy.

These attitudes were specifically blessed by Jesus in the Sermon on the Mount. By them, we become equipped to discern and disarm unseen tempters—our enemies and His.

41

YIELD TO VERBAL INTIMACY

Our Creator is very verbal and encourages us to converse with Him. An immediate symptom of true meekness is a vigorous interaction with the Bible. The entire *Unseen* Series of books and resources is predicated on the truth of God's Word. The Bible is the objective standard to which we submit, not vice versa. The meek Christian takes God's Word at face value, and constantly sees God validating what it says.

The Spirit lives in us when we are born as spirits by faith in Jesus. When Scripture enjoins us to pray continually, it is referring to a non-mental, internal dialog with Him. Jesus described it with a shepherd analogy: *"The sheep follow him, for they know his voice"* (John 10:4). He communicates by words, pictures, thoughts, circumstances, and impressions of various kinds.

YIELD TO THE EQUIPMENT

As we mature in pursuit of Him, we learn to distinguish His voice from the stranger's, and from our own. *"Yet they will by no means follow a stranger, but will flee from him, for they do not know the voice of strangers"* (John 10:5). We can test spirits, as Apostle John tells us to in 1 John 4:1.

God's Spirit within us happily equips us with revelation gifts that Apostle Paul describes in 1 Corinthians 12: speaking in and interpreting tongues, prophetic words, and words of knowledge and wisdom.

Not all Christians agree about the revelation gifts of the Spirit. Doctrine differs as well as practice and protocol. These powerful gifts have a propulsive effect, and past proponents and opponents have both evidenced repulsive behaviors.

These gifts help us live as spirits, in a world that He created and birthed us into when we believed. The meek crave these gifts. In contrast, self-reliance rationalizes the revelation gifts out of existence. Instead of disarming our enemies, refusing His ordained gifts disarms Christians from full function as human spirits.

Jesus also ordains maturing Christians into the fivefold offices. With meekness, they execute Jesus' ongoing ministry to the church, and the meek recognize God's authority through them.

When He ascended on high,
He led captivity captive,
And gave gifts to men. (Ephesians 4:8)

And He Himself gave some to be apostles, some prophets, some evangelists, and some pastors and teachers. (Ephesians 4:11)

YIELD TO THE RIGHTEOUSNESS

Meekness submits to the righteousness Jesus earned for us. God graciously considers us justified with Him, because we believe and yield to the One who deserves us to be forgiven. Jesus' own justified standing then transfers to us.

The meek recognize the arrogant futility of trying to earning our own righteousness.

For they being ignorant of God's righteousness, and seeking to establish their own righteousness, have not submitted to the righteousness of God. (Romans 10:3)

Meekness yields to our high status without arguing over our self-image and hiding behind the skirts of false modesty. God says He exalted us, period (Ephesians 2:6–8). We are also meek when we submit to His transformation, so Jesus can grow His righteous character in us. Like Mary, the yielded Christian spirit says to God:

Behold the maidservant of the Lord! Let it be to me according to your word. (Luke 1:38)

YIELD TO LOVE FOR THE LOST

God's home on earth is in us, and rivers of His Spirit flow through us to everyone we meet.

If anyone loves Me, he will keep My word; and My Father will love him, and We will come to him and make Our home with him. (John 14:23)

"He who believes in Me, as the Scripture has said, out of his heart will flow rivers of living water." But this He spoke concerning the Spirit, whom those believing in Him would receive. (John 7:38–39)

Something in each Jesus lover invites others to enjoy it also, and it never ceases to amaze me that people resist that. Unbelievers have persecuted Christians for two millennia despite offering the greatest deal in history. Not everyone welcomes the love.

Jesus explained it as the convicting presence of a Holy Spirit with us. We repulse people who prefer to be lost and damned because we carry His convicting presence, as Jesus told His disciples.

> And when He has come, He will convict the world of sin, and of righteousness, and of judgment. (John 16:8)

> If the world hates you, you know that it hated Me before it hated you.... If I had not come and spoken to them, they would have no sin, but now they have no excuse for their sin. (John 15:18, 22)

Yet despite the pushback, the force of love within us compels us. In meekness, we yield to it and brave the potential rejection to express God's loving provision in the gospel of Jesus.

> For the love of Christ compels us, because we judge thus: that if One died for all, then all died. (2 Corinthians 5:14)

YIELD TO COURAGE

Meekness is not cowardice. When the unseen spirit realm manifests itself, both the holy and the unholy, every human adequacy withers. Yet we do not retreat from this; faith is courageous to face and mourn our poverty of spirit.

> "I take no pleasure
> in the one who shrinks back."
> But we do not belong to those who shrink back and are destroyed,
> but to those who have faith and are saved. (Hebrews 10:38–39 NIV)

People have seen Jesus and angels throughout history and report the deep dread. Daniel, Paul, and John all became like dead men. Apostle Paul described how unequal he felt for the revelation he received and how brave his faith had to be (2 Corinthians 2:16, 4:13, 11:30).

A saved person is a living spirit and directly interacts with God, who is *much more* overwhelming than our enemies. He sometimes overwhelms us on purpose, to expose and end our misguided attempts to keep Him at a safe distance. We don't turn back from Him, but answer the heavenly call for courage—preferring His intimacy over our comfort.

YIELD TO LORDSHIP

Our Father's ambition is a governing love relationship with each one of us. Jesus expressed a clear expectation that we obey Him, not vice versa. *"Why do you call me 'Lord, Lord,' and not do the things which I say?"* (Luke 6:46).

YIELD TO DISCOMFORT

When we speak in tongues or receive words of knowledge, that communion can make us feel like bursting. In worship, His glory reduces us. In prayer, travail or weeping can interrupt our agenda. In resistance from others, we can feel rejected or inadequate.

But we do not shrink from these, as costly as they feel. God arranges these for our momentum, and we do not look back.

> But Jesus said to him, "No one, having put his hand to the plow, and looking back, is fit for the kingdom of God." (Luke 9:62)

> I press toward the goal for the prize of the upward call of God in Christ Jesus. Therefore let us, as many as are mature, have this mind. (Philippians 3:14–15)

MEEKNESS THREATENS THE PROUD

Our enemies are dreadful and they pump themselves up against us, like boxers prior to a match. Although they know us to be their replacements, they fight to the last moment. These unseen angelic opponents devote all their capabilities to evil. They are coming out of hiding in our time.

With intimidating destruction, their chokepoints of authority gleefully support the darkest agendas. These bottlenecking henchmen blackmail entire cultures, industries, and nations. The kingdom of darkness threatens us with the costs of being in God's kingdom rather than theirs.

But we, the faithful, courageously discern their threats as an attempt to dominate their own replacements. Faith accepts the Bible's revelation that we threaten satan's kingdom, not vice versa.

It's tempting (key word) to withdraw from confronting the invisible, threatening spirits. Christians often justify a retreat from discerning or confronting satan's ways. This retreat is the complete opposite of being blessed.

MEEKNESS IS BOLD

The blessed meek bravely hunger and thirst for righteousness, just as Paul pressed toward the goal for the prize. Beatitude people do not tolerate the shadows of evil within them, and God blesses us for that.

Instead, discerning these enemies, we rely upon God to transfuse boldness into us. One such transfusion was when the apostles denounced Jesus' crucifiers to their faces only a few weeks later. The bravery of meek faith grows in confidence.

> Now, Lord, look on their threats, and grant to Your servants that with all boldness they may speak Your word.... And when they had prayed, the place where they were assembled together was shaken; and they were all filled with the Holy Spirit, and they spoke the word of God with boldness. (Acts 4:29, 31)

> Therefore do not cast away your confidence, which has great reward. (Hebrews 10:35)

MEEKNESS WAS ALWAYS THE WAY

Jesus saw these truths in His Bible, our Old Testament. Far from irrelevant, it described God's way for Him and for us. He taught God prizes humility, yieldedness, and meekness.

> Take my yoke upon you, and learn from Me, for I am gentle and lowly in heart. (Matthew 11:29)

Apostle Paul wrote the same truth in different words from the same Old Testament. The purpose of the law was to induce within us a meek sorrow for sin and a craving for God's mercy in Christ Jesus.

Now we know that whatever the law says, it says to those who are under the law, that every mouth may be stopped, and all the world may become guilty before God. Therefore by the deeds of the law no flesh will be justified in His sight, for by the law is the knowledge of sin. (Romans 3:19–20)

But the Scripture has confined all under sin, that the promise by faith in Jesus Christ might be given to those who believe. But before faith came, we were kept under guard by the law, kept for the faith which would afterward be revealed. Therefore the law was our tutor to bring us to Christ, that we might be justified by faith. (Galatians 3:22–24)

The New Testament states what God had already revealed hundreds of years before, through His prophets. Moses explained that Israel's wilderness troubles were God's test of their meekness. Isaiah's plain statement is another.

...to humble you and test you, to know what was in your heart, whether you would keep His commandments or not. So He humbled you, allowed you to hunger, and fed you with manna which you did not know nor did your fathers know, that He might make you know that man shall not live by bread alone; but man lives by every word that proceeds from the mouth of the LORD. (Deuteronomy 8:2–3)

For thus says the high and exalted One
Who lives forever, whose name is Holy,
"I dwell on a high and holy place,
And also with the contrite and lowly of spirit
In order to revive the spirit of the lowly
And to revive the heart of the contrite." (Isaiah 57:15)

ALL DISOBEDIENT, ALL UNDER MERCY

God bound us all to disobedience. Adam and Eve chose poorly, but like you and me, they were bound to disobedience. We'll shortly find that God did not warn Adam and Eve to resist the devil. He forced a choice situation.

For God has committed them all to disobedience, that He might have mercy on all. (Romans 11:32)

Revelation 13:8 directly states that the Lamb was slain before the foundation of the world. The implications reveal the history before history began. Jesus had atoned for sin even before He created our first parents. It required that people must exist and be sinfully aligned with enemies of God.

Their sin, your sin, and my sin were all baked into reality before God created any of it.

> For there is no difference; for all have sinned and fall short of the glory of God, being justified freely by His grace through the redemption that is in Christ Jesus, whom God set forth as a propitiation by His blood, through faith.... (Romans 3:22–25)

Every human being freely repeats the choices of the first two human beings. Each of us is responsible and will be judged by the Son of God. God's standards tutor us into an awareness of our abject poverty of spirit. We mourn it, and we meekly hunger and thirst for His righteousness. Meekness that yields to Him is the only approach God welcomes. That's why Jesus said they are the blessed package of attitudes.

NONE PERFECT

God described Lucifer as the seal of perfection, perfect in his ways (Ezekiel 28:12–15). Lucifer had a closer proximity to God than any other being. Surely these privileges would prevent Lucifer's fall? One would think so, and be wrong. God had decreed everlasting wrath *before* He made the angels or Lucifer.

Lucifer's perfection went to his head. God identified what happened within the archangel through the seedbed of his trading:

> Your heart was lifted up because of your beauty;
> You corrupted your wisdom for the sake of your splendor. (Ezekiel 28:17)

God is Perfection personified. If even Lucifer could fall, what hope is there for a meek mortal like me? The Lamb who was slain before the world began: the only hope. He can pass His perfection on to me, the only perfection heaven allows.

We turn now to Eden and the background knowledge we need to discern and disarm them.

EDEN

CHAPTER 4

THE CREATION OF COVENANT MULTIPLICATION

And the Lord God formed man of the dust of the ground, and breathed into his nostrils the breath of life; and man became a living being. (Genesis 2:7)

In the beginning, the new human race was only one person. His name *Adam* means "man," and he was alive in spirit, soul, and body. He was in God's image and likeness with no impairment.

The Bible doesn't say what knowledge or wisdom Adam started with. We don't know if he needed education, or had knowledge when created. However, judging from the record of his actions and choices, knowledge was not his issue.

A REPLACEMENT IN GOD'S IMAGE

Consider satan's perspective on Adam, who appears on the last of Earth's first six days. During them, God reclaimed Earth from the dominion of satan and his angelic rebel partners. The six days were God's terroristic assault upon their empty, formless comfort zone in Genesis 1:2.

Witnessing the end of the sixth day, the kingdom of darkness is introduced to an unprecedented being.

Then God said, "Let Us make man in Our image, according to Our likeness...." (Genesis 1:26)

God made no angel in His image. Lucifer was the highest of them all, but he wasn't in God's likeness. On days five and six, God made the birds, fish, and animals, but none of them were in His image and likeness. There were creatures everywhere, but Adam alone was God's image-creature.

We often hear about being made in God's image, but that was beyond any angel's imagination. For all satan knew, God had created a new improved model to fill his place. It's possible that Lucifer, the would-be replacer, would only notice his own replacement.

COVENANT MULTIPLICATION

The kingdom of darkness would acutely perceive another distinctive about the new image-creature. The human race embodies a new declaration about the Almighty, one never visible to the angelic hosts before our creation: He is a God of love.

Relationship and intimacy are values with their origin in His nature as Three-in-One. He manifests the love of the Trinity through His covenants with us. Our status with Him is based on relationship rather than religion or ritual. He wants to covenant with people and live in them.

> He who has My commandments and keeps them, it is he who loves Me. And he who loves Me will be loved by My Father, and I will love him and manifest Myself to him.... If anyone loves Me, he will keep My word; and My Father will love him, and We will come to him and make Our home with him. (John 14:21, 23)

In the Bible, God only makes covenants with humans, not angels. His love would cover the Earth, once the first image-creatures reproduced more image-creatures. They would all be under their covenant with Him.

God is love, Apostle John wrote. James wrote that God is unchanging. He has always been love, and He has always been holy.

The angels had seen God's holiness in action when the rebels were filled with fire and expelled eternally, with no opportunity to repent. But how would the angels perceive His love nature? The Bible reveals He is not personal with angels as He is with people. Angels can't reproduce and do not marry, Jesus said. Covenants are not part of their existence in the Bible.

When only angels existed, there was no multiplication of covenant love. God's covenant love only multiplied after our creation. When our race was made, that possibility became a reality.

Look how God created Adam, befitting a God of love. God can simply give the word, and what He wants, happens; that's how every other action occurred during the six days. With man, it's different. God placed Himself nostril to nostril with the creature made of dust. He breathed His life into Adam's nose. That's intimate, full of promise.

Ultimately, all the heavenly hosts would see God's love in action, incarnating and dying for the very people who failed His covenant.

MORE DETAIL

In contrast to the one-sentence creation in 1:26, our creation in Genesis 2:7–25 occurs in two steps. God makes the male first; only later does He form the female.

Are there really two Creation accounts, as they say? Some people say this to undermine the authenticity of Scripture, disregarding the simpler explanation: the second account provides more detail.

We have many summaries in our lives, far more often than details. Go shop online where you will see the summary of an item. If you want more detail, you click *Read more* or scroll down. Likewise, God first reveals the summary of our creation, and then reveals His detailed steps in creating us.

Genesis 1:27 says on the sixth day, "*He created them male and female.*" That's accurate, but incomplete, because it is a summary. What Genesis 1 lacked in details, Genesis 2 provides. First, the sixth day event is summarized, and then the sequence and conversation of the event are described in the next chapter.

> Since the only member of the Trinity with a body is Jesus, breathing into Adam's nostrils would have been Jesus' first recorded appearance on Earth. He won mercy and approachability for us on the cross. Nose to nose with the man, it was on full display.

We were the only created beings in God's six days to have a more detailed account. Genesis 2 is the *Read more* of Genesis 1.

COVENANT NORMS

"Not good to be alone" is a general principle unique to our race. Not everyone marries. God calls some to be unmarried—but being single doesn't mean being alone. Everyone seeks companionship. Close friendships exhibit the covenant-seeking quality that God installed into us, such as Jonathan's with David.

> Now Jonathan again caused David to vow, because he loved him; for he loved him as he loved his own soul.... So the two of them made a covenant before the LORD. And David stayed in the woods, and Jonathan went to his own house. (1 Samuel 20:17, 23:18)

Angels possess the capacity for solitary existence, but it is not the norm for human beings.

> Therefore a man shall leave his father and mother and be joined to his wife, and they shall become one flesh. (Genesis 2:24)

During Jesus' ministry, He cited that verse as the basis of marriage (Matthew 19:5). God's love nature causes the replication of His image on Earth through the covenant intimacy of His image-creatures.

God made us as His image-bearers on Earth. He is multi-personal unity; therefore, we are as well. Just like the Persons of the Triune God commit to each other, so do man and wife. As three Persons are One God, so also husband and wife are one flesh.

> So God created man in His own image; in the image of God He created him; male and female He created them. (Genesis 1:27)

INTIMACY MULTIPLIED

The Triune God produced two image-creatures like Himself. Likewise, our marriage covenants produce more like ourselves. God instructed the first two people, *"Be fruitful and multiply; fill the earth and subdue it"* (Genesis 1:28). Like God's love multiplies into us, so does ours; thus intercourse leads to babies, described in Genesis 2:24 above.

He made animal reproduction sexual, but it is not characterized by pleasure as ours is. People can indulge sexual activity without marriage. It is one way we debase the pattern of God's image.

His pattern for relationships is the unity within His Triune being, an intimate covenant love. Father, Son, and Holy Spirit take unimaginable pleasure in one another, as one God in three Persons. In His trinity, He personifies agreement, commitment, and mutual honor.

The pleasure pattern is reflected in the covenant between a man and woman in their sexual relationship. The ecstasy of intimacy is not a bonus, nor is it a devilish temptation. Our marriage intimacy is a screenshot of the covenant intimacy within the Three Persons of the Triune God.

Our pleasurable intimacy in covenant love is the photographic image of His Own. In fact, He created our marriage covenants of man and woman as the supreme image of Him on Earth—right in the former territory of His enemies.

CHAPTER 5

GOD'S FATHERHOOD

Genesis 1:1 says, *"In the beginning, God created the heavens and the earth."* The heavens included the host of angelic beings repeatedly mentioned throughout Scripture. The verse does not elaborate on the content and character of original Earth. We know it only by implication from God's imaginative power of beauty.

SATAN AS HOMEWRECKER

The kingdom of darkness failed in their misguided attempt to replace God. He implanted His fiery wrath into their physique (Ezekiel 28:18). Aflame within, Lucifer and his partner angels were exiled to original Earth in their physical bodies. All this occurred between Genesis 1:1 and 1:2.

Cast down to original Earth, the fallen enemies enjoyed free rein. To cool the relentless fire within their bodies, they ruined God's original Earth into the condition of Genesis 1:2. That's why Earth was empty, formless, watery, and dark—a giant cooling pool that relieved their inward physical burning. This ruination occurred prior to the six twenty-four-hour days that began in Genesis 1:3.

GOD AS HOMEWRECKER

But God forcibly dislocated satan's comfort zone with staccato terror over those six days. He blasted darkness with light, formed and shaped the surface, and raised dry land. His reformation deprived the kingdom of satan of their accustomed free rein.

Restricted into seas by the boundaries of dry land, they were then crowded with living things. Compared to their free-rein cooling pools, the teeming seas would feel like confining puddles. Their relief became scarcer. God had ended their uncontested dominion.

Think of the rebels' jealousy to hear God's instructions to Adam and Eve: *"Multiply, fill the earth, and subdue it"* (Genesis 1:28).

GOD AS HOMEMAKER

In contrast to the enemies' confinement was God's expansive homemaking for our first parents in their garden home. Wherever the two image-creatures looked, they beheld verdant plants and fruitful trees. Every spot they stood, the thundering sound of the giant spring would match with the aromatic and bejeweled waters it spewed in every compass direction.

Eden was abundantly full of delights, privileges, intimacy, and security—twenty-eight distinct benefits, last I counted. In the garden, Adam and Eve had the liberty to go anywhere and eat from any tree, except for one.

God placed our first parents into abundance, not into scarcity. Adam and Eve now had the same freedom that darkness used to have. God's restrictions were aimed at satan, not people.

For those rebels in darkness, exiled on Earth, any multiplying by these human invaders would be completely foreign and threatening.

ADAM'S DEFICIENCIES

This amazing man was in God's image with God's breath in Him. Yet Adam still had three deficiencies. God created Adam with these inadequacies because He intended to supply them. Whether that would occur depended upon the choices of Adam and Eve.

The first inadequacy was dependent existence. God exists on His own, needing nothing. Adam was in His image but lacked this independence. Adam had needs. For instance, for unending physical life, he required fruit from the tree of life.

Adam's second deficiency was human companionship. God intentionally created Adam alone, to teach him through the animal-naming process.

God provided for Adam's third deficiency by placing tree two in downtown Eden: the tree of knowledge of good and evil. Prior to eating its fruit, Adam and Eve had room to become more like God. As Adam had been incomplete without a human companion, so also their original likeness to Him had been incomplete. This fruit would be useful at the proper time.

Why were these deficiencies created into Adam, who had the very breath of God in him? Because a maturing process was required, a learning curve in which the choices of Adam would be authoritative.

THE AUTHORITY OF ADAM

The names he gave the animals were authoritative, and the names he gave the woman were authoritative. Right from the start, Adam mirrored God's authority by possessing the ability to make choices and take consequential actions. God's statements and actions leave no doubt: Adam was responsible because he had choice.

A human was responsible to work the garden and harvest its food. The fruit from the two central trees had to be plucked and eaten, when God so directed. Standing uneaten, the significant trees had no effect otherwise. A human had to choose and act.

We still have to. Our authority to subdue and fill the Earth is unabated. Slowed and impaired, certainly—yet the blessing to do it remains on our race.

This authority preceded the pair's maturing process. Authority was not based on knowledge, expertise, or wisdom, because Adam had little (as events soon revealed). The Creator God had blessed them and authorized them to subdue and exercise dominion. All Earth was under our authority—except one tree.

ONLY ONE HUMAN?

Eight times in the six days of creation, we read His phrase, *"according to their kind."* Each creature reproduced according to their kind, sexually. God conceived the sexual mating of male and female before making Adam. Every other creature was paired male and female.

But the first human is solitary. The woman arrives after a while.

Adam being the only one wouldn't surprise the devil and his minions. Angelic beings were not made in pairs. Lucifer had no wife or helpmate. Adam, a solitary being, embodied the only known pattern in the unseen world. God was the only one who was multiple, as a Trinity.

Why was Adam the only one made? God's plan was exquisite. No angels knew He was a loving God with a Father's heart. By creating us in two steps, He presented His character of love in a dramatic flourish, visible and shocking to all the solitary spirits of the unseen world.

STEP TWO BEGINS

During Adam's time as the only human, God's father-love verbally initiated three love actions. With each one, the heavenly host beheld His relational nature more fully.

> And the LORD God said, "It is not good that man should be alone; I will make him a helper comparable to him." Out of the ground the LORD God formed every beast of the field and every bird of the air, and brought them to Adam to see what he would call them. And whatever Adam called each living creature, that was its name. So Adam gave names to all cattle, to the birds of the air, and to every beast of the field. But for Adam there was not found a helper comparable to him. (Genesis 2:18–20)

NOT GOOD?!

First, God verbally pinpointed an inadequacy in what He had made. Adam was created in God's image, yet a gap remained: *not good*. Earlier, God had pronounced over all His work, *"It was good"* (Genesis 1:4). We now hear Him say that it is not good.

What would satan and his exiled partners think when they heard that? The six-day series had just stripped darkness of their formless, void domain. An unpredictable sequence would continue with the unpleasant sound of *not good*.

God's *not good* might sound to his disrupted enemies like "not finished yet?" Imagine the spectating rebels: "Not good? What is He talking about? What will He do to us now?" If you were manhandled as

AS WE SEE TODAY

Have you considered that the *not goods* and *alones* of your life have been His customized discovery process for you? With such a meek attitude, we can receive even our hardest trials with thanksgiving.

We too require training. Some people intimidate us for what we do not know or cannot do. This may be an alert to darkness.

God had no problem with Adam's incomplete knowledge. Why should we be ashamed for ours?

The training process of God shows His father-love.

"I will bless the LORD who has given me counsel; my heart also instructs me in the night seasons" (Psalm 16:7).

they had been, with such abject helplessness, wouldn't you brace yourself for more such divine attacks? God rested on the seventh day; we know it, but darkness didn't.

Or darkness may have rejoiced. Possibly they construed God's *not good* as admitting a mistake. If so, they would gloat with mockery over His so-called perfection, like mockers among people.

"It is not good that man should be alone"—this implies an alternative to aloneness. Suppose a fish could talk intelligibly. You ask him how the water is, and he replies, "What's *water?*" Without knowing an alternative to water, the word means nothing to the fish. Likewise, when God uses the word *alone,* He has an alternative in mind. Angelic beings couldn't imagine anything but being alone. All other possibilities would be foreign, impossible to imagine.

WORK AND LEARN

Second, God engaged Adam in work—and then shared in it.

In His soliloquy about Adam's solitary existence, God also said what He would do: *"I will make him a helper comparable to him"* (Genesis 2:18). Judging from the account itself, Adam did not know that until later. It doesn't appear that God explained to Adam why this animal-naming was important.

God physically led animals, pair by pair, to Adam, who named them. The primary purpose was not the naming. That's one reason we don't know the names Adam gave them, or the language he used. We only know Adam's conclusion: none of the animals were like him.

The naming of the animals was a customized discovery process in which Adam and God worked together. Working with others is normal for us, but only one human lived then. God tenderly mentored Adam to impart understanding to him. He wanted Adam to agree: *"I am alone and it is not good."* Thus, Eve's creation resulted from an agreement between God and the man.

Satan may have felt this was all wrong for at least two reasons. First, God never mentored Lucifer or the angels in such a way. Nowhere in Scripture is this suggested. Second, God created a creature in His image and actively worked alongside the man.

After all, God had named the light and seas and everything formed during the six days. He could have easily named the animals. But like a partner, God brings the animals and the man does the naming.

Not only was there delegation; there was education as well. It's a contrast to our expectation. After all, God Himself had breathed into Adam, nostrils to nostrils. What a way to start life! Then God walked with him in the garden.

What possible needs could we have after that? We feel that being closer to God makes us more like Him, and life easier. Yet, even after the most intimate physical interaction with God, Adam had to learn, just like we do.

Education might feel wrong to Lucifer; there is no record that any angelic being required training or education. For the man to require this mentoring meant he wasn't instantly smart like God. Instead, Adam had to learn gradually.

The creature, although made like God, was oblivious to his own state: solitude was not desirable. For him to realize it required a training process. From the proud Lucifer's viewpoint, Adam would look unexpectedly dumb.

NO LONGER ALONE

And the LORD God caused a deep sleep to fall on Adam, and he slept; and He took one of his ribs, and closed up the flesh in its place. Then the rib which the LORD God had taken from man He made into a woman, and He brought her to the man. (Genesis 2:21–22)

God's love nature was evident in a third way: He created the comparable companion. Using Adam's body parts, the Divine Physician crafted woman. It was the first time a new creature emerged from another creature. It took place before the first woman gave birth.

No instruction to Adam is recorded, but none was needed when we read how her mere presence aroused the man. God brings to Adam the last animal type for naming, producing the man's first recorded utterance to capture the moment.

This is now bone of my bones
And flesh of my flesh;
She shall be called Woman,
Because she was taken out of Man. (Genesis 2:23)

Adam gave her two names after all: "Woman" because of her origin in his body, and next according to her role: *Eve ... the mother of all living* (Genesis 3:20).

The picture of intimacy expands, and relationships multiply. The Second Person of the Trinity took Eve physically and brought her to Adam. With the vulnerable image-creatures, God Almighty engaged intimately as no angel ever enjoyed in Scripture.

GOD'S FATHERLY WAY

With the naming process, Adam also received training for some level of knowing about good and evil. Between the animal-naming and Eve's arrival, the man felt dissatisfaction and lack. This taught him the meaning of *not good.*

When he saw Eve, he could feel the opposite as well. *"This is now bone of my bones and flesh of my flesh"* (Genesis 2:23). Adam expressed relief. He distinguished between *not good* and *good.*

Through resolving Adam's companionship deficiency, God fathered him and activated his sense of *not good* and *good.* Training us is something fathers love to do. Even poor fathers justify their actions as teaching the children something.

How many topics could God the Father train into our early parents? His training might have included a proper time to eat the knowledge fruit. God's evident plan was a gradual increase in their knowledge of good and evil, a maturing process under His tender fatherhood.

CHAPTER 6

GOD FORCES US TO CHOOSE

Most teaching about Eden involves the tree of the knowledge of good and evil, right in the center. Near it was the tree of life as well.

But zoom out from those two trees. Imagine yourself and your five physical senses, plopped down in the garden of Genesis 2:8–20. Every natural thing happening would be sensible for you. Slowly read the passage with your physical imagination for smells, sights, sounds, tastes, and feelings. Which would you experience in God's garden of pleasure?

The LORD God planted a garden eastward in Eden, and there He put the man whom He had formed. And out of the ground the LORD God made every tree grow that is pleasant to the sight and good for food. The tree of life was also in the midst of the garden, and the tree of the knowledge of good and evil.

Now a river went out of Eden to water the garden, and from there it parted and became four riverheads. The name of the first is Pishon; it is the one which skirts the whole land of Havilah, where there is gold. And the gold of that land is good. Bdellium and the onyx stone are there. The name of the second river is Gihon; it is the one which goes around the whole land of Cush. The name of the third river is Hiddekel; it is the one which goes toward the east of Assyria. The fourth river is the Euphrates.

Then the LORD God took the man and put him in the garden of Eden to tend and keep it. And the LORD God commanded the man, saying, "Of every tree of the garden you may freely eat; but of the tree of the knowledge of good and evil you shall not eat, for in the day that you eat of it you shall surely die."

And the LORD God said, "It is not good that man should be alone; I will make him a helper comparable to him." Out of the ground the LORD God formed every beast of the field and every bird of the air, and brought them to Adam to see what he would call them. And whatever Adam called each living creature, that was its name. So Adam gave names to all cattle, to the birds of the air, and to every beast of the field.

Let your senses take in everything. Animals unimpaired by sin are moving and making sounds all around you. Birds fly and perch, all with their unique calls. Feel the wind of the newly created atmosphere, whispering in the leaves of the trees. Hear their fruit dropping to the ground near you. Taste every nourishment Eden offers you.

Moisture is everywhere. Smell the ground. The mist rising from the ground might smell like fresh flowers, or grass, or dirt—what do you imagine?

Four major rivers all had their headwater springs in Eden. Imagine the roar of that giant volume. Taste the pure water. Their mists carry the smell of aromatic resin to you. The gushing springs sparkle with gold and onyx—in their highest concentration there from the depths of the earth, pushed out into distant riverbeds by the forceful springs.

This was our parents' home every day. Adam and Eve enjoyed this bounty without any scarcity or impairment whatsoever. Everything God intended for them, they enjoyed to the fullness of their ability.

CENTRAL ON PURPOSE

The tree of knowing good and evil was in the unavoidable hub of the garden. It's a mistake to think it was in the center to tempt them. Would the tree of life be there as well, if the central location was intended to tempt? A more plausible explanation of the central *location* is the central *role* God intended their fruit to play in their lives.

Being in downtown Eden offered an advantage, just like the center of a city: easy and frequent access. Not only the trees but also the springs were in the hub. Departing Eden in all four directions, all their roar, jewels, and aromas were centralized in the garden. The water, the bounty, the tree of life and the knowing tree, all in downtown in Eden. The centrality was conducive to frequent visits and resupply, both from trees and springs.

NOT A PERMANENT PROHIBITION

Was God's prohibition of that fruit an everlasting one? Did He not *ever* want Adam and Eve to know good and evil?

I believe it was a timing issue. He could someday lift the prohibition.

With good choices, perhaps their permission level would increase; it's quite plausible the tree would speed their advance through levels of knowledge. Maybe He would have allowed one, then a few, then any quantity. Maybe after *allowing* them to eat the knowing fruit, with time He might have *encouraged* it.

From a practical standpoint, if the tree was like our fruit trees, a knowledge of ladders would be needed from one of the fruits.

We do not know what would have happened with the knowledge tree, because our first parents ate of it so readily. Had they resisted satan, we might have had a Bible that recorded increasing permissions to the fruit. The tree of knowing good and evil might even still be available.

> As a child, I asked my father why people didn't invent the internal combustion engine sooner. Even my eight-year-old thinking understood his explanation of it.
>
> That might have happened, if Adam and Eve had chosen to resist satan's lie. Maybe one fruit was labeled ENGINEERING.

TEMPTATION RIGHT AT HAND

Adam and Eve enjoyed complete innocence; this is not true for us. Apostle Paul described how closely sin clings to our lives: "I find then a law, that evil is present with me" (Romans 7:21). All of us have sin within us and ever-present, except three only: Adam, Eve, and Jesus. We are all born sinners, except those three people.

Our parents Adam and Eve could experience only one temptation, concerning only one single tree. From the viewpoint of satan, he had only one human choice to work with.

But ever since, people have provided the enemy with many opportunities to tempt our choices. Temptations surprise us wherever we turn. We experience our enemies only slyly and occasionally, but on Jesus, these temptations were piled with no subtlety at all. Even the devil himself took charge of tempting Jesus. The Son of Man ran the gauntlet of temptation during His thirty-three years.

He was in all points tempted as we are, yet without sin. (Hebrews 4:15).

To discern and disarm our temptations from darkness, we must understand human choice—our choice.

CHOICE POWER

People alone in all Creation are in God's image, which includes the freedom to choose between alternatives. Although a maturing process is required from our infancy, everyone has some form of power to choose.

Adam was the first of us, then Eve. Their partial knowledge of good and evil was not yet adequate to resist the tempter. They were confronted with a choice for which they were unknowledgeable. They chose poorly, as the ancient Crusader said to Indy in *Indiana Jones: The Last Crusade*.

God Almighty submitted His ideals to Adam's poor choice. As the Lamb who was slain, God also suffered the consequences. Likewise, the consequences of our choices are imposed upon Him, as well as ourselves.

Our choices exert a domination over all that happens subsequently. God's ideal possibilities are eliminated by every substandard choice a person makes. Consistently, we go our own way, stifling the ideals conceived by God's father-love, for which He created us. The very race He created for love, He must now treat with unrelenting holiness. This was not His choice. It was ours.

INTERROGATE THE BIBLE

The invisible rebels encourage us to evade God's ways with willful blindness. The first way to defeat their effort is to interrogate the Bible. The hunger of meekness wants to know God; our questions unearth its truths.

It is the glory of God to conceal a matter,
But the glory of kings is to search out a matter. (Proverbs 25:2)

WHY NOT MORE EXPLANATION?

This God forces us to choose. His "tree choices" raise many disturbing questions.

And out of the ground the LORD God made every tree grow that is pleasant to the sight and good for food.

The tree of life was also in the midst of the garden, and the tree of the knowledge of good and evil....

And the LORD God commanded the man, saying, "Of every tree of the garden you may freely eat; but of the tree of the knowledge of good and evil you shall not eat, for in the day that you eat of it you shall surely die." (Genesis 2:9, 16–17)

> Try speaking the passage aloud. It makes your mind slow down; your spirit can fully engage and perceive. It also helps to verbalize it several times, accentuating it differently each time. Look at the forced choice.

Here are two central trees of dramatic power, but you just read the sum total of what God told Adam. Why didn't God give more explanation? If it were me, I would sell him on eating the tree of life first; wouldn't you? But the record of Eden gives no hint that God did so.

WHY NOT MORE WARNING?

Maybe instead, you would scare Adam from disobeying by painting a really frightful picture. God did use the word *die*, but since Day One when God made light, death had not occurred. No animal or human had yet died nor seen death.

The word *die* was meaningless for an Adam with no experience. You or I might explain what the death meant. Why didn't God? Imagine this:

Adam, this is a tree for knowing good and evil. I'm not ready for you to eat it yet. If you eat its fruit before I say you are ready, here's what will happen.

You will get kicked out of this garden, with the woman I'm about to make for you. Food won't grow on trees; instead you'll have to dig it out of the ground. Your fingernails will come off; your skin will dry and crack.

You and the woman will make more people like yourselves. Then your first son will murder your second son. All your children will kill each other. You will see all this.

You will live a very very long time with withering flesh, witnessing the result of one bite of that fruit, and then you will die, your woman will die, your children will all die, and everyone ever related to you will live with all this sorrowful destruction.

Worst of all, you and I will not be close again.

But you can eat the fruit, if that's what you want.

69

Lord God, why didn't You say that, and warn Adam and Eve with more detail? Why didn't You equip them to resist the serpent?

Adam, I made you in My image, like Me, the only creature ever. There are spirits that I exiled here to Earth who are not like you and Me. In fact, I created you as part of their penalty. I put you here to rule Earth instead of them.

They hate Me and now they hate you. Especially watch out for their leader. He is an ancient being of great power who hates Me. He disguises himself as a serpent, and he will do everything in his power to make you eat the one fruit I put off limits for now.

You can eat it if you choose, but you have another choice: you can trust Me. I am on your side. Whatever that serpent says, he will make you think that I am only interested in Myself, while he is on your side against Me.

He is a liar which means that you should ignore him. In fact, if he comes to you, just call out for Me and I will explain the truth to you.

THIS IS FOR US

The trees of life, and of knowledge of good and evil, are an example of a mystery. We can think it through and ask any question. But we yield to the uncertainty God imposed, since He never mentioned it again.

Reason cannot succeed when He has not released truth to our understanding. But we should hold our puzzles in the back of our minds. He likes us to search things out (Proverbs 25:2), and rewards our inquisitiveness about His Word.

Maturing as a Christian is a constant process of receiving better explanations of the Bible, and our puzzles open the door for them.

Why didn't You say those things, Father?

As long as we are at it, why did You even put us in the same place where You exiled the devil and the rebel angels? You spent time with Adam while he named the animals, but wouldn't it be more effective to warn Adam about the tempter? At least, before diverting time to animal husbandry?

Wasn't there adequate justification to send those deceivers to Hell first thing? right away? What conceivable reason made You leave evil spirits on the loose after you made Adam? Why exile these powerful rebels to Earth and then put Your dearest, most fragile creature here as their victims?

Why didn't You protect our race? Truly, Lord, it looks like You *wanted* our race to fall prey to satan.

We need not fear these questions. God can take it. This is how we interrogate the Bible. That's where He has revealed the answers—truths He wants us to understand, if we will to.

> The secret things belong to the LORD our God, but those things which are revealed belong to us and to our children forever. (Deuteronomy 29:29)

THE TEST OBJECTIVE

The test of Adam and Eve did not depend on understanding the two trees, nor on vigilance against the tempter. We shall soon see the only question: Would they trust their Creator?

Themselves left vulnerable to the ancient evil one, they would have only one refuge available. It was not knowledge. It was not warning. It was trusting their Creator.

If they had chosen that, they would have been immune to temptation. Even had they eaten and repented, they could have yet trusted Him for remedy. After all, the remedy had already been slain before the foundation of the world.

GOD CONTRIVED THE TEST

God Himself created the tree's qualities which Eve saw: *good for food, pleasant to the eyes,* and *desirable for gaining wisdom* (Genesis 3:6). God named it *"the tree of the knowledge of good and evil"* (Genesis 2:9). He Himself had placed it in *the middle of the garden.*

The serpent did none of these things; God did. The warnings we would give, the pitches we would make, God did not do. Thus, He contrived the situation. Adam and Eve would be forced to choose.

He forces our choice as well. We would prefer to be done with temptation, and walk in holy intimacy with Him at all times. Christians often wish they could go to heaven already. But His purpose is our testing and maturity. We may not remain stagnant. Each temptation and each choice can advance us toward our maturity, if we so choose.

For our first parents, there was only one choice, and it was at a tree. Our lives are not so simple. Temptation is a constant reality for us, because God is adamant that we mature to discern and disarm enemy tempters.

TREE NUMBER TWO

God Himself identified tree two as the source of knowing good and evil, but how? Did its fruit actually impart such knowledge when eaten? Did its chemical composition have a binary spiritual component: wisdom if eaten second, but death if eaten first?

This knowledge tree never appears again in the Bible. In fact, the phrase, *"knowledge of good and evil,"* appears in only one other place in the Bible. Moses (who received and recorded the revelation of Eden) used the phrase to tell God's explanation for the forty-year wandering penalty.

> Moreover your little ones and your children, who you say will be victims, who today have no knowledge of good and evil, they shall go in there; to them I will give it, and they shall possess it. (Deuteronomy 1:39)

That tree of knowledge was the only limit our first parents knew. Their Creator had made it unavoidable and inescapable, in the hub of their existence.

TREE NUMBER ONE

The tree of the knowledge of good and evil receives most attention in preaching about Eden. But it was not the only tree in the center area, nor was it the first one God mentioned. *The tree of life* was also there, close by the knowing tree. Tree number one was free for the taking: no restrictions, no unintended consequences.

The Bible authors refer to it several times over the next fifteen hundred years. Sometimes the tree of life is metaphorical, such as the Word of God (Psalm 1:2–3). It is actual in Revelation 22:2, where it is not one but a whole promenade of trees bordering a fruitful river. In that setting, its leaves are for the healing of the nations, so long stained by the principalities claiming them.

WHAT THE TREES DID

What was the effect of the two downtown trees? God says, after Adam and Eve first sinned. We can reverse engineer their effects from His statement.

> Then the LORD God said, "Behold, the man has become like one of Us, to know good and evil. And now, lest he put out his hand and take

also of the tree of life, and eat, and live forever"—therefore the LORD God sent him out of the garden of Eden to till the ground from which he was taken. (Genesis 3:22–23)

From God's statement, we know the pair did not eat of the tree of life. The campaign of satan started before they had eaten either tree. Two marvelous trees were before them, but our parents chose satan's guidance over God's restriction. Adam and Eve both ate from the wrong tree first.

When they died spiritually, the tree of life became a tree of eternal death. They and their progeny would have been fixed forever. To prevent this, God banished our race from Eden.

You and I would be souls without hope, in bodies unable to die, never able to be reborn as spirits. To eat from the tree of life second would have been undying hellishness; every human being would be irredeemable sinners. The tree of life is not here now because God subsequently removed it from Earth—so great a danger it posed.

God protected our race from an eternal death without repentance and restoration. By preventing our race from ingesting fruit from the tree of life, He ensured that we could be reborn as spirits. That's when the tree of life can fulfill its intended purpose: when we are reconciled to the Spirit of life.

SAME WAY TODAY

Imagine if you could never escape life as a sinner. If they had eaten the tree of life, that may have been exactly what you and I would experience.

The Picture of Dorian Gray, the 1890 novel of Oscar Wilde, captures the horror: existing forever, with inescapable damnation within. Dorian Gray was able to end the torment, by stabbing the picture of himself.

Neither Adam and Eve, nor you and I, could have ever died or been restored to God, had they eaten from the tree of life. The horror!

This is the action of a loving Father in response to our first parents' poor choice.

TWO-TREE DISTRIBUTION

If humankind had multiplied without sin, would there have been only one life tree and one knowing tree? Would they both be limited to Eden? How would a burgeoning population have enough?

He created every tree with seedbearing fruit for reproduction according to its kind (Genesis 1:11). The tree of life and the knowing tree were no different. Thus Revelation 22 depicts a spreading tree of life bearing fruit constantly. This was God's plan for an Earth ruled by unfallen humanity.

God might have taught them how to distribute the two trees globally. The knowing fruit, eaten by obedient people, would easily include transplantation and plant-grafting. My wife and I have transplanted rose stems; could we be transplanting trees of life everywhere?

Scarcity is the foundation of all economics in a fallen world. A limited supply of goods drives up costs and always leaves some people without. But if Adam and Eve had trusted God, there would be no scarcity. An abundant supply of life fruit and knowledge fruit would leave no one excluded.

That is why such abundance will characterize the new heavens and the new earth.

> In the middle of its street, and on either side of the river, was the tree of life, which bore twelve fruits, each tree yielding its fruit every month. The leaves of the tree were for the healing of the nations. (Revelation 22:2)

Our premise is that *both trees* were intended for our use, in the correct sequence and proper time. Imagine if they were now available to people everywhere.

Mothers would nurse their children as we do now. Instead of vitamin drops, only droplets of the tree of life would be needed. What we call child prodigies now would be commonplace once moms added drops from the tree of knowledge. School might take two or three years instead of the twelve, sixteen, and twenty it now requires.

There are so many possibilities if Adam and Eve had eaten from the tree of life first.

SATAN

CHAPTER 7

MUTUAL
REPLACEMENT

Read between the lines of Scripture. What unspoken reality must be true, in order for its direct statements to be true? We did this in Book Three, *Nobody Sees This Creation: The Origin of the Devil and His Replacements*.

In Ezekiel 28, Isaiah 14, Luke 11, and Revelation 12, we found the origin of satan and his kingdom of darkness. In those and Genesis 1 lay the root causes of the war we experience constantly. That one conflict has always defined all created reality. God decreed it before the foundation of the world, and its comprehensive impact pervades all human experience until the end of this world.

God's kingdom is in attack mode against the kingdom of darkness.

On this rock I will build My church, and the gates of Hades shall not prevail against it. (Matthew 16:18)

SATAN'S REPLACEMENT GRID

Lucifer was jealous of God's authority and wanted to wield it himself. The covering archangel wanted to replace God on the throne of heaven.

Every person has a grid for making sense of their existence. To disarm our unseen enemies, we must discern how they think. The devil's grid of existence is replacement, and the Scripture reveals his attempt to replace God.

Consider the foolish bravado of Lucifer.

Your heart was lifted up because of your beauty;
You corrupted your wisdom for the sake of your splendor. (Ezekiel 28:17)

He lost both his wisdom and his splendor. After all, no angel was in a better position to understand God. The exalted cherub would have known about God's omnipotence (power over everything), omnipresence (presence everywhere), and omniscience (knowing everything). Yet even knowing these things, his heart held the five *"I wills"* of Isaiah 14. The top angel wanted to unseat God and replace Him as ruler of all. Replacement is satan's grid for interpreting existence.

REPLACEMENT INITIATED

The archangel engaged in trades with other angels. God identified those trades as the seedbed for their jealousy (Ezekiel 28). When he was ready to seize God's throne, Lucifer called in IOUs from his angelic trading partners (Isaiah 14). But their rebellion failed at the hand of the archangel Michael. Lucifer was cast down to Earth and exiled from God's favor (Revelation 12). Into him and his rebel partners, God installed His inescapable, inexhaustible searing fire (Ezekiel 28).

THE COUNTERFEIT & THE REAL

It's like the Superman story. Lex Luthor has one grid for his entire life: defeat Superman. Luthor is constantly cooking up some scheme. Superman always wins in the end.

The futility of Luthor's plans are evident to everyone except himself. All readers know without any doubt that Superman always wins in the end.

The devil is the model for all such futile efforts. Our many tales of heroic figures like Superman are parables of us who follow Jesus.

We always win in the end over the Lex Luthors of darkness.

Ever since, to find rest from their inner burning, they crave moisture and water (Luke 11:24). So they murdered all the life in original Earth (John 8:44, 10:10). They ruined it into a dark, formless, and void chaos (Genesis 1:2).

God's beautiful Earth had become satan's giant cooling pool with no dryness to be found. The archangel finally established his own dominion to replace God's. The kingdom of darkness had free rein with no restrictions.

The devil himself described it to Jesus during the wilderness temptation in Luke 4:6.

All this authority I will give You, and their glory; for this has been delivered to me, and I give it to whomever I wish.

On Earth at least, Lucifer had successfully replaced God as ruler. He only forgot one thing:

But God.... (Ephesians 2:4)

GOD'S REPLACEMENT GRID

Replacement was in the air, and God got into the action as well.

In six twenty-four-hour days of terror attacks on darkness and their cooling dominion, God restored the Earth. As the crowning goodness, He placed a brand-new pair of creatures here. Their mandate was to reclaim it for His dominion, so He gave them the authority to subdue the entire Earth. To do that, He gave the pair the ability to multiply themselves and fill it (Genesis 1:28).

God's new image-creature was mortal, not angelic. God replaced Lucifer with us. Human beings replaced His unseen enemies as the ones in charge.

He created us right where satan had been exiled: Earth. This dramatically escalated the war of two kingdoms. But unable to withstand God's ever-spreading replacement, the gates of satan's kingdom are in continual retreat.

For the earth shall be full of the knowledge of the LORD, as the waters cover the sea. (Isaiah 11:9)

For Yours is the kingdom and the power and the glory forever. (Matthew 6:13)

PLAN A THROUGH PLAN Y

In *The SpongeBob SquarePants Movie*, the title character naively and repeatedly steps on Plankton, arousing his hatred and enflaming him to steal the Krabby Patty recipe from Mr. Krabs. Plankton tells his computer wife that he has tried everything from Plan A to Plan Y.

She helpfully replies, "What about Plan Z?" Plankton thought Plan Y was the last one, and is overjoyed to find one more in his dastardly file cabinet. That Plan Z provides Plankton his greatest success in the Bikini Bottom universe.[3]

Like Plankton, our tireless, angelic opponent persists in rebellion. This is what he has always done. He gains power over others with seemingly innocuous IOUs. It worked with a third of heaven's angels, and it works against all of us.

The devil's power pattern is using implied obligations against others. His native language is lies. His bloodthirsty motive is to destroy and kill. Can we imagine this powerful liar terminating his efforts to derail God's plans for people?

THE MEEK INHERIT

As cartoonish as SpongeBob and Plankton are, they truthfully depict our superiority to satan. We were created by God to replace the exiled Lucifer as Earth's dominator. As such, we would serve as the wardens of exile for his entire kingdom of darkness.

Like SpongeBob was naive to Plankton's evil, we are naive compared to the sinister enemy. As SpongeBob was meek and lacking, so are we in our mortal nature. Yet God exalts us over His enemy, satan. No wonder the serpent's animosity was targeted at Adam and Eve.

SNIPER ATTACK

Imagine Adam and Eve, living forever after resisting satan's ploy. Matured in their knowledge they would resist satan with increasing effectiveness.

Even after eating from the wrong tree first, they still lived nine hundred years. The devil would have had endless opportunities to dog them, to wear them down into succumbing. We know this well; it's what darkness does with us today.

SOMETHING IS BETTER THAN NOTHING

If Adam and Eve ate from the tree of life first, they would have had eternity before them, on Earth as God's warden for satan. They would have multiplied with no pain in childbirth, and all their children would be born godly. The ancient tempter might then deploy a *divide and conquer* strategy.

Our rapidly increasing population would provide the tempter with an ever-larger target, more and more candidates to tempt. If Adam and Eve were holy, satan and his fallen angels would attack their children.

If only one descendant heeded the lies and trusted satan over God, a new line of descendants would begin. That lineage would include the death and sin now common to all of us. The Earth would be full of two distinct human races: the spiritually alive and the spiritually dead. As we'll see, the Flood occurred because of a similar two-race division.

POWER MEETS INTIMACY

Where the archangel of envy thought replacement, the God of love thought relationship. Lucifer and his partners had no concept of intimacy and the vulnerability it required. Scripture shows instead, the only variable in their replacement grid was power.

We look back on the accounts of Genesis 1 and 2 with our hindsight that everything reproduces sexually. The kingdom of darkness had never seen sex; such intimacy was unheard of in the heavenly realms. Even more striking, they had never seen one creature come out of another. Imagine the strangeness when Eve came out of Adam, and new people came out of her.

The distinctions of our race multiplied right before the envious eyes of darkness. Now God had creatures in His own likeness, and He actually walked and talked with them in Eden.

Fast forward to our present time. Living human spirits sit with God in heaven, in physical bodies like the resurrected Jesus who achieved this privilege for us. We are closer than Lucifer ever was. There we show God's nature of love to all the heavenly hosts.

> [God] made us sit together in the heavenly places in Christ Jesus, that in the ages to come He might show the exceeding riches of His grace in His kindness toward us in Christ Jesus. (Ephesians 2:6–7)

CHAPTER 8

THE WAYS OF THE DEVIL

Our unseen enemies are powerful but they dread us more than we dread them. That's why they sneak. To fulfill our dominion mandate requires us to know how they operate.

When a human being becomes a living spirit by faith in Christ, the image of God is reactivated. The restored dominion makes satan's replacement inevitable, and it fills him with fury (Revelation 12:12).

But the unseen opponents do not escalate immediately into direct attack. They sneak like serpents, emerging from their cooling refuges onto hostile territory, as their founder did to meet Eve in Eden.

To disarm them, we must discern them.

> ...lest Satan should take advantage of us; for we are not ignorant of his devices. (2 Corinthians 2:11)

UNAFRAID TO KNOW

Many church circles say we shouldn't know too much about the devil and demons. It's no wonder Christians are such easy prey for the deceptive enemies.

Cowardly neutrality is not possible in the war of the two kingdoms, because that conflict governs all reality. We the vulnerable have angels for enemies, fallen though they be. Either we replace them, or they replace us. God has declared that retreat and cowardice make us His enemies.

He who is not with Me is against Me, and he who does not gather with Me scatters. (Luke 11:23)

But the cowardly ... shall have their part in the lake which burns with fire and brimstone, which is the second death. (Revelation 21:8)

Any Christian who fails to engage with God's kingdom army is at great risk. However compliant or accurate the beliefs of such a person may be, the defining war of existence renders cowardice a vote for the other kingdom. Attempts at neutrality reveal secret covenants with God's enemy. We already saw His wrath and its consequences; we do not want God as our enemy.

People can only know about the kingdom of darkness because God revealed it in Scripture. It is for us to know, and we do not shrink from the pervasive conflict.

With brave faith and meek hunger, we can know satan's ways, just as Jesus and the New Testament writers knew them.

Get behind Me, Satan! You are an offense to Me, for you are not mindful of the things of God, but the things of men. (Matthew 16:23)

Satan himself transforms himself into an angel of light. Therefore it is no great thing if his ministers also transform themselves into ministers of righteousness, whose end will be according to their works. (2 Corinthians 11:14–15)

Resist him, steadfast in the faith, knowing that the same sufferings are experienced by your brotherhood. (1 Peter 5:9)

Resist the devil and he will flee from you. (James 4:7)

This is the spirit of the Antichrist, which you have heard was coming, and is now already in the world. (1 John 4:3)

JEALOUSY

First arising in Lucifer, long before people were created, jealousy is an original motive. That ancient origin makes it powerful and pervasive. With twisted fecundity, jealousy spawned a close cousin: envy. To discern darkness, we must understand how envy works and how jealousy can be identified.

The duo are known by their effects. Jealousy poisons all perception. It produces a feeling of threat. Whether alone or in combination, jealousy and envy prompt all-consuming action.

So you can imagine the jealousy of this once-exalted archangel on Day Six. God created a new creature in His own image. No such creature like us had ever been seen. God bestowed on us the privileges Lucifer had once enjoyed. That day, the fire of satan's original jealousy of God was suddenly stoked with jealousy of the new race.

God replaced an eternal angelic being with vulnerable mortal human beings.

> You have made him a little lower than the angels,
> And You have crowned him with glory and honor.
> You have made him to have dominion over the works of Your hands;
> You have put all things under his feet. (Psalm 8:5–6)

The event overturned all expectations of the heavenly host, whether holy or enemy. Every norm they knew was upended.

ANGELIC NORMS

The Scripture never shows God being friendly or conversational with an angel. They were not created for relationship. Although His love nature and holiness are unchanging, Scripture says they are ministering spirits (Psalm 104:4; Hebrews 1:7, 14). Their every appearance reveals a singular function: to execute His commands and serve those He favors.

God and angels in Scripture relate like a military command structure. It is always formal; there is no casual. They stand before Him (Luke 1:19) and they worship Him (Revelation 4–5). Some, but not all of them, can see His face (Matthew 18:10). Revelation reveals many distinct angels, more than any other Bible book. In it, each one executes their exclusive assignment from God—and nothing more.

Seeing the Holy and Almighty God as they do requires a capacity for eternal discipline. The angels must constantly respond as God deserves. The eternal severity of Lucifer's penalty stems from this requirement. In contrast, the speech and songs of the holy angels all express honor for God and His worthiness.

The Bible reveals no angelic capability for covenant, nor for physical love, nor for multiplying. The vulnerability and personal intimacy of covenant love was foreign to the angelic host.

No angel, rebel or otherwise, had ever witnessed anything like they saw on the sixth day. God made a creature out of dirt. Never had that been done. Between God and the new race of spirit-creatures, there was proximity and intimacy. He even got nose-to-nose, and breathed into the new creature.

SATAN'S CORRUPTED THINKING

God's Word is knit together with relationships, intimacy, and agreement; satan's thematic patterns are replacement and IOUs. By identifying satan's thought patterns, we are better equipped to disarm his efforts.

Although satan's entire nature is now ablaze with God's holy retribution, he does not repent. Angelic in nature though satan be, his thinking was corrupted when he rebelled. The devil's angelic mind is still corrupted even today; he still hopes to win against God.

The devil never wearies of opposing God at every turn. The fruit of tree two was not the primary issue. If God had said, "Don't eat dirt," satan's pitch would have been, "The dirt is good to eat!" The devil need only replicate his own motive into the new humans: replace God.

PLANS NEEDED?

Ample experience teaches us how frail human holiness is. However, we can't assume that satan knew that. In hindsight, it's abundantly clear that Adam and Eve showed no discernment—but before that, what would a rational observer have expected?

We would have heard God bless the people, His own image-creatures. Right before our eyes, we would hear His intimate breathing into Adam's nostrils. Wouldn't we expect that Adam and Eve had everything needed to function like God on the Earth they were told to subdue? After all, the pair had two superior qualifications: created in God's image, and then breathed into by Him.

What God breathed into Adam was life-breath, the Bible reveals. But the rebels didn't have that revelation. The kingdom of darkness could not be certain that His breath didn't include power and holiness as well as life.

The devil would reasonably expect the new race to have God's same alertness and discernment. It would not be surprising for the new creature to recognize enemies immediately and treat them with wrath as God had.

JEALOUSY PLANNING

> Now the serpent was more cunning than any beast of the field which the LORD God had made. (Genesis 3:1)

Our first Bible introduction to satan says he is more cunning than any other beast God made. Rational beings make plans. An angelically rational schemer would naturally ready an arsenal of persuasive arguments, prior to attacking a creature in God's own image.

Human history of kingdom and family usurpers provide a powerful witness to this sneaky replacement thinking. Tyrants both ancient and current all manifest the grid of the original replacement strategist.

The pair had an advantage that satan lacked: they were in God's own image and likeness. Who better to replace God than the creature made in His own image? Maybe he thought Adam and Eve could succeed where his rebellion had failed. Did satan think he could ride their coattails? After they replaced God on the throne, he might consider replacing them more doable.

1. I should be ruler of everything, not Him.
2. I failed because God is a higher order than me.
3. Now He has foolishly made a creature in His image and likeness.
4. One day, this image-creature is going to try to replace God.
5. I will get in on the ground floor with the humans, so I'm not left out.
6. I'll help them replace God, and then I'll rebel against them after they are on the throne.

In Eden, the serpent introduced the idea of replacing God. By telling Eve, "You will be like God" (Genesis 3:5), satan subtly offered his own motive: to be like God, to replace God, to render God unnecessary.

COOL AND WET

> A mist went up from the earth and watered the whole face of the ground. (Genesis 2:6)

The two races met at a certain tree in Eden: archangel and man. Lucifer was in the form of a serpent. Revelation 12:9 affirms that this serpent was the cast-out Lucifer, become satan. Serpents slither along the ground; that doesn't seem very proud. Have you ever wondered why he is a serpent? How was it cunning?

Isaiah 14 and Luke 11 reveal that the fallen Lucifer still commands his fellow rebels, although latent division simmers beneath their kingdom's hierarchical structure. What was their general attitude, watching their leader become a snake and leave the deep for the garden of Eden on dry land? Possibly it was the only physical manifestation he could muster at that time.

On Day Three, God specifically raised up land as dry. What if satan feared the dryness, burning with God's fiery wrath within? Jesus revealed they crave moisture for rest, and find neither in dry places (Luke 11:24). That explains why Lucifer and his ilk had ruined original Earth into a dark and formless watery void (Genesis 1:2).

The newly-created air would dry out the enflamed body. Thus, the misty, cooling ground was preferable over the sunlit air and its warming effect. Humidity rising from the ground would cool a ground-slithering body. A serpentine body would be safe.

Another possible benefit of his serpentine physique was to appear harmless. Maybe it camouflaged the burning devil. Without any experience of fire, the humans might have been alerted by the burning body of satan. Cunningly, he wanted to be as innocuous as possible.

DEVIL EVOLUTION

Evolutionary theory applies to satan, not us. He is the one who crawled from the so-called "primordial soup."

Never again in the Bible does he interact with anyone as a snake. By the time of Apostle Paul, satan had even learned how to appear in disguise as an angel of light (2 Corinthians 11:14).

If he was cunning, why didn't he try to look like a person? Adam and Eve knew the Second Person of the Trinity; He walked in the garden with them and made sounds of walking (Genesis 3:8). Was satan afraid to try to mimic such a body?

The serpent spoke. This element causes many to designate this as myth or fable because animals don't talk today. That's like saying it has never rained because it is not raining right now. In fact, if enduring human fiction and pet ownership is any indicator, we expect animals to talk. Is that a vestigial instinct from Eden, when they could converse?

In any case, no surprise is recorded when Eve and Adam heard the serpent speak. Clearly, he spoke in a language they understood.

We are told the serpent was cunning. Whatever his reasons for appearing as a snake, it worked.

THE EVIDENT SUCCESS

The Bible doesn't say what the corrupted Lucifer expected from creatures in God's image. It simply, elegantly declares that they did not resist him. The evidence is all around us and throughout our history.

The two parents of the new race complied with no resistance; no elaborate arguments were necessary to persuade them. This raises important questions to be considered in the coming chapter, "The Law of Consequences."

LIFE-HATER

Jesus warned His persecutors they were exhibiting satan's motives.

He was a murderer from the beginning, and does not stand in the truth, because there is no truth in him. When he speaks a lie, he speaks from his own resources, for he is a liar and the father of it. (John 8:44)

The thief does not come except to steal, and to kill, and to destroy. (John 10:10)

Jesus would have seen that in Genesis 1:1–2, where the exiled rebels ruined original Earth into the formless, watery darkness, void of anything living. That murderous destruction is why Jesus described Lucifer the liar as *"a murderer from the beginning."* Tempting Adam and Eve was not satan's first wickedness, or Jesus would have called him "a liar from the beginning."

The devil had killed, and knew what *die* meant when he heard God tell Adam, *"In the day that you eat of it you shall surely die"* (Genesis 2:17).

The opponents in Eden were his replacement, actually created in God's image and likeness. They had God's breath for their life-force. But if satan the life-hater could produce death again, what a sweet victory he could savor over God.

CHOKEPOINTS

The kingdom of darkness focuses its efforts on chokepoints and bottle-necks which are strictures on free movement. No one can escape confine-ment under their kingdom because would-be escapees cannot get past the tight bottleneck.

The free movement of darkness was restricted by God in the six days. The dry land and division of the watery deep into seas formed bottlenecks on His enemies.

This principle has amazing explanatory power for discerning the actions of unseen tempters. With bottlenecks and chokepoints, they can control large numbers of people by controlling a few.

At Babel, God created every ethnic group, nation, and tribe when He confused language. The chokepoint pattern of satan's hater-kingdom has been replicated in every one (the fourth strategy of darkness, to be explored shortly).

But if satan could dominate the first two human beings somehow, every child would be influenced by that one chokepoint. Possibly no other would be needed. One success with the first two people would impart success over all people ever. No human being ever would escape the influence.

CHAPTER 9

STRATEGY ONE: HEREDITARY CORRUPTION

The *Unseen* Series explores nineteen distinct strategies which satan devised to replace us as Earth's dominators. The first: introducing corruption to infect all human multiplication. Apostle Paul described its success in Romans 5:12–14.

> Therefore, just as through one man sin entered the world, and death through sin, and thus death spread to all men, because all sinned—For until the law sin was in the world, but sin is not imputed when there is no law. Nevertheless death reigned from Adam to Moses, even over those who had not sinned according to the likeness of the transgression of Adam, who is a type of Him who was to come.

What benefit did satan and his kingdom derive from people dying? What would have happened if his strategy had failed? Don't all people die whether the devil is involved? How can hereditary death be a strategy of the fallen Lucifer?

The Bible provides answers that leave

The value of these questions is to consider the event from many different perspectives. Such inquiry is never wasted with God's Word. Puzzles lead us deeper into it. There are many plausible reasons that satan didn't lure them to the tree of life. Any or all could be true. Some mysterious Scriptures may be solved by considering satan's possible reasons.

you in awe of God's wisdom. What He permitted at the very beginning of humanity was not accidental.

WHY NOT THE LIFE TREE?

Tree one was the tree of life. Why didn't satan tempt them to eat from it before or after tree two? For us to live eternally stuck as irredeemable sinners would have been to satan's liking. Why didn't the devil follow such a plan? The pitch would require only a slight change: "God knows that when you eat of these two trees together, you will be like God."

> And the LORD God commanded the man, saying, "Of every tree of the garden you may freely eat; but of the tree of the knowledge of good and evil you shall not eat, for in the day that you eat of it you shall surely die." (Genesis 2:16–17)

God's warning to Adam did not mention the tree of life. Presumably, its function was unknown to Adam and Eve. The serpent could not know about it if his source was God's verbal statement. Instead, satan knew only about the tree God mentioned.

The concept of a tree of life may have eluded Lucifer. He would assume creatures in God's image would be eternal like Him. In hindsight, we know what happened, but the devil may have genuinely believed that God was lying about Adam and Eve's mortality.

LISTENING NO MORE

The devil knew about the knowing tree because God had described its effect of death. Satan may have been unaware of the tree of life.

Another possibility: the serpent knew about the life tree, but feared its fruit would protect them from him. Maybe it would open their eyes to their glory, rather than their nakedness as tree number two would do. Any such outcome would forever stymie his corruption plan.

After their first bite, satan couldn't convince them to eat the life fruit, even if he tried. Tree two brought recognition of their nakedness and perception of the deceiver. *"The serpent deceived me, and I ate"* (Genesis 3:13). The serpent was present when God came; God spoke the punishment directly to him (Genesis 3:14–15). Further complicity with the liar would never be possible.

Maybe he may actually wanted their bodies to die. Isaiah 14 talks about satan's prison; did he relish the humans' death so he could incarcerate their souls there? Shortly we will discover that satanic pattern with the Genesis 6 half-breeds on Earth prior to the Flood.

ONE DISOBEDIENCE ONLY

All these are only possibilities. The Scripture doesn't state why satan neglected the tree of life, but the fact remains: he did. God allowed the life fruit; the devil's perpetual "opposite day" found no value there.

Scarcity was required for the IOU strategist to have leverage, yet Eden had none. Like a veteran trader and armed with IOUs, satan could only use tree number two to offer some inducement Adam and Eve didn't already have.

One disobedience was enough for satan's purposes. The tempter's goal was for them to distrust God.

Our parents never ate fruit from the tree of life. God removed them from it, and then removed it from Earth. We are very glad.

IN THE DARK

We have the Bible revelation about Adam and Eve, their limits, and the results of their sin. In contrast, satan was in the metaphorical dark. He may not have known what to expect.

God had commanded Adam and Eve to multiply—a foreign concept to every heavenly citizen. Angelic beings like satan and his partners are non-sexual and don't reproduce. Whatever *multiply* meant, it was part of people filling and subduing Earth. Such an outcome would make Earth very uncomfortable for the exiled kingdom of darkness.

Would satan have expected childbearing? Human reproduction had not occurred when our parents were banished from Eden and the tree of life. At that time, no sexual intercourse had occurred for our extremely fertile parents.

We know what *multiply* meant, but would satan? Retaining an archangel nature, satan plausibly would be a quick study. Perhaps he watched the birds and the bees, as we say—or better yet, his new Day Five neighbors in the seas, whales and fish.

SATAN INVENTS ABORTION

Preventive action had to be taken to prevent any more image-creatures on Earth—or at least to spoil their ability to replace him. What strategies does a murderer employ to avoid their replacements multiplying?

Corrupting the parents would either abort the reproduction of God's image, or fill Earth with poison copies of Him. Tempting Adam and Eve was the first chokepoint strategy of satan: influencing many through a few, or only two.

If the fallen archangel reached Adam and Eve, it would impact all their multiplication. What did he expect to happen if he could succeed?

POSSIBLE RESULTS

The devil could only guess what God would do. Consider this: rebellion by beings in God's image would be far worse than the rebellion of a mere archangel like Lucifer.

As an angelically rational being, he might have ranked his preferred results, just as we do. He had painful experience to draw upon: God's instance justice upon him.

Best-case scenario: Adam and Eve would both sin, and God would destroy them and forget the whole affair. If that occurred, the leader of darkness could rebuild his disrupted exile and restore his preferred cooling deep. After all, satan had it the way he liked it before Day One.

The earth was without form, and void; and darkness was on the face of the deep. (Genesis 1:2)

However, the heavenly host had never seen such a response. The Bible does not document any instance of God destroying a race, not even the rebel angels.

Second-best scenario: God could exile them somewhere, as Lucifer had been. Maybe God would even fill the pair with the fire of God's wrath. After all, that's what God had done to the angelic rebels.

Next best: God could stop the multiplication. Certainly God would not want the spoiled humans to multiply, would He? Satan spoiling them might eliminate any further competition.

Also acceptable: if only one of the pair had distrusted God and eaten the fruit. Had not Adam and Eve eaten it together, their division would be profound. Nine hundred years of marriage lay ahead for them before her death.

One would be alive in spirit, free from shame; the other would be dead in spirit, shamed about nakedness, wearing unnecessary clothes, and unable to walk with God in the garden. Intimacy would be elusive. Apostle Paul used the phrase *"unequally yoked"* (2 Corinthians 6:14). What a mess their children would be.

Worst best-case scenario: even if God multiplied the humans, spoiling the parents would spoil all their copies. In that case, satan's later work would be much simpler. If Satan triumphed in Eden, all image-creatures would share the same vulnerability.

Whatever occurred, satan could pollute God's image-multiplication. If darkness could induce spirit death in Adam and Eve, their spirit death would multiply. So much for filling the earth with God's image.

As we know, the worst-best-case happened. Our first parents multiplied and filled the Earth with copies of their deathful selves. That's why Adam and Eve were the first chokepoint used by darkness. That bottleneck of inherited corruption stands between every person ever born and God our Creator.

God placed our first parents within reach of the master tempter—and vulnerable.

THE MOMENT OF CHOICE

Now the serpent was more cunning than any beast of the field which the LORD God had made. And he said to the woman, "Has God indeed said, 'You shall not eat of every tree of the garden'?"

And the woman said to the serpent, "We may eat the fruit of the trees of the garden; but of the fruit of the tree which is in the midst of the garden, God has said, 'You shall not eat it, nor shall you touch it, lest you die.'"

Then the serpent said to the woman, "You will not surely die. For God knows that in the day you eat of it your eyes will be opened, and you will be like God, knowing good and evil." (Genesis 3:1–5)

CHAPTER 10

DISCERNING
TEMPTATION

The Bible never describes love and covenant between God and angelic beings. When we say God is love, it's only evident in His dealings with us. One result of creating us is manifesting His nature of love. In ways that the rebels had never imagined, people can enjoy covenant intimacy and partnership with God Almighty.

He welcomes our race. He breathed into our father's nostrils and hand-crafted our mother from the man's rib. The resurrected Jesus, now outside our timeline, intimately engaged with us and walked with us. And He knits together every one of us in our mother's womb.

Seeing this intimate engagement would be completely foreign and deeply threatening to the devil and his rebel partners. What a humiliation: those who thought to replace God are themselves replaced by a meek creature, formed from dirt, in God's image.

The cunning satan began his takedown with a question. The sinister question seems innocuous enough, merely a matter of facts. Yet his unspoken premise of God's untrustworthiness imposes its pattern on every one of us. Now all our instincts are to replace God by trusting ourselves.

Look, all you who kindle a fire,
Who encircle yourselves with sparks:
Walk in the light of your fire and in the sparks you have kindled—
This you shall have from My hand:
You shall lie down in torment. (Isaiah 50:11)

Only Jesus maintained the integrity of obedience against satan's sneaky questions. As He described Himself, *"I am meek and lowly"* (Matthew 11:29). That's why He could challenge His worst enemies to point out any sin in Him (John 8:48).

FREE REIN VERSUS RESTRICTED ZONE

The free rein of satan was gone after the six twenty-four-hour days of Genesis 1. Instead of cooling themselves wherever they pleased, cooling shrank to one restricted zone, the seas. They supposed themselves qualified to replace Him, and rebelled. Yet here they were, imprisoned in a newly crowded sea, their venerable leader barely able to venture onto dry land as a snake.

God's homemaking for our first parents was a very noticeable contrast to the newly confined kingdom of darkness. The verdant garden was the home for the two image-creatures, with lush fruit and giant springs, aromatic and lined with sparkling jewels. Adam and Eve could eat from any tree but one (Genesis 2:17). Theirs was a situation of abundance, not scarcity.

Now, Adam and Eve could do as they pleased. The restrictions targeted Satan, not them.

Discern the pattern in yourself where you feel restricted, clamped down, restrained, and limited. Only satan oversees a prison, the ultimate symbol of restriction. Jesus' mission was to release people from it.

Your voluntary discipleship to Jesus may be restrictive for you. David described feeling hemmed in by God's hand (Psalm 139:5). Jesus chose His limiting submission to the Father (John 8:26). But within the boundaries of obedience to His love, the truth sets us free.

If you abide in My word, you are My disciples indeed. And you shall know the truth, and the truth shall make you free. (John 8:31–32)

PROJECTION

But the king of darkness projected his plight upon them. He suggestively unnerved *them* with what only *he* suffered.

Has God indeed said, "You shall not eat of every tree of the garden"? (Genesis 3:1)

God said no such thing, not even close. God said, "You may," and satan quotes it as, "You shall not." Think of the fabled Little League baseball dads. The overzealous one kept yelling at his child at the plate, "Don't strike out!" In contrast, the positive dad encouraged his batter: "You can hit it!"

Compare satan's caricature with what God actually said to the pair.

Satan: Has God indeed said, "You shall not eat of every tree of the garden"? (Genesis 3:1)

God: "Of every tree of the garden you may freely eat." (Genesis 2:17)

The devil purposely worded his question with a sneaky, hidden assumption that they are restricted. It presumes the two people suffer prohibitions and boundaries similar to his own.

Think of where you believe scarcity over abundance. Running about or worrying shows your agreement with satan, who needs you to believe scarcity so he has leverage in your life. Compare that to our Father's promise to provide; He needs no leverage and makes no threat.

> To understand temptation, we can examine the wording of satan's question. Our first clue: it is at odds with reality. To entertain his questions requires us to discount or even ignore the plain reality that is before us.

Therefore do not worry, saying, "What shall we eat?" or "What shall we drink?" or "What shall we wear?" For after all these things the Gentiles seek. For your heavenly Father knows that you need all these things. But seek first the kingdom of God and His righteousness, and all these things shall be added to you. (Matthew 6:31–33)

Scarcity is at the very core of his inquiry. The question, *as satan worded it,* prevents any answer containing abundance. The premise that satan wants to implant: God is miserly, withholding from them to benefit Himself.

SHE SAW WITHOUT SEEING

So when the woman saw that the tree was good for food, that it was pleasant to the eyes, and a tree desirable to make one wise, she took of its fruit and ate. She also gave to her husband with her, and he ate. (Genesis 3:6)

Each quality Eve observed was God's work; He made those desirable qualities and declared them good (Genesis 2:9). Her observation was accurate. Like the undeniable fact that the serpent was not dead, the tree's benefits were undeniable.

But tree number two was the wrong thing to examine. Neither she nor her mate scrutinized the serpent or his claims. God had given them everything else in abundance, but never mind that. Instead, they adopted the lie that God was really out for Himself, and they had to take care of themselves.

Eve's study of the tree confirmed what little truth satan's lie contained. The lie organized all the truthful evidence into a wrong action. Jesus used the eye parable to alert us to this.

> The lamp of the body is the eye. If therefore your eye is good, your whole body will be full of light. But if your eye is bad, your whole body will be full of darkness. If therefore the light that is in you is darkness, how great is that darkness! (Matthew 6:22–23)

The sociological term for this is *confirmation bias*. Once a person adopts a premise or belief, everything evidence confirms the belief. Adam and Eve now believed that God had lied.

They multiplied that premise into you and me. We more readily see what we lack than what we have, our limits more than our freedoms. You may see no reason for God to withhold something from you. You can believe He is holding back, keeping something for Himself and away from you—like Adam and Eve believed.

Sadly, our own assessments repeat this logic around the clock. No wonder we struggle with doubt; we adopt the devil's premise. So much for believing God is a God of love; we give the lie to that pablum in all our self-reliance.

Temptation is often disguised within God's good. The miracleworking, demon-delivering prophets of Matthew 7:22 fell for it. The satanic super-apostles of 2 Corinthians 11:13–15 were seducing people from the gospel. Like the Judaizers that Apostle Paul cursed in Galatians 1:7–8, all these couched their temptation in the cloak of prized spiritual or religious benefits.

BLACK OR WHITE?

> Then the serpent said to the woman, "You will not surely die. For God knows that in the day you eat of it your eyes will be opened, and you will be like God, knowing good and evil." (Genesis 3:4–5)

The enemy of humanity now switches to assertive statements. Eve opened the door by responding to his question.

Was satan accurate to say they would not die? Would their eyes truly open? Would they really be like God? Did the first humans even understand these ideas?

It's often said that satan trades in half-truths, and we must be alert to the false mixed with the good as we resist him. However, penetrating beneath the surface, we admit satan is fully truthful, within the encyclopedia of his own existence. His assertions are accurate, in a world defined by his egocentric vanity. Let's examine his implied lies.

AS SEEN REPEATEDLY

The enemies use words whose definitions they create within their own outlook. Reality turns on words. "Through the Word of God was everything made that has been made.... He upholds all things by his powerful word" (John 1:3; Hebrews 1:3). Darkness uses words also. Their words are accurate—within the closed universe of their own miserable existence.

"DIE?"

Lucifer and his partner angels rebelled; now look at them. The serpent's question uses a distorting vocabulary. It is the very glossary of hell's so-called life. As angels, the fallen cannot die. His statement is accurate.

We know now, these rebellious spirits only *live* as in *exist*. Within their bodies are the fiery stones of holiness which once surrounded God's throne (Ezekiel 28:14, 18). Like the bush Moses saw, they burn without being consumed. They exist with permanent insufficiency and inward burning.

Adam and Eve lacked discernment for these different nuances of *die* and *live*. Whatever fire raged within the serpent was not meaningful to them. The newest Christian today knows more about living and existing than that first pair, who had no warning.

We would consider him, cut off from the Bread of Life forever, to be quite the fool for talking about "life" in any form. Yet satan discerns the new image-creatures won't notice his brazen bravado. They did not ask the simplest questions such as, "What do you mean by 'die'?"

"SEE?"

Would their eyes be opened? This was satan's claim, using God's own phrase: *"in the day you eat of it."*

They did not ask questions of satan. Any scrutiny at all would have consoled us about our first parents, but they applied none. If God had warned them about satan (as Scripture warns us), they could have chosen several comebacks to rebut satan's sales pitch:

What are you hiding? Why are you telling me? What's in it for you? What could go wrong for me? Opened to what? What will we see? Who says it will be desirable to see it? Are you saying we don't see now? Tell us what we are missing.

Our parents weren't warned about satan, but we are. Yet people still accept their hollow promises without scrutiny; we willfully subject ourselves by agreeing with them. Examining temptation disarms the misdirection and exposes the unseen practitioners.

Adam might have looked unintelligent to satan during the animal-naming process. Whatever doubt remained would vanish after satan saw how easy it was to fool them. The devil did the first one-time close, thanks to Adam's passivity while Eve entertained satan's assertions.

> The devil used the word day, revealing his adaptation to the timekeeping, imposed by God's Day One division of light and night. Being eons older than the people, and at least seven days older on the schedule of days, satan knew the meaning of day before the pair did.

"LIKE GOD?"

The pitch to the pair included a nuclear attack: *"You will be like God."*

Perhaps this is the saddest of all the ploys they fell for, because they were *already* like God, made in His image and likeness. He had breathed into them. No other creature in heaven or earth was so like God as they were. The devil is totally unlike God, but Adam and Eve were far superior.

Yet the burning blindness of satan's seduction convinced Adam and

Eve they were not, in fact, like God. They were missing something. God had withheld something desirable from them and lied to them so they wouldn't desire it.

Despite walking with God in the garden, despite working together on naming animals, despite filling Adam's insufficiency with Eve, the two still believed the enemy. They agreed with satan that they could be *more* like God, and that God had restricted them to protect Himself.

Ironically, satan's attractive weapon was exactly what he sought: to be like God. What they already were, he desired and attempted, never to attain. God quotes the ambition of Lucifer in Isaiah 14:14:

I will ascend above the heights of the clouds,
I will be like the Most High.

Unseen enemies try to replicate their replacement grid in us. Consider where you feel pressure to be or do something only God can. What lack do you feel they are using for leverage? Consider how available our abundance from God still is.

Ho! Everyone who thirsts,
Come to the waters;
And you who have no money,
Come, buy and eat.
Yes, come, buy wine and milk
Without money and without price.
Why do you spend money for what is not
  bread,
And your wages for what does not satisfy?
Listen carefully to Me, and eat what is good,
And let your soul delight itself in abundance.
  (Isaiah 55:1–2)

We Christians have the same birthright as Adam and Eve. Jesus told everyone watching when Zaccheus came out of the tree, *"The Son of man came to seek and to save that which was lost"* (Luke 19:10). Jesus had read about Adam and Eve's fall, just like we have. One of His prime motives as Redeemer was to recapture what was intended for the Edenic life of covenant and stolen by satan's success.

In two short sentences, meeting at a tree, this prince of evil projected his restrictions upon the free Adam and Eve. With his scarcity, he obscured their abundance. He offered them hell's sunglasses to replace their unimpaired sight. Blinding them to their own God-likeness, satan imparted an unsatisfiable, impossible ambition—just like his own.

"GOD IS OUT FOR HIMSELF"

The reactor that produced satan's nuclear deception for our first parents was in three words: *"For God knows."* Within that simple phrase, the devil offers them his universe of self-interest, insecurity, and betrayal.

Projecting his own definitions upon God, satan is right. "God will not give me what I want; He is reserving status for Himself; when I challenged Him, He cast me onto earth with fire in my nature."

So satan suggests God is holding out that same way on Adam and Eve. The devil projects the God whom he knows and suffers. For the rebellious angels, it is accurate. True, they conveniently dismiss their own responsibility in the matter, but the status is the same.

His dark armies project their plight upon you and me as well. They repeat the same lie to every human born: God is out for Himself at your expense.

God forgive us for believing them.

"FOR GOD KNOWS"

If satan had stopped with the tree question, God's supposed unfaithfulness would be about that tree only. They could avoid the issue: "He gave us all so many good trees; we don't need this one."

But by saying, *"For God knows,"* satan is talking about habits. Whether it's one tree or many, today or tomorrow, satan insinuates that God *habitually* holds back, limits, restricts, and otherwise prevents anyone from encroaching on His self-interest. That's true in satan's universe. It is not true in ours.

This ploy is a frequently used logical trick, from small to large. Often, you can find unseen tempters where one problem gets magnified into a problematic life. "Eat any tree but one" becomes "don't eat any tree."

The falsity at the one tree in Eden invades many people's lives. Unknowingly using the devil's deluding definitions, we can conclude that God does not love.

Like Job, we too can endure a few losses and still trust God's management. But when losses mount, inner turmoil rages, and impossibility looms everywhere, our unseen enemies try to persuade us that God *habitually* withholds from us, betrays our interests, and serves His own. We can even consider God our victimizer, as Job likened Him to a dog, and himself as God's chewbone.

Adam and Eve illustrate the multigenerational cost of believing such a wicked persuasion. Thank God we can repent, as He helped Job repent.

"GOD ALWAYS DOES THIS"

A successful sleight-of-hand artist diverts your attention from his actual actions. The devil also did that to Adam and Eve. The trick worked, so the kingdom of darkness keeps using it.

Technically, the devil is addressing privileges centered on only one tree. He cannot compete in the matter of the other trees; the humans know they are free to eat them.

Nor can the devil debate any scarcity in their existence. Their garden is full of food and beauty. Gushing aromatic springs flow into glistening riverbeds. The neighboring tree of life was right at hand. "Let's eat that one instead," Adam could have replied.

Sometimes one issue can color everything else; one worry can steal the joy from all the good. Our tempters encourage such mono-focus, giving them control over every issue through the one.

The disarming occurs by separating the problem issue from the good. Apostle Paul used that separating principle for a doorway to God's peace. Distinguish the troubling issue in prayer and let God know (Philippians 4:6). Meditate on the good in everything else (4:8). The result of both is God's peace filling us.

In order to compete, the devil must keep them focused on this one tree. He must make it an issue of scarcity and obscure their abundant supply of other trees. Through that controlled focus, satan drives a truck of lies about God's habits: *"For God knows."*

"YOU'RE ON YOUR OWN"

By accepting that lie about God, we must embrace its corollary: we must take care of our own interests. We deeply welcome this lie; consider the symptoms.

Doubt plagues many Christians because they do not trust God to care for their interests like His own. They believe what satan says, that God is out for Himself at our expense. The devilish words span the generations, penetrate our minds, and cripple our faith. They haunt us in every impulse and decision. The only remedy is the Word of God, both in writing and within us by His Spirit.

People might verbally parrot 1 John 4:8: *"God is love."* But it just papers over our agreement with satan, because we deeply suspect God is holding out on us somehow. We accept the lying belief that the pressure is on us.

It's one reason we fear going all out for Jesus; we believe God is out for Himself at our expense. To put it another way: we agree with satan. As a new Christian in the 1970s, the fear was being called to be missionaries to Africa instead of pursuing the yuppie dream. Africa might have been safer for my friends, who became distracted by the cares of this life.

> Do not love the world or the things in the world. If anyone loves the world, the love of the Father is not in him. For all that is in the world—the lust of the flesh, the lust of the eyes, and the pride of life—is not of the Father but is of the world. (1 John 2:15–16)

Adam and Eve swallowed the poison pill premise: *God is out for Himself. I've got to take care of myself.*

Seeing, dying, knowing, and being like God were not decisive for the pair. When they permitted the possibility that God was holding out on them, they passively complied with what satan said.

Watch your own thoughts and behaviors with this discernment. Where do you behave as if you're alone? There lies your hidden covenants or agreement with darkness. Disarm them with confession and repentance. The lying belief will quickly lose its grip; you will quickly see how safe it is with your Father.

This is the first documented use of the popular political trick: accuse your righteous enemy of what you did wrong, before he can expose you for it. Then, when he exposes what you really did, it just seems like sour grapes and makes the good guy look like the bad guy.

Adam and Eve opened the door to all their offspring when they passively agreed with satan.

> Through one man sin entered the world, and death through sin, and thus death spread to all men, because all sinned. (Romans 5:12)

IT COULD GO EITHER WAY

Notice: satan did not elaborate on the tree of knowledge with Eve. He may not have known its properties and may not have cared. His standard of success was low. They need only disobey God by trusting themselves, as he had done.

Lucifer was never omniscient; the exiled satan does not know everything. God's counsels are unknown to him. The serpent ironically comes to the knowing tree with ignorance. He was talking with the first two creatures ever in God's own image. There were no patterns to draw upon, except for what had occurred to him and his rebel partners.

Why did the tempter choose that particular tree? Because God audibly spoke about the restriction on the fruit of that one tree. Adam and Eve's limits and capabilities were unknown to the devil. When God walked with them, satan was not privy to their communion.

Nor can he eavesdrop on our private times with the Spirit of God who indwells us. That's a reason we have daily quiet times with God. With time and maturity, the habit neutralizes pervasive and internal sneaky lies.

The devil may well have expected a far greater challenge from a creature in God's image. He may have expected several rebuffs, and planned multiple attacks upon the obedience of the pair. It's plausible that the devil was ready to deploy analytical logic and persuasion. His arsenal may have included far more complex schemes to use—if needed.

None were—so easily did the two people agree with satan.

DEVIL VICTORY

Perhaps to satan's surprise, Eve bought the pitch immediately, as did her husband. The Bible reports no scrutiny by either of them. The passivity of their compliance is complete.

Even children nowadays would say, "You go first." After all, God had prohibited nothing but eating the fruit. The tree itself was not forbidden. Smell it, touch it, use its fruit to play catch or go bowling—everything was fair game except eating it.

This is easy behavior; we do it all the time. Scrub your ovens; you know not to eat the acidic cleaner. Put medicine in your eyes that becomes poison if ingested. At the gas pump, easily avoid the fuel type that ruins your engine.

It's easy to imagine how much glee satan found in the easy, quick fall of the two. He might have been prepared for at least some argument, some pushback, some skepticism. After all, God had dominated Lucifer at every turn, and they were in God's image.

Instead, the wicked archangel finds the two quite amenable to his suggestions:

God is out for Himself, not them;
God is holding out on them at their expense;
God is restricting them as He had satan.

SATAN'S VENGEANCE

Seeking shade, Satan emerged as a serpent on the cool ground. Compared to his perfect pre-fall glory, his appearance was unimpressive. Yet he found that the creature God created actually listened to him.

Satan's rejoicing and vengeance against God would have been immense. The ugly snake had spoiled God's image forever. The eternal souls were created to dominate the earth and overcome satan's rule. Instead, they now occupied satan's universe of misery.

This is a victory for darkness, a revenge upon God. All alone, Satan obliterated any possibility of what could have been. He poisoned all that God intended. By introducing corruption, an Earth dominated by man in God's image and on His behalf would never happen.

CHAPTER 11

THE LAW OF CONSEQUENCES

The serpentine satan successfully replicated his motive in Adam and Eve. In the one bite, they replaced God with their own wisdom. Distrusting God's warning about dying, they cast Him off. They expected to be wiser. They replaced God with themselves.

The devil soon learned the consequences his trickery had earned for Adam and Eve, and so did they.

WHAT DID THEY KNOW?

Did they know they were replacing God as Lucifer had attempted? Did they knowingly replace their covenant with God in favor of a covenant with satan? The account doesn't say that Adam or Eve had such understanding.

They had not fully grasped the concepts of good and evil. In fact, the word *sin* appears nowhere in the passage—not in satan's pitch nor in God's judgment nor in their admission.

An age-old principle of law undergirds the gospel of Jesus. Whether Adam and Eve consciously disdained God or knew what they were doing is of little consequence. Their action disdained Him.

UNINTENDED

The law of unintended consequences became Adam and Eve's accuser when God confronted them. They admitted being deceived, but they didn't plan on it being this painful.

Then the LORD God called to Adam and said to him, "Where are you?"

So he said, "I heard Your voice in the garden, and I was afraid because I was naked; and I hid myself."

And He said, "Who told you that you were naked? Have you eaten from the tree of which I commanded you that you should not eat?"

Then the man said, "The woman whom You gave to be with me, she gave me of the tree, and I ate."

And the LORD God said to the woman, "What is this you have done?"

The woman said, "The serpent deceived me, and I ate...."

To the woman He said:

"I will greatly multiply your sorrow and your conception;

In pain you shall bring forth children;

Your desire shall be for your husband,

And he shall rule over you."

Then to Adam He said, "Because you have heeded the voice of your wife, and have eaten from the tree of which I commanded you, saying, 'You shall not eat of it':

"Cursed is the ground for your sake;

In toil you shall eat of it

All the days of your life.

Both thorns and thistles it shall bring forth for you,

And you shall eat the herb of the field.

In the sweat of your face you shall eat bread

Till you return to the ground,

For out of it you were taken;

For dust you are,

And to dust you shall return." (Genesis 3:9–13, 16–19)

AS SEEN TODAY & YESTERDAY

The ill-begotten "wisdom" from the tree is visible throughout human history. Our race habitually falls for the strategies of darkness.

This wouldn't be the case if Adam and Eve had acquired real knowledge of good and evil. But they corrupted their wisdom, just as Lucifer's had been.

What our race has done since Eden is even worse than the sin of Adam and Eve. Unlike them, we have historical proof of evil's destruction—centuries and centuries of proof. Yet humanity agrees with satan ever more tightly.

A BAD UNIVERSE

Just as readily as our parents agreed with the serpent, they also learned that the so-called life on their own was quite an unpleasant one. The issue wasn't just the nakedness. It was the broken relationship with God.

Adam and Eve adopted the premise of satan's universe, that God restricted them and told them something untrue because He habitually restricts others and protects His own position. So Adam and Eve strike their own path along the corollary: "If it's to be, it's up to me." They disdain God's only prohibition.

Seeing their shame, living in fear, broken from God, and exiled from the garden of free food to the ground of hard labor—what a nasty universe they entered.

BACKFIRE!

Little did satan realize, God purposely created the pair so vulnerable as He did.

Our susceptibility to satan's deception resulted from God's eternal decree even before angels existed. Our sin was a step to the intended consequence: the death of the Second Person in a body descended from the original pair.

The Lamb was *"slain before the foundation of the world"*—in an eternal NOW that is independent of our sequential time (Revelation 13:8).

EXILE

God had exiled Lucifer from his original heavenly home. Now the image-creatures also suffered God's exile: cast out of Eden.

The Lord God sent him out of the garden of Eden to till the ground from which he was taken. So He drove out the man; and He placed cherubim at the east of the garden of Eden, and a flaming sword which turned every way, to guard the way to the tree of life. (Genesis 3:23–24)

Lucifer's exile is eternal. But God wants people back and provided Jesus to propitiate His wrath. Everyone who chooses Him will see the tree of life again.

The Son of Man has come to seek and to save that which was lost. (Luke 19:10)

In the middle of its street, and on either side of the river, was the tree of life, which bore twelve fruits, each tree yielding its fruit every month. The leaves of the tree were for the healing of the nations. (Revelation 22:2)

HONOR FOR IMAGE-CHOICE

We talk about glory, righteousness, truth, and covenant. They each presume honor in relationship. Earlier, we saw how God forces us to choose. By creating us with choice power, He honored our choices. Many difficult Scriptures become clear when we recognize His respect for human choice.

The Bible confirms what experience reveals: we select among alternatives without even knowing it. Our choices may be both actions and failures to act. We determine our attitudes. We willfully hold beliefs about ourselves and reality, whether taught or inherited. A choice in line with God's revelation is always available, but we may be unaware we are choosing at all.

Consequences directly result from God's honor for our choice power. If we select what pleases Him, He will honor it. If our choice disdains Him, He will honor it. His choices have eternal consequence—and so do ours. Each little choice we make influences the attitude of God Almighty. It is a weighty glory to bear, this power of choice.

Our minds are powerful. Eve's reasoning led to her choice.

So when the woman saw that the tree was good for food, that it was pleasant to the eyes, and a tree desirable to make one wise.... (Genesis 3:6)

A watchful eye on our reasoning helps us discern rationalizations. "It won't matter. It's just a white lie. Just one bit, as an exception." These rationalizations are tempter-encouraged. *The heart chooses and the mind excuses.*

Disarm them by yielding your alternatives to God, right in the moment. "Holy Spirit, what do You say about this?" Simply asking is a choice to welcome His partnership.

THREE CHOICES

Apostle Paul wrote about three possible choices we can make, in Romans 2:4–11. The first is doing good, and when a person—Christian and otherwise—chooses good, God honors that choice.

[He renders] glory, honor, and peace to everyone who works what is good, to the Jew first and also to the Greek. For there is no partiality with God. (Romans 2:10–11)

The second choice includes our self-seeking, disobedient, and immoral choices, a.k.a. sin.

To those who are self-seeking and do not obey the truth, but obey unrighteousness—[He renders] indignation and wrath, tribulation and anguish, on every soul of man who does evil, of the Jew first and also of the Greek. (Romans 2:8–9)

The third choice is to repent of our ungodly choices. As we saw earlier, neither Adam nor Eve expressed a recorded repentance. But we can, and we do.

The goodness of God leads you to repentance. (Romans 2:4)

REPENTANCE PERSISTS

True repentance manifests in following Jesus. We meekly accept that God desires our friendship. We also respect His right to set the terms, and submit to His requirements. Such repentance includes its own persistency.

Consider the goodness and severity of God: on those who fell, severity; but toward you, goodness, if you continue in His goodness. Otherwise you also will be cut off. (Romans 11:22)

Since we are receiving a kingdom which cannot be shaken, let us have grace, by which we may serve God acceptably with reverence and godly fear. (Hebrews 12:28)

Remember therefore how you have received and heard; hold fast and repent.... As many as I love, I rebuke and chasten. Therefore be zealous and repent. (Revelation 3:3, 10)

Repentance is also comprehensive. The poor-in-spirit mourner recognizes that our own nature welcomes disobedience. We give opportunity to the ancient evil spirits.

Draw near to God and He will draw near to you. Cleanse your hands, you sinners; and purify your hearts, you double-minded. Lament and mourn and weep! Let your laughter be turned to mourning and your joy to gloom. Humble yourselves in the sight of the Lord, and He will lift you up. (James 4:8–10)

CONSEQUENCES PERSIST

Repentance does not override the consequences of our poor choices. In Isaiah 50, God warned about trusting in ourselves. When we light our own fire, torment can result.

Do not be deceived, God is not mocked; for whatever a man sows, that he will also reap. For he who sows to his flesh will of the flesh reap corruption, but he who sows to the Spirit will of the Spirit reap everlasting life. And let us not grow weary while doing good, for in due season we shall reap if we do not lose heart. (Galatians 6:7–9)

For there is nothing covered that will not be revealed, nor hidden that will not be known. Therefore whatever you have spoken in the dark will be heard in the light, and what you have spoken in the ear in inner rooms will be proclaimed on the housetops. (Luke 12:2–3)

For we must all appear before the judgment seat of Christ, that each one may receive the things done in the body, according to what he has done, whether good or bad. (2 Corinthians 5:10)

Exhort one another daily, while it is called "Today," lest any of you be hardened through the deceitfulness of sin. (Hebrews 3:13)

REPENTANCE IS NOT TRADING

The consequences of one poor choice have ruined many people's ambitions and blocked off their ideal lives. Repentance may be faster when we see the destruction of our decisions. But true repentance is not bargaining. We don't negotiate as if repenting gives us usable credit; we don't use God to get out of the jams we make for ourselves.

We repent out of respect for Him and what He deserves from us. The law of consequences is the reality He created. The true mourner yields to it.

He honors our choices with their consequences. This is a powerful motive to mature in our relationship with Him, so we can choose well.

CHAPTER 12

PATTERNS OF CONSEQUENCE

An infinite variety of times, places, and personalities characterize human life. In contrast, the patterns of our consequence are consistent and simple. The following patterns equip you to discern unseen tempters far more quickly.

SELF-CENTEREDNESS

God Himself handcrafted the parents of our race. He worked and walked and spoke with intimate attentiveness to them. They had abundance without scarcity.

Yet they showed more love for their own interests. What was prominent in Eve's reasoning about the tree? Only benefits for themselves, absent any hint of love for their Creator.

This result-pattern signals how highly we prioritize our interests—and how little His. Consider all the signs of His love: He saved us, filled us with His Spirit, and gave us the promises in His Word. Yet we panic so readily, and scramble to take care of our own interests.

People often opt for a spiritual solution. It's good to be and act Christian, but even then, we can use God for our own self-interests. It's self-centered to *use* anyone, particularly Him. We must mature from this babyish disrespect for God.

We disarm this self-centeredness with Scriptures that impart a passion to know God. There are many; we have cited Paul's passion in Philippians 3:7–11. A sampling of the Psalms provides these.

But his delight is in the law of the LORD,
And in His law he meditates day and night. (Psalm 1:2)

O my soul, you have said to the LORD,
"You are my Lord,
My goodness is nothing apart from You." (Psalm 16:4)

Oh, taste and see that the LORD is good;
Blessed is the man who trusts in Him! (Psalm 34:8)

Create in me a clean heart, O God,
And renew a steadfast spirit within me.
Do not cast me away from Your presence,
And do not take Your Holy Spirit from me. (Psalm 51:10–11)

Whom have I in heaven but You?
And there is none upon earth that I desire besides You. (Psalm 73:25)

How sweet are Your words to my taste,
Sweeter than honey to my mouth! (Psalm 119:103)

RIGHTS

An unseen pattern closely related to self-centeredness is to demand our rights. In the Western world, our founding documents, won by blood and hard work, enshrine human rights.

Yet no one talks much about Creator rights. Our rights dominate our thinking and conversations. We even use rights in attempted bargains with spiritual beings, God and satan alike.

Darkness will feign respect for your rights and sucker you by promising to honor them. They welcome misguided efforts to claim your rights with them.

God cleanses us of this pattern. To do it, He will leave you apparently abandoned, to expose every false belief that He owes you. *Owe* is the key word, the O in IOU. "I tithe, I go to church, I submit to leaders, I study the Bible, I ... I ... I...." Have you ever felt He didn't act as you expected? It can reveal your hidden IOU patterns.

When you see this in yourself, quickly confess what it is: focusing on your rights rather than His. Jesus told us the disarming attitudes in the Beatitudes, and illustrated it with the parable of Luke 17:7–10. The power of our faith lies in our submission to the rights of God.

> And which of you, having a servant plowing or tending sheep, will say to him when he has come in from the field, "Come at once and sit down to eat"? But will he not rather say to him, "Prepare something for my supper, and gird yourself and serve me till I have eaten and drunk, and afterward you will eat and drink"? Does he thank that servant because he did the things that were commanded him? I think not. So likewise you, when you have done all those things which you are commanded, say, "We are unprofitable servants. We have done what was our duty to do."

JUDGMENT

God's respect for our choices says, "Go right ahead and see what happens." The judgment of consequences lets us have more of what we choose.

As we age, our innumerable small choices come home to roost. Decades of small decisions produce a tsunami of irresistible proclivities. The youthful adaptability gives way to the aged rigidity of our most frequent choices.

Our first parents accepted satan's premise. Suddenly, they had a newfound knowledge of good and evil. But they were no wiser.

> Professing to be wise, they became fools. (Romans 1:22)

In Ezekiel 28:17, Lucifer corrupted his wisdom to secure his own splendor. Adam and Eve chose likewise, as do we when choosing sin. This always separates us from God, as it did them with awfully destructive consequences.

> Even as they did not like to retain God in their knowledge, God gave them over to a debased mind, to do those things which are not fitting; being filled with all unrighteousness, sexual immorality, wickedness, covetousness, maliciousness; full of envy, murder, strife, deceit, evil-mindedness; they are whisperers, backbiters, haters of God, violent, proud, boasters, inventors of evil things, disobedient to parents, undiscerning, untrustworthy, unloving, unforgiving, unmerciful; who, knowing the righteous judgment of God, that those who practice

such things are deserving of death, not only do the same but also approve of those who practice them. (Romans 1:28–32)

SHARED CONSEQUENCES

Like dogs are bolder in packs, people derive encouragement to sin from each other. They also have to face the consequences together.

Then the eyes of both of them were opened, and they knew that they were naked. (Genesis 3:7)

Despite eating in sequence, neither Adam nor Eve, the head and first disobeyer respectively, was the first to see their nakedness. They shared the eye-opening. The consequence was common and instant to them both.

Discerning our unseen tempters requires alertness to group sin as well. Without vigilance, we quickly become a mob of sinners, egging each other on.

Coming chapters reveal how our unseen enemies influence our people groups through bottlenecks and chokepoints. The net effect of that strategy is that groups share the same sin patterns, like families share genes.

SUDDEN PERCEPTION

Genesis 3:7 above uses two parallel statements: eyes opened, nakedness known. How closed were their eyes before they ate it? How open were their eyes afterward? And what eyes, anyway?

Their bodies weren't obscured. Adam was well aware of Eve's body when God brought her to him. He could see that her body was like his in kind, unlike the animals.

The nudity wasn't new, but the judging perspective was. Open eyes implies suddenly noticing the importance of something previously taken for granted. Having our eyes opened is a pattern of consequence. Like theirs, it can be very unpleasant.

The disciples who walked with resurrected Jesus to Emmaus experienced such an eyeopening (Luke 24:31). We all experience our eyes being opened as a burst of new perception. We do not mean that we were blind beforehand, but rather unperceptive of something now unavoidably evident and significant.

However, we can entrust our perception to God, the great revealer. When we partner with Him, it makes our eye good.

> The lamp of the body is the eye. If therefore your eye is good, your whole body will be full of light. But if your eye is bad, your whole body will be full of darkness. (Matthew 6:22–23)

Jesus opened the eyes of the blind man in John 9. He next warned that the seeing can be blinder than the blind.

> Then some of the Pharisees who were with Him heard these words, and said to Him, "Are we blind also?"
> Jesus said to them, "If you were blind, you would have no sin; but now you say, 'We see.' Therefore your sin remains." (John 9:40–41)

The shocking shame made Adam and Eve attach great significance to their nakedness. No return was possible; they couldn't *not* see their nakedness. Their only way forward was confession and meekness, which Jesus said was blessed. The same is true for us.

STERILE WISDOM

Eve saw that the fruit was good for making one wise, and rationalized the gain would be worth the disobedience. But after eating it, how wise did they become, and how much did they know?

Was it total, or limited? Was it all good, or all evil, or mixed, and in what proportion? The text does not answer specifically, but their behavior shows only a partial knowledge increase, and undesirable at that.

The promise of wisdom and greater control of our lives can be a tempter tactic. Discern their presence by the suggested independence from God, doing it yourself, lighting your own fire. Disarm their tactic with the repeated biblical guidance to ask God and await His answer.

> God gives wisdom and knowledge and joy to a man who is good in His sight. (Ecclesiastes 2:26)

> Trust in the LORD with all your heart,
> And lean not on your own understanding;
> In all your ways acknowledge Him,
> And He shall direct your paths. (Proverbs 3:5–6)

If any of you lacks wisdom, let him ask of God, who gives to all liberally and without reproach, and it will be given to him. (James 1:5)

But self-smarting ourselves has a nasty pattern of consequence: more awareness of our deficiencies. Their eyes being opened didn't give understanding of God's grace. The knowing fruit did not yield character, responsibility, or meekness. They were only wiser about their shameful nakedness. All the knowledge gained was self-centered and fear-driven, so they hid.

SHAME, FEAR, CONTROL

I heard Your voice in the garden, and I was afraid because I was naked; and I hid myself. (Genesis 3:10)

Adam and Eve were not ashamed until they disobeyed. They had walked naked with God in their garden paths, but no more. Nakedness is not bad; their bodies were not dirty. But disobedience steals our feeling of safety. Their eyes opened, they suddenly perceived a shameful deficiency.

That awareness of deficiency is shame. Guilt lights up our wrongdoing, but shame concerns our unfixable nature. In his nakedness, Adam exhibited that self-judgment and dislike for something inescapable about yourself which you can't help or change.

Shame is common and very fearful to acknowledge. People and circumstances can threaten to confirm the dreaded, lurking accusation: we are unfixable. It hurts so badly and seems so irreversible that we fear it.

The first pair's meager cover-ups felt like escapes—until God called them. They indulged in any effort to avoid dealing with God in their shame. The fear of exposure motivated two self-protective efforts: fig leaves and hiding.

We feel shame (*naked*) about ourselves, albeit in different ways and intensities. Dreading its discovery and confirmation (*afraid*), we adopt controlling coping mechanisms (*hid*). These consume our energies and stall our maturity. Fig leaf coverups explain much that we do.

There is an escape from this cycle: birth as a living spirit by following Jesus as Lord. In the maturing process, the Holy Spirit replaces our shame, fear, and control. He restores what was lost: security, peace, and receptivity with God.

You and I inherited this fig-leaf instinct. Discerning it requires meek candor about our behaviors and their motive. "Am I hiding? Is this my control mechanism to avoid my shame?" Cover-ups prevent the exposure and confirmation we fear, and have deep roots in our identity.

Confession of our sin and meekness about our nature is a Christian virtue. We are not bargaining with God when we confess. Instead, we disarm the temptation to shame, fear, and control. Call temptation what it is, and pour the daylight antiseptic.

> But if we walk in the light as He is in the light, we have fellowship with one another, and the blood of Jesus Christ His Son cleanses us from all sin. (1 John 1:7)

God didn't address their fear or shame at all. Instead, he immediately addressed the disobedient action and got them to admit to it. He pronounced and executed their consequences. When we confess, we still face consequences, but He has favor on those who are contrite.

> I dwell in the high and holy place, with him who has a contrite and humble spirit, to revive the spirit of the humble, and to revive the heart of the contrite ones. (Isaiah 57:15)

FEELING SHAMEFULLY WRONG

Have you ever kicked yourself over and over for a poor decision? We can only imagine how many times Adam and Eve must have done that. Child after child would show the fruit of their choice. For all the joy, each one would uniquely show how costly disobedience was. Memories of Eden-walks with God would be haunted with regret.

How often would our first parents kick themselves inwardly when they rebuked their children? "Why didn't you do what I told you?"

PARENTING TO HEAL SHAME

Parenting is a constant reminder of how we didn't listen to God, and the consequences we have to endure. The child displays the same disobedient and foolish tendencies as our first parents.

Our cultural priority on self-esteem disallows guilt for wrongdoing and shame of sinfulness. This prevents confession and restoration. Thus, the younger generation manifests levels of despair, violence, and suicide, which mark greater demonic oppression. Despair increases when shame is suppressed.

Parents disarm the bent to disobedience by punishing children's misdeeds and rewarding confession. The mother and father must show both God's holiness and fatherhood. A child's behavior can be destructive and shameful; parents must impose consequences. Like our Heavenly Father, we disarm shame, fear, and control by helping the child to admit their sin and its consequences. Simultaneously, we encourage them that God has a good destiny for them.

> But we were gentle among you, just as a nursing mother cherishes her own children. So, affectionately longing for you, we were well pleased to impart to you not only the gospel of God, but also our own lives, because you had become dear to us. (1 Thessalonians 2:7–8)

> We exhorted, and comforted, and charged every one of you, as a father does his own children, that you would walk worthy of God who calls you into His own kingdom and glory. (1 Thessalonians 2:11–12)

SELF-JUSTIFYING BLAME

Their new knowledge of good and evil did not include the wisdom to say, "I'm sorry," or "Will you please forgive me?" To the contrary, each of the pair shunted responsibility onto another.

Adam blamed Eve and indirectly blamed God; she blamed the serpent. Like criminals cornered by evidence, they admitted their wrongdoing with a *but*. Each blamed everyone but themselves.

Their blame game comments are telling. The knowledge tree at least included words Adam and Eve could never have spoken before. God asked where they were, and suddenly they have a new vocabulary: *afraid, naked, hiding, deceived.*

As they found, our pattern of consequence is that deep fear of owning up. To avoid it, we throw our beloved ones under the bus. Blaming them is but another fig leaf for our shame.

Confessing our own sin and forgiving one another in Jesus' name disarms this blame game. "I'm sorry, I was wrong. Will you forgive me?" Confession never ends with an excusing *but*, or a blaming *but they.*

Their so-called open eyes now found fault everywhere but themselves, and the vocabulary to match. So much for their wisdom.

BELIEF, EXPECTATION, AND FULFILLMENT

One prominent consequence pattern is the belief-expectation-fulfillment cycle. We believe life should be a certain way for us, and the beliefs produce expectations.

Voilà! What we expect occurs, fulfilling the expectation and reinforcing the original belief. The cycle becomes more entrenched in our lives, like a car's wheels spinning us deeper and deeper into wet mud.

This pattern is simple and easy to spot, once you learn it.

God had asked no belief of the freshly created human beings. He gave them a completely free scope of thought, movements, and sustenance. They had only one restriction, slight in comparison.

The serpent, in contrast, was selling a belief: they could not trust God with their welfare. Likewise, satan and his delegates are constantly selling us beliefs that spin our wheels ever deeper into their damnation.

The belief satan sold included an expectation: *"You will be like God."* Whatever that meant to them, they bought it. He packaged two fulfillments inside that expectation, both unstated. They would enjoy everything they already had, without loss. Second, they would be wiser, better fed, and less restricted.

The expectations were false, and the promised fulfillments did not occur. The only fulfillment was what God imposed. Adam and Eve saw their naked helplessness. Without trust in God, they felt vulnerable and exposed. All the food was lost when He exiled them from Eden. They could eat anything they could grow through hardscrabble labor.

For nine centuries, they each lived that way, populating Earth with each painful birth. Would Adam and Eve agree with Jesus that satan was the father of lies? The lying belief he sold them and the expectations they bought started a cycle of fulfillment: all their progeny were born dead in spirit.

Our remorseful parents could not disarm the cycle of belief, expectation, and fulfillment. Their action also installed that consequence fully for our race. God's solution is to impart His Holy Spirit to us. With His help to mature, we gain the beliefs and expectations He wants to fulfill.

But the Helper, the Holy Spirit, whom the Father will send in My name, He will teach you all things, and bring to your remembrance all things that I said to you. Peace I leave with you, My peace I give to you; not as the world gives do I give to you. (John 14:26–27)

DEAD SPIRITS

God had warned, *"In the day you eat of it, you shall surely die"* (Genesis 2:17). The tempter disputed this: *"You will not surely die"* (Genesis 3:4). Which was truthful? Both.

Adam and Eve possessed a tripartite nature, mirroring the image of the triune God. Like the Second Person outside of time, they were spirits, with souls, in bodies. They *did* die the day they ate: their spirits.

Existing solely in their souls and bodies, the pair died physically nine hundred years later. That's what satan meant; he defined *die* by his own experience: "I rebelled, and I'm still here."

He conveniently omitted that he had eternal fire in his physical body and that God was wrathful to him. The devil did not disclose that God's *die* included all spiritual function and intimacy.

When their spirits died, they lost every enjoyment that requires a living spirit. They didn't have to wait the entire day; it happened immediately. God could have said, *"In the second you eat it you will die"* (if they had known the word *second*).

Book One of the *Unseen Series* is *Nobody Sees This You: How to Live as a Spirit in the Unseen Realm*. Its many Scriptures provide daily applications for maturing as living, functioning spirits.

God intended preeminence for His Earth-dominators. But our bodies and souls are quite unsuited for it without living spirits.

After satan's corruption victory, our parents multiplied only souls in bodies. The entire human race is born dead in spirit, completely vulnerable to demonic oppression.

How can we ever escape the bottleneck of our hereditary corruption?

CHAPTER 13

GOSPEL THROUGH SATAN

Thanks to satan's success, we have the gospel of reconciliation with God as living human spirits, through faith in Jesus Christ and His substitution for us on the cross.

> For the judgment which came from one offense resulted in condemnation, but the free gift which came from many offenses resulted in justification. For if by the one man's offense death reigned through the one, much more those who receive abundance of grace and of the gift of righteousness will reign in life through the One, Jesus Christ. (Romans 5:16–17)

By ordaining that Jesus should be crucified for our sin, God ambushed the kingdom of darkness. They could never imagine God dying willfully, as Apostle Paul wrote. The success of His ambush led to the outpouring of God's Spirit to live in any and everyone.

> We speak the wisdom of God in a mystery, the hidden wisdom which God ordained before the ages for our glory, which none of the rulers of this age knew; for had they known, they would not have crucified the Lord of glory. (1 Corinthians 2:7–8)

UNCERTAINTY ABOUT GOD

Upon Lucifer and his allies, God had imposed a terrible fate—exiled from the heavenly courts and bodily transformed with inescapable, eternal burning. So great was the physical torment that Lucifer first ruined God's beautiful Earth into a giant cooling pool.

Now God had created Lucifer's replacements, who quickly fell prey to the deceiver's guile. After Adam and Eve ate the fruit, what actions would the fallen archangel anticipate from God? It's a guess, but Bible truths guide the guessing.

Until our creation, God's covenant love was not central to angelic perception. The songs in Revelation 4–5 reveal what is most evident in heavenly courts: God's worth. Isaiah 14 reveals that Lucifer's ambition gives no value to love, completely unmentioned.

> For you have said in your heart:
> "I will ascend into heaven,
> I will exalt my throne above the stars of God;
> I will also sit on the mount of the congregation
> On the farthest sides of the north;
> I will ascend above the heights of the clouds,
> I will be like the Most High." (Isaiah 14:13–14)

The God of holiness became wrath personified for Lucifer. Would the serpent expect the same result for Adam and Eve? Quite plausibly so.

Lazy Bible readers think the Old Testament God is a god of wrath, but the New Testament God is a god of love. How would a wrathful god punish Adam and Eve? I daresay he would blast them into oblivion and start over. A god of wrath might condemn them to tormented lives. Just like the gods of mythology, he could command crows to devour their livers day after day.

GOD'S GRACE FIRST REVEALED

Contrary to that willfully simplistic view of the Old Testament, the true God did none of these things. He who responded to Lucifer with holy wrath instead protected Adam and Eve from undying sinfulness. Where the rebellious archangel received a wrath-filled body from God, the sinful mortals received coverings of animal skin.

Lucifer received no favor or help in the biblical record of Ezekiel 28,

Isaiah 14, and Revelation 12. But for the sinful people, God manifested tenderness. He even helped Eve through her first pregnancy.

> Now Adam knew Eve his wife, and she conceived and bore Cain, and said, "I have acquired a man from the Lord." (Genesis 4:1)

Whatever expectation the successful tempter had, it would not include God's grace. God decreed painful childbearing painful and laborious food production. These would seem like slaps on the wrist to the fallen Lucifer.

In the unbiblical mythology of many Christians, satan is all-knowing and all-powerful. Instead, the Bible reveals an enemy plagued by uncertainty, outsmarted by God at every turn.

God's response to us does not follow the patterns of God's response to Lucifer and his allies. The actual response of tender grace for the sinful pair was unimaginable for an enemy whose grid is replacement, measured by power.

GOD WASN'T PROTECTING HIS POSITION

Adam and Eve had believed satan's premise about God, that He was habitually holding out on them to protect His position. Now they knew it was not true, and confessed: *"The serpent deceived me, and I ate"* (Genesis 3:13).

God had restricted them from the knowing tree to protect them, not Himself. The penetrating shame they felt immediately was not His desire for them. If He was holding out on them, it was for their good, not His. As if to punctuate this, He Himself clothed their shame with the skins of animals He killed.

The initial animal sacrifice for human sin was carried out by the Second Person of God. He who once walked physically with the pair now slaughtered animals and stripped hides to clothe them. That first sacrifice foreshadowed what we did to Him. The clothing symbolized the robes of righteousness He would earn for us.

> I will greatly rejoice in the LORD,
> My soul shall be joyful in my God;
> For He has clothed me with the garments of salvation,
> He has covered me with the robe of righteousness. (Isaiah 61:10)

GOD'S REAL PLAN

Our first parents distrusted His love and ate the fruit in the wrong order. By eating from tree two first, Adam and Eve gained a premature, half-formed knowledge of good and evil. Their spirits were dead; and their children's spirits were all dead. To protect our race from living forever that way, God banished us from Eden with its trees, and posted an unpassable cherub at its entrance with a flaming sword.

But it was not left unremedied in God's purposes. He often promised to reverse and replace the immature knowledge at the right time. Jeremiah 31:33–35 gives this great news:

> I will put My law in their minds, and write it on their hearts; and I will be their God, and they shall be My people. No more shall every man teach his neighbor, and every man his brother, saying, "Know the Lord," for they all shall know Me, from the least of them to the greatest of them, says the Lord.
>
> I have not written to you because you do not know the truth, but because you know it. (1 John 2:21)

That's the knowledge we want—not half-baked and self-smarted. Jesus condensed it further in John 17:3.

> This is eternal life, that they may know You, the only true God, and Jesus Christ whom You have sent.

PROMISE

As dark as human promise became, God was working His plan. The law of unintended consequences worked not only against Adam and Eve. It worked against satan as well.

God's plan required satan to succeed against the pair, and impose death onto every human being. If that's all it was, satan would happily oblige. But there was more to the plan, which the kingdom of darkness could never imagine. If they had, satan might even have stayed away from Eden permanently.

God would let people repent and be saved. He would actually come live in us (which Adam and Eve did not have). The saved human spirit would be more powerful against darkness than Adam and Eve. Jesus pronounced this about us in Matthew 16:18–19. The rebels in darkness would shudder to hear it.

> I will build My church, and the gates of Hades shall not prevail against it. I will give you the keys of the kingdom of heaven, and whatever you bind on earth will be bound in heaven, and whatever you loose on earth will be loosed in heaven.

DECREES BEFORE TIME

Jesus sourced His revelation about this new pattern of men and devils. To do so, He coined a Greek phrase which the New Testament writers followed carefully: ἀπὸ καταβολῆς κόσμου, transliterated *apo kataboles kosmou* and translated *"before the foundation of the world."* Jesus and His followers used the phrase for God's three decrees before time began. The Triune God verbalized them when only He existed, before creating any heavens and earth.

> Decree One: God chose us who are saved and prepared a kingdom for us.
> Decree Two: Jesus was crucified.
> Decree Three: An eternal fire was prepared for all God's enemies, angelic and human alike.

Those verbal decisions foreordained the outcome of all existence. That's why God could tell the future to the serpent after His response to Adam and Eve.

> So the LORD God said to the serpent ...
> "And I will put enmity
> Between you and the woman,
> And between your seed and her Seed;
> He shall bruise your head,
> And you shall bruise His heel." (Genesis 3:14–15)

GOD THE AMBUSHER

> However, we speak wisdom among those who are mature, yet not the wisdom of this age, nor of the rulers of this age, who are coming to nothing. But we speak the wisdom of God in a mystery, the hidden wisdom which God ordained before the ages for our glory, which none

of the rulers of this age knew; for had they known, they would not have crucified the Lord of glory. (1 Corinthians 2:6–8)

God's plan required people to sin, and the Lamb to be slain, so He kept it a mystery. Lucifer was unaware of the decrees as he had not been created yet. If he had known that Jesus' death reversed damnation, he would have preferred for Jesus never to die. For darkness, Jesus physically on Earth forever was preferable to the reconciliation of God and man.

But the devil behaved as expected and stepped into God's ambush. His kingdom of animosity produced what God had planned all along.

For truly against Your holy Servant Jesus, whom You anointed, both Herod and Pontius Pilate, with the Gentiles and the people of Israel, were gathered together to do whatever Your hand and Your purpose determined before to be done. (Acts 4:27–28)

Now, because of Jesus' death, we can reconcile with God. The devil's scheme released such comprehensive propitiation that God Himself pours out His Spirit into every Jesus follower. The intended spread of living human spirits dooms all satan's strategies to failure. It is his gates that retreat, not ours.

WHEN SPIRIT IS ALIVE

Physical conditions, even nakedness, are less fearful when our spirits are alive. The peace of God arrests attention away from our bodies' shortcomings. With living spirits, Adam and Eve enjoyed the all-sufficient One.

His companionship absorbed all their attention. But the day they died, attention became available for their shame and exposure.

This pattern is throughout the Bible. One striking example is Moses after his intimate fellowship with God on Sinai, in Exodus 34:29–35.

Moses did not know that the skin of his face shone while he talked with Him. (Exodus 34:29)

Jesus alone gives birth to living human spirits. By His ministry, our spirits are born again, as He said to Nicodemus.

That which is born of the flesh is flesh, and that which is born of the Spirit is spirit.... The wind blows where it wishes, and you hear the sound of it, but cannot tell where it comes from and where it goes. So is everyone who is born of the Spirit. (John 3:6, 8)

Only living spirits can subdue our bodies and souls. When our spirits mature, our bodies and souls do not rule us or determine what happens to us. They are simultaneously subdued and fulfilled.

Walk in the Spirit, and you shall not fulfill the lust of the flesh.... Those who are Christ's have crucified the flesh with its passions and desires. (Galatians 5:16, 24)

So significant is our reborn Christian spirit, that *"the things of earth grow strangely dim,"* in the words of Helen Lemmel's hymn, "Turn Your Eyes Upon Jesus." Our maturing spirits restore God's image in us—with the commensurate glory one might expect.

Now the Lord is the Spirit; and where the Spirit of the Lord is, there is liberty. But we all, with unveiled face, beholding as in a mirror the glory of the Lord, are being transformed into the same image from glory to glory, just as by the Spirit of the Lord. (2 Corinthians 3:17–18)

God is spirit. Maturing as spirits, we learn everything needed is right at hand, in Him. To begin, we admit and mourn our poverty of spirit, and through faith in Christ Jesus, we meekly hunger for His righteousness (Matthew 5:3–6). His Holy Spirit fills the poor in spirit—to God be the glory.

Many people vouch for the breadth of His substitution for our poverty. Jesus trades His righteousness for our sin; He also trades His resurrection health for our ailments and aging. I have experienced this in multiple medical emergencies. When my body's service was uncertain and waning, my living spirit received all that my body needed, both with and without medical intervention.

The Christian can function as a living spirit, among other spirits and flesh, unseen and seen alike. We are far more advanced than our first parents.

SPIRIT-DISCERNING

Discerning unseen tempters is a subset of discerning spirit realities. Earth, angels, God Himself, and our own spirits become more recognizable. We grow into the full spirit function described in the Bible.

We can't disarm the tempters on our own. All of us are born on their side, in their kingdom. This admission that we are poor spiritually is the first blessed condition of the Beatitude nine in Matthew 5:3–12. The second is to mourn it, and there is much to be sorrowful about. Consider how easily satan's henchmen victimize and oppress us; mourning comes easily.

When we are born in spirit, we emerge into a perceptible spirit world. God's Holy Spirit pours into us. With His partnership and tutoring we can mature into disarmers of the dark.

Cain refused such tutoring. The first partner to be released from satan's prison successfully disarmed him.

SIN

CHAPTER 14

THE UNCERTAIN KINGDOM

The devil wants to destroy the most people with the fewest partners. Isaiah 14:17 describes him as the ruler *"who did not open the house of his prisoners."* That's why his first strategy used no partners. With only two people on the entire earth, satan himself dealt with Adam and Eve.

He succeeded, but uncertainties remained. The grace God had shown was only the first surprise.

WOULD THEY STILL MULTIPLY?

God judged Adam and Eve, applied consequences, clothed, and protected them. Yet included in God's judgment was the promise that Eve would still bring forth children.

To the woman He said:
"I will greatly multiply your sorrow and your conception;
In pain you shall bring forth children." (Genesis 3:16)

Adam and Eve had not yet borne children. Whatever they knew about childbearing and childrearing was not experience-based. Nor did satan have a precedent to set expectations.

God said nothing in His judgment about the children's nature, their inheritance, their prospects. Many uncertainties remained for satan, requiring a close eye on the offspring of God's image-creatures.

WHAT KIND OF CHILDREN?

Would Eve's babies be born dead in spirit? Long hindsight as a race of sinners makes it hard for us to imagine otherwise, but satan would not have known from God's judgment on our parents in Genesis 3:16–19.

Nothing said in God's judgment imposed their fate on their offspring. God had breathed into Adam directly, and fashioned Eve personally. Plausibly those origins would replicate.

For satan's kingdom, the human race was a bigger puzzle than before. Would the multiplied people be living spirits, requiring darkness to deploy an increasing tempting army?

Plausibly, the Creator would cause them to reproduce godly children. The devil could not rule out that the offspring would get another chance at Eden and its two trees. Maybe the cherub at the gate would permit entry by some but not others.

The devil couldn't assume that the parents' corruption would influence other human beings. After all, satan's rebellion had not corrupted all angels. The preference of darkness is clear for the corruption to pass on. Then satan's tempting at the tree would undercut the entire human race.

But the destroyer had to watch and wait.

The biblical record next records three children of Adam and Eve. Genesis 4 is solely concerned with the offspring. Adam and Eve fulfill the multiplication mandate, and the events of their lives pass from the biblical record after Genesis 5:5.

THE ORGANIZATION OF DARKNESS

Ezekiel 28, Isaiah 14, and Revelation 12 reveal the origins, the prison, and the policies of the kingdom of darkness. At the time of Genesis 1, Lucifer and a third of heaven's angels rebelled, and were exiled to earth, by God. They had a fixed population, with no reinforcements.

The fallen angels comprise satan's management levels active on Earth today, named by Apostle Paul in Ephesians 6:12 cited elsewhere. But satan only gradually released them from his prison as needed. The nine-book *Unseen* Series traces his gradual release of partners and the historical flow of his strategy development.

God identifies Sin in Genesis 4, its first Bible mention. Sin was the second strategy of darkness after satan's corruption of multiplication. Sin was the first partner satan released—but why?

INTIMACY CONTINUES

The birth of Cain and his younger brother resolved one uncertainty: God was proceeding with His plan to multiply people and fill the earth. The devil's replacements would definitely multiply, and it clarified the *how*: birthing children.

Fertile Eve would be the mother of all the living, as Adam recognized. The Scripture succinctly says, *"Adam knew Eve"* (Genesis 4:1). He knew her often enough to populate the world. Their intimacy continued, every time displaying the covenant multiplication that God originally intended. That must have vexed the lying, murdering devil.

God restrained His wrath over the rebellion of Adam and Eve, showing a grace not seen before by the heavenly host. The contrast between God's punishment of Lucifer and the humans was unmistakable.

DEATH UNCERTAINTY

Human reproduction was an unpleasant discovery for the kingdom of darkness, yet more uncertainty lingered. Could their children die? God had said that Adam and Eve would die and return to dust; did that include Cain and Abel? Remember, satan may have known nothing about the tree of life and its properties. He also defined *die* differently. After all, Adam and Eve did not stop existing.

We have the Word of God plus experience to learn from, but satan had neither. Inherited death is obvious now, but not then. When satan released his partner Sin, no physical human death had yet occurred on Earth.

So, for all satan knew, Cain, Abel, and all the children would live forever. The offspring could still fulfill the original intention.

The accuser could not rule out that every child would be a brand new Adam or Eve, born as God had created them: without sin. He had to assume that every child would require individual attention, corrupted from scratch. Even brief human multiplication would stretch the rebels thin.

THE WORSHIPER

The dark kingdom's uncertainty demanded close scrutiny of the offspring. Immediately, they witnessed a disturbing threat. Adam and Eve taught their firstborn to worship the LORD.

And in the process of time it came to pass that Cain brought an offering of the fruit of the ground to the LORD. (Genesis 4:3)

A potential disaster loomed for satan upon seeing this. Maybe the corruption that the parents suffered was not transmitted to the children.

Cain, not Abel, is the Bible's first recorded worshiper. Cain worshiped God.

THE FIRST PARTNER RELEASED

When the population doubled from two to four, all initial indicators were unfavorable to darkness. Cain was worshiping satan's enemy, as his brother Abel did afterward.

The satan gave an assignment to one partner: Sin. God Himself described satan's partner in darkness and its habits, when He spoke directly to Cain.

CHAPTER 15

STRATEGY TWO: RELEASE SIN

The human race has indeed multiplied and filled the earth, as God intended. But satan is only one place at a time; he does not have omnipresence like God does. He requires henchmen.

DELEGATION IN DARKNESS

God is not limited to one place, but the devil is. God delegates to honor and elevate others, but satan delegates out of necessity. He only releases the fallen angels from his prison if necessary, with specific assignments. The strategies of darkness revealed in Scripture (and compiled in the *Unseen* Series) all affirm the delegation habit of satan.

In the biblical record, satan only acts directly in four periods: Adam and Eve, Job, David (1 Chronicles 21:1), and the three-year ministry of Jesus (Matthew 4, Luke 4, and Luke 22:3). How do we explain the abundant evil in the world and trouble in our lives? The delegation system in darkness authorizes evil principalities to conduct destructive activity on satan's behalf.

Christians correctly attribute troubles to the devil's malevolence, the driving force of darkness. Peter wrote that satan prowls around looking for people to devour (1 Peter 5:8). However, the devil is not free from limits to time or place. Jesus spoke of satan having a throne in Pergamum (Revelation 2:12–13). By necessity, therefore, the subordinates of satan are the ones we encounter. That is why Apostle Paul does not list the devil in his list of opponents in Ephesians 6:12.

DELEGATION IN HEAVEN

The exiled archangel learned delegation from God Himself. Lucifer egotistically believes he deserves God's throne. Mimicking God, satan operates likewise in his kingdom of darkness.

When Lucifer had mounted his original rebellion, God did not contest him. Instead, God entrusted the battle to Lucifer's peer archangel.

> And war broke out in heaven: Michael and his angels fought with the dragon; and the dragon and his angels fought. (Revelation 12:7)

Fast forward from that heavenly rebellion to Genesis 1:2, when satan's dominion has ruined original Earth into a watery, dark void. God's response in six twenty-four-hour days unveils His new delegate in His own image.

MULTIPLICATION PROMPTS DELEGATION

Sin is unmentioned in satan's work against Adam and Eve. No dark delegate was needed. With only two people, the devil's serpent form was sufficient and accomplished the goal.

But the birth of new human beings laid one uncertainty to rest: yes, the multiplication of the image-creatures was proceeding. Despite the apparent success of strategy one in Eden, Adam and Eve would reproduce.

The devil's limits rendered it impossible for him to tempt all the multiplying people. In order to stem the tide he feared, satan released one prisoner when Cain began worshiping God. To nip it in the bud, Sin was the first partner released upon Earth.

Whatever the dark rationale, satan does not approach Cain directly. Instead, he delegates to Sin, the personal entity, the first parolee of darkness.

That's when God spoke to Cain directly.

GOD DESCRIBES SIN

Our centuries of experience have proven that Sin sneaks at the door of all people, so we read God's statement about Sin in Genesis 4:7 without thought, as old knowledge.

Are you surprised that God spoke with Cain? People rarely include this detail in the frequent retelling. The first mention of Sin in the Bible is the Lord's warning to Cain.

We identify sinfulness as a force or inherited inclination. God's warning to Cain, like Romans 7 and other Scriptures, exposes Sin as an unseen but active entity from the kingdom of darkness. God describes Sin in personal terms, with a definite identity, manner, and desire: to have Cain and rule him.

So the Lord said to Cain, "If you do well, will you not be accepted? And if you do not do well, sin lies at the door. And its desire is for you, but you should rule over it." (Genesis 4:7)

God's statement to Cain is a fresh revelation not recorded for Adam and Eve. The first biblical mention of a door introduces the concept of control in our lives, specifically the door of one's life.

God says Sin's *"desire is for you,"* introducing the concept of darkness *having* a person. His wording suggests a possessive invasion, implying ownership, domination, subjugation, and slavery. Like a slave owner, Sin demands, commands, and dictates.

In Eden, no such terminology described satan *having* Adam and Eve. God's warning reveals the ambition of darkness to enslave His image-creatures through sneaky Sin.

SNEAKY PLEASURE

God also revealed Sin's mannerism of sneaking and evading attention. Sin didn't say hello to Cain, and didn't knock on the door of Cain's life. When he did not heed God's warning, Sin would oblige Cain's choice.

Included in the surreptitious deception is Sin's false promise of reward. Sin can appear very alluring. This isn't a reference to religious codes designating pleasures that are sinful. Many adherents sneak those pleasures to avoid public disapproval.

STUPID PLEASURE

When we are tempted by Sin, a choice stands before us. We act in agreement with either our Lord, or with darkness. When you boil it down so simply, you see how dumb it is to choose Sin over God. Yet we are allured by the benefits falsely promised by sneaky Sin. Like our first parents, we fail to exert scrutiny—because we *want* the benefits, and we want them *apart* from God.

In the coming chapter we will review the benefit that Cain coveted. His own desire led him to open the door to Sin. It's the same with us. How many times do we kick ourselves for choosing a stupid sin for a reward that proved to be hollow?

James explained why we fall for it, and described the sequence. Unless we discern and disarm the allure of Sin, it grows within us and produces death.

Let no one say when he is tempted, "I am tempted by God"; for God cannot be tempted by evil, nor does He Himself tempt anyone. But each one is tempted when he is drawn away by his own desires and enticed. Then, when desire has conceived, it gives birth to sin; and sin, when it is full-grown, brings forth death. (James 1:13–15)

TWO AT YOUR DOOR

Behold, I stand at the door and knock. If anyone hears My voice and opens the door, I will come in to him and dine with him, and he with Me. (Revelation 3:20)

Like Sin, Jesus also is at our door. But instead of lying in secret, He knocks and waits for our opening. He honors our choice, whether we open to Sin or to Him. With God, there is intimacy rather than invasion, fellowship instead of subjugation.

God's description of Sin warns each of us. Like Cain, you and I have doors to our lives, which our choices open. Two are at your door: Jesus and Sin.

Whichever you open to, they will assert a right based on your welcome. Jesus describes His right in Revelation 3:20 in intimate terms of fellowship—eating together. Jesus stands erect and knocks. Everyone hears His knock despite their poverty of spirit because every person has a door to their life. If they open to Him, they know they are opening to the Son of God and He is coming in.

The other is sneaky and does not announce its presence. God warns us as He did Cain, maybe through others or by our own sense of righteousness. But we can ignore the warnings. We may not realize we opened the door to Sin, because Sin is sneaky.

When we choose our own way, we willfully break agreement with God. Sin gains the foothold of a right because refusing God's leadership strengthens our agreement with darkness.

Two are at our door. It's a continual experience, not a one-time event. By repeatedly choosing to align with Jesus, we build a discipline and habit. These can support us during challenging choices. A valuable resource in our later years is the habit of attentiveness to Jesus' knock and voice.

But each time we open our door to Sin, we also practice a habit. As James said above, it leads to death. The devil who released Sin to sneak at our doors wants to kill, steal, and destroy (John 10:10). If fast isn't possible, slow will do. A habitual yielding to Sin is destructive, because when it is full-grown, it brings forth death and eternal damnation.

Beware, brethren, lest there be in any of you an evil heart of unbelief in departing from the living God; but exhort one another daily, while it is called "Today," lest any of you be hardened through the deceitfulness of sin. (Hebrews 3:12–13)

See that you do not refuse Him who speaks. For if they did not escape who refused Him who spoke on earth, much more shall we not escape if we turn away from Him who speaks from heaven. (Hebrews 12:25)

The Lord's voice can be hard to discern. A process of trial and error is part of Christian maturing. But it is not an elective process, nor to be indulged lightly. Hearing Him speak to us is our birthright as the sheep of His flock (John 10:4–5). However, He expects us to grow on purpose, to take advantage of training and improve our listening. The proof is doing what He says, rather than opening the door to Sin.

I will raise up for Myself a faithful priest who shall do according to what is in My heart and in My mind. (1 Samuel 2:35)

Why do you call Me "Lord, Lord," and not do the things which I say? (Luke 6:46)

Even the smallest disdain for His leadership reinforces habits of disobedience and strengthens our bonds with the kingdom of darkness. That has an enormous cost. In contrast, passionate habitual attention to His leadership builds our defenses against Sin and strengthens our intimacy with God.

THE CHOICE WITH SIN

What was Cain's choice with Sin? God warns with a two-part statement, in which neither clause contradicts the other. His warning implies an either/or but requires us to fill in the unspoken alternatives. The Book of Proverbs also uses this technique frequently. Once we include them, in italics below, the full message is plain.

> And its desire is for you, *to enter your life and rule you.*
> But you should rule over it, *prevent it from entering the door of your life, keep it outside, be alert to its crouching sneakiness, and resist its control.*

On the one hand, He describes Sin's lustful desire to enter Cain's life. On the other, God warns Cain that he must dominate Sin.

MASTER OR BE MASTERED

We, like Cain, face the same choice. We have victories against Sin; maturing as a living spirit renders Sin more obvious. When we discern it, its sneakiness is disarmed; indulgence is less compulsive. The Holy Spirit within us functions like an early warning system and empowers us to avoid sins. As David sang in Psalm 18:23, *"I was also blameless before Him, and I kept myself from my iniquity."*

But Sin, the unseen entity, continues its persistent efforts to insinuate the habits of darkness into our lives. Whether it is our thinking, emotions, or actions, Sin crouches at our door, just as God warned Cain. We must master it, or Sin will master us.

Knowing this strengthens you for discerning and disarming Sin. Awareness of sneaky, evasive Sin as an unseen being explains Apostle Paul's warning in Romans 6:12–14. His logic anticipates a supply-and-demand equation in the mind of his capital city recipients: "More sin, therefore more grace." He warns them, as God alerted Cain, Sin wants to rule.

> Therefore do not let sin reign in your mortal body, that you should obey it in its lusts. And do not present your members as instruments of unrighteousness to sin, but present yourselves to God as being alive from the dead, and your members as instruments of righteousness to God. For sin shall not have dominion over you, for you are not under law but under grace.

WARNING, NOT PREVENTION

Why did God only warn Cain? God could have stepped in, prevented Cain's transgression, and saved Abel's life. After all, had He not blessed mankind? He intended for us to replace darkness, not be ruled by it. If we were God, would we tolerate an entity from darkness ruling one of our image-creatures? And think how Abel would have trained his children, and started a godly line.

All people were created with the power to choose. God forced Cain's choice and honored it. He didn't override it, prevent it, or hide it. He presented the choice to Cain personally and clearly.

THE ASSIGNMENT OF SIN

Like Cain, we can actually place ourselves under the rulership of Sin. This is why Apostle Paul wrote:

> Therefore do not let sin reign in your mortal body, that you should obey it in its lusts.... For sin shall not have dominion over you.... (Romans 6:12, 14)

The rule of Sin is destructive. It is a slave owner, having us, using us, and blinding us. Sin gets its power from God's holiness. Sin induces us to choose actions of rebellion against God. It is His own righteous judgment against us which Sin uses for our shackles.

We can know Sin's patterns. Apostle Paul said in 2 Corinthians 2:11, *"We are not unaware of his schemes."* Apostle Peter wrote, *"Be sober, be vigilant"* about our adversary the devil (1 Peter 5:8). They saw those truths in our Old Testament, such as Genesis 4.

SIN IS PERSONAL AND GLOBAL

We understand Sin little, but are overly familiar with its effect. Sin as an entity is distinct from our individual acts, called sins. The Bible is full of peoples' sins and liberally reports the sins and flaws of its heroes, which other religions cover up.

We sin in individual acts and choices, and mature beyond their compulsion. But the unseen Sin persists, lying at our door, as even the Apostle Paul described it so eloquently in Romans 7:15–20.

What I am doing, I do not understand. For what I will to do, that I do not practice; but what I hate, that I do. If, then, I do what I will not to do, I agree with the law that it is good. But now, it is no longer I who do it, but sin that dwells in me. For I know that in me (that is, in my flesh) nothing good dwells; for to will is present with me, but how to perform what is good I do not find. For the good that I will to do, I do not do; but the evil I will not to do, that I practice. Now if I do what I will not to do, it is no longer I who do it, but sin that dwells in me.

Apostle Paul wrote earlier in Romans 3:9 that all people are under Sin. In Romans 7 above, he attributes personal qualities to Sin. It deceives and kills, dwelling in a person and infecting deeds. It makes our most frequent word *I*. The result is behavior that is contrary to our actual desires and allegiances.

MUCH MORE WARNED

God warned Cain directly. Compared to Cain, we have many more alerts. We are warned by the history of our race, by personal experience, and by the Word of God. If Cain was without excuse, how much less excusable is it when we allow Sin to sneak in?

Our choices to cooperate with Sin only increase the wrath we deserve. We, God's own image-creatures, choose agreements with Sin over our identity in Him. We must discern and disarm this unseen force of wickedness.

DISARMING SIN

Confession names Sin and maims it. Daylight is the best antiseptic, a principle that most of us resist. But if we relent and repent with loyalty to Jesus' name, if we hunger and thirst for righteousness, God forgives us and cleanses us.

If we say that we have no sin, we deceive ourselves, and the truth is not in us. If we confess our sins, He is faithful and just to forgive us our sins and to cleanse us from all unrighteousness. (1 John 1:8–9)

By walking with Jesus persistently, we strengthen our habit of choosing Him and rejecting Sin. We die daily to Sin's false promises of hollow rewards. Each obedience erodes and terminates Sin's authority over us; we are freed.

> For he who has died has been freed from sin.... For the death that He died, He died to sin once for all; but the life that He lives, He lives to God. Likewise you also, reckon yourselves to be dead indeed to sin, but alive to God in Christ Jesus our Lord. (Romans 6:7, 10–11)

We also strengthen one another with alertness and supportive exhortation.

> And let us consider one another in order to stir up love and good works, not forsaking the assembling of ourselves together, as is the manner of some, but exhorting one another, and so much the more as you see the Day approaching. (Hebrews 10:24–25)

THE CHOICE IS OURS

Thus, the Scripture identifies the crucial element in our relationship with the entity of Sin. Do we open the door of our lives to Sin? Do we let it have us? Do we give it authority?

After dying to ourselves in Christ, we only return to Sin's dominion by choice.

> Therefore do not let sin reign in your mortal body, that you should obey it in its lusts. And do not present your members as instruments of unrighteousness to sin, but present yourselves to God as being alive from the dead, and your members as instruments of righteousness to God. For sin shall not have dominion over you, for you are not under law but under grace. (Romans 6:12–14)

CHAPTER 16

ABEL AND CAIN

Cain was the first human baby on earth. He was the first to suckle at his mother's breast. He was the first to be potty-trained (not suggesting they had potties, of course). He was the first to teethe.

When you list everything commonplace about babies growing into adults, Cain was the first on every one. First cold, first vomit, first earache, first wetting the bed—that was Cain's life. Like firstborns today, the first older brother had no hand-me-downs.

He was also the first person mastered by Sin. All that Apostle Paul described in Romans 7 above, Cain experienced first.

LITTLE ABOUT ABEL; MUCH ABOUT CAIN

Most people learn about Cain and Abel early on. Genesis 4 devotes one verse to Abel's qualities. For understanding Abel, Hebrews 11:4 provides more insight than Genesis 4.

In contrast, the chapter allocates twenty-four verses to Cain and his line. Cain's descendants show the success of satan's Sin strategy with an entire family line. Genesis 4 foreshadows our entire race using Cain's line.

Our frequent retellings make the story about murder; it's safe to do that because few of us murder. To be precise, it pertains to worship, which affects a greater number of people on a personal level. If the second strategy was to release Sin on Earth, its first expression was to corrupt Cain's worship. The murder arose from that.

WORSHIP ANGER

Cain's worship lacked the quality of Abel's worship.

And in the process of time it came to pass that Cain brought an offering of the fruit of the ground to the LORD. Abel also brought of the firstborn of his flock and of their fat. And the LORD respected Abel and his offering, but He did not respect Cain and his offering. And Cain was very angry, and his countenance fell. (Genesis 4:3–5)

Notice that Cain was measuring the results of his offering, and comparing with Abel's results. The text doesn't say how God's respect was communicated. The simplest explanation is that He was present, displaying respect on His face and with words.

Much has been written about the shortfall in Cain's sacrifice. Even if not compliant with Mosaic law, God wouldn't reject a sacrifice due to a later regulation. Maybe the key is Cain's *some* versus Abel's *firstborn*. Was Cain's sacrifice less passionate, more perfunctory? But Cain was in fact so passionate about some expectation that he got angry.

GOD TUTORS CAIN

Cain was a human being like us. Although he was dead in spirit, he was alive in emotions. God asked Cain, *"Why are you angry? And why has your countenance fallen?"* (Genesis 4:6). These questions were to the point; the door where Sin was crouching was being governed by Cain's emotions.

Cain was asked these questions not to educate God, but to challenge Cain himself. The same God who walked Adam through the animal-naming education tutored Cain through these questions. God's third question appealed to a common understanding: *"If you do well, will you not be accepted?"* (Genesis 4:7). It definitely implies that Cain had not done well. What fault in the sacrifice—a fault known to Cain—displeased the Lord?

WELL-DONE WORSHIP

God's statement presumes Cain's understanding of a well-done sacrifice. Cain didn't argue with God about that assessment. The common knowledge of the four living human beings included the definition of a well-done offering.

One place Cain could learn it: watching his younger brother Abel. Another source of knowledge would be his parents, Adam and Eve.

A third source of tutelage would be Jesus Himself. Eve said the Lord had helped her deliver Cain; when grown, the angry Cain hears His audible voice. All the evidence suggests that the pre-incarnate Jesus was active physically on Earth, even after their expulsion from Eden.

AS LITTLE AS NEEDED

Cain rejected what his sources taught him. Cain offered a sacrifice, but knew it was not done well. Why do that? He illustrates what to discern within ourselves about our own worship.

Cain was working a reciprocal deal to God. He was exchanging something for a similar response from the Lord.

The shame-fear-control consequence pattern made Cain more afraid of what he would lose with a well-done offering. In Cain's value system, what he held back was worth more to him than pleasing God with true worship. In Cain's plan, he could escalate the offer on an as-needed basis.

This negotiation system plays right into the hands of darkness. Our extensive study in previous books of the *Unseen* Series amply demonstrates that the kingdom of darkness runs on negotiated exchanges.

These IOUs are appropriate among people in the course of trading, which God loves. But Cain planned a limited exchange with God, who needs nothing. Divine worthiness should be the top priority, but Cain valued something else he withheld. The Bible calls it idolatry when we value something more than Our Creator, His blessing, and our relationship with Him.

This negotiation approach of Cain is replicated in all of us. It sounds like this: "God, if you save my mother from dying, I'll attend church every Sunday." The bargain we offer has a *some* quality. We want a *some* from God, and offer Him as little *some* as we can get by with.

This age-old human pattern dies when we are reborn as living human spirits. *"But the hour is coming, and now is, when the true worshipers will worship the Father in spirit and truth; for the Father is seeking such to worship Him. God is Spirit, and those who worship Him must worship in spirit and truth"* (John 4:23–24).

Sin walked through the door of Cain's life. He himself created a door for Sin when he attempted a *some/some* negotiation with God. Likewise for us: when we apply our habits of negotiated exchange to God Almighty, it gives Sin the door to rule us. Nowhere is it clearer than in religion.

EXPECTATIONS IN WORSHIP

The source of Cain's anger was religious. He made an offering to God, and God did not respect it. Cain expected that his *some* would elicit a *some* from the Lord, but none was forthcoming.

Emotions are closely tied to expectations. Cain got onto the belief-expectation-fulfillment cycle. When God didn't live up to Cain's expectations, Cain became angry. With hindsight, we review Cain's attitude as demanding and petulant. "God, here is what I offer You; now take it and be glad."

NEGOTIATED WORSHIP

We see this today in churches. At times, the Lord Jesus is near, and His presence is perceptible. We cannot imagine it ever ending, but it does, because that is not our maturity. He habitually withdraws to inspire our pursuit and hunger for the maturity He intends.

Still, we can hesitate when faced with the costly pursuit of maturity and make minimal efforts. Resorting to the methods that produced the former feeling, we misuse our corporate worship to feel close to God. Our individual disciplines can have the same negotiated exchange that Cain attempted.

Pastors and church leaders are especially susceptible to falling into these traps, even more so than other Christians. They feel many pressures, such as paying church bills, placating major givers, avoiding embarrassment, and earning growth by popularity.

Uncovering the hidden manipulators of this IOU system of worship and religion is a challenge. Most of us can tell when we feel like murdering someone, but we rarely notice or describe our inclination to religious negotiation.

Understanding the IOU system in people's worship expectations is the first step to discerning the subtle insinuations of darkness. The contemporaries Isaiah (in the southern kingdom) and Hosea (in the northern) each had prophetic insight into the corruption of tit-for-tat religious observances. Apostle Paul was equally vigorous in exposing it. He summarizes the contention among the apostles in Galatians 1–2, and even confronted Apostle Peter before an entire church.

As they showed, bravery is required to challenge negotiated worship and its secret expectations. Deference to tradition has its value until it permits the worship of Cain.

LOVE VERSUS JEALOUSY

Closely associated with these base motives for religious worship is judgmental jealousy. In order for God to accept our *some*, we feel pressure to worship correctly. Anyone worshiping differently is a threat to our acceptability. If they are blessed, we easily conclude we are doing something wrong. Doubtless this is a motive behind much church gossip, which is an uncontestable assassination of someone else's character.

Jealousy identifies someone else as a threat. Cain became jealous of Abel, murderously jealous because Abel's righteous worship made Cain's look bad. Just because we are worshiping doesn't mean we are worshiping God, or that we love Him. Apostle John saw the tie of love and murder.

> For this is the message that you heard from the beginning, that we should love one another, not as Cain who was of the wicked one and murdered his brother. And why did he murder him? Because his works were evil and his brother's righteous. (1 John 3:11–12)

Apostle John wrote that to a church. Don't doubt that Christians can fall prey to Sin lying at the door—even in their worship and religious expectations. Be alert to discern your own jealousy in worship, and disarm it immediately so you don't become like Cain.

MORE EXCELLENT WORSHIP

The author of Hebrews had a revealed understanding. Hebrews 11:4 is the one of three New Testament references to Cain.

> By faith Abel offered to God a more excellent sacrifice than Cain, through which he obtained witness that he was righteous, God testifying of his gifts; and through it he being dead still speaks.

Hebrews 11:4 uses the comparative *"more excellent,"* meaning *"more in value or quality."*

WORSHIP BY FAITH

How was Abel's offering better? We are told: it was *"by faith."* Abel and his offering are the first entry in the Hebrews 11 Hall of Fame. Abel is the first person in the Bible to please God.

Abel's offering by faith included trust in God. Consider the risk he faced to make his offering. Sheep reproduction was a new and uncertain process. Does each sheep have only one lamb? To bring the firstborn required a faith that more sheep would be born.

Genesis 4 says nothing about faith; this is a New Testament revelation to the author of Hebrews. Abel's comparative excellence over Cain's was not for what was offered, but for the pleasing quality of Abel's faith. Hebrews 11:6 further emphasizes this by saying, *"Without faith it is impossible to please Him."* Through Abel's faith is how he learned he was righteous, *"God testifying of his gifts"* (Hebrews 11:4).

The implication is that Cain's worship was unacceptable because it lacked faith. He performed worship acts, but didn't believe God as Abel did. Therefore, Cain was holding back something of more value to him. God appeals to Cain's existing knowledge, that the well-done offering is worship by faith, not by negotiation. But Cain refused to do it, for lack of faith. He did not trust that if he pleased God, God would care for him.

> Like Abel, we know God accepts us by faith. God testifies within us that we are righteous in His sight. Everything we do with God requires faith because He is unseen. He is spirit, and of the unseen realm.
>
> *"Though now you do not see Him, yet believing, you rejoice with joy inexpressible and full of glory, receiving the end of your faith—the salvation of your souls"* (1 Peter 1:8–9).

BRINGING OFFERINGS

Cain brought offerings, and Abel did as well. It's one thing to *bring*; it's another thing to *bring to*. The latter shines the spotlight on the recipient, and thus Hebrews says, *"Abel offered to God"* (Hebrews 11:4). The gospels repeatedly use this same word; people are physically *brought to* Jesus.

Very familiar passages use the same Greek word, when the offering is something we bring to God or to others.

Christ also has loved us and given Himself for us, an offering and a sacrifice to God. (Ephesians 5:2)

A sweet-smelling aroma, an acceptable sacrifice, well pleasing to God. (Philippians 4:18)

Therefore by Him let us continually offer the sacrifice of praise to God. (Hebrews 13:15)

Worship is personal, between me and God. I bring to Him all that I am; myself is all I can offer. Such an offering tells the unseen witnesses, both friend and foe, "I hold nothing more dearly than my God."

O my soul, you have said to the LORD,
"You are my Lord,
My goodness is nothing apart from You." (Psalm 16:2)
Whom have I in heaven but You?
And there is none upon earth that I desire besides You. (Psalm 73:25)

WORSHIP HABITS

God affirmed Abel's *gifts*. Using the plural indicates more than one gift. Genesis 4 describes Abel's habitual worship, not a single event.

Hebrews describes a complete assurance that Abel had. It's similar to the feeling of being saved. We know we are, and we know it by faith; an assurance appears within us. Our spirits become alive, reshaping our entire existence.

TWO-WAY WORSHIP

But Hebrews 11:4 describes an ongoing process when it says, *"God testifying of his gifts."* God actively and continually affirmed Abel's gifts. Abel had a habit and God responded habitually. Abel made offerings, and God testified about them. Hebrews 11:4 describes a verbal interaction of spoken words between God and Abel, just as God spoke with Cain.

Short of murder, whatever designs satan had on Abel and his worship, they were ineffective. If Sin was lying at Abel's door, that door remained closed to it. Likewise, our two-way worship with God closes our door and disarms the Sin crouching there.

ONE TO KILL

After God verbally warned him, Cain murdered Abel. How can we explain this action? He opened his door to Sin. Its presence manifested in three patterns. We can discern from such patterns when Sin is crouching at our door.

1. Cain was attempting IOU negotiation with God.
2. He compared himself to someone else.
3. He harmed the one who made him look bad.

WHAT CAIN HAD TO BELIEVE

Several willful beliefs were required for Cain to think and act that way—not accidental but deliberate. First, he disdained God's warning about Sin. He also ignored God's identification of his anger's source. Nothing God had said to Cain received any credence.

Ignoring God's Word like Cain is a habit throughout our society. It opens the door to our lives and welcomes Sin in, where it can dominate us.

Jesus defended his door against Sin, and retorted to satan, *"Man shall not live by bread alone, but by every word that proceeds from the mouth of God"* (Matthew 4:4). As the Holy Spirit was in Jesus, He is also in us. The Bible in our habits, hearts, and minds activates His power and keeps our door closed to Sin.

Second, Cain willfully identified Abel as the problem. He decided that eliminating Abel would cause God to respect his offering. Once Abel's more excellent offering didn't make Cain's offering look so bad, God would respect Cain's offering.

This thinking assumes that God is lacking in worship and settles for whatever He can receive.

Third, Cain willfully believed that God would not know he murdered Abel. Like babies who think you can't see them when they cover their eyes, Cain supposed he could return to worshiping God.

The thinking behind Cain's beliefs is another evidence that the preincarnate, post-resurrection Jesus was on Earth. Cain and Abel knew a physically present God, not just a voice. To them, God was a physical person who performed significant actions and was worthy of offerings.

Cain concluded that God wouldn't know because He wasn't physically nearby. He didn't think God knew his thoughts, so he planned the murder. Cain killed Abel while God wasn't close by, because God wouldn't see him doing it. He then hid the body because he didn't think God would smell it. And he could protest, *"I don't know,"* because God would believe him and move elsewhere to locate Abel.

THE CAIN-EYE IN US

Cain and Abel were spiritually dead. Their parents chose it, but the boys were born with it. We might look down on Cain's juvenile beliefs, but we repeat the pattern when we are not alert to Sin's tricks for ruling us. We criticize our religious leaders, then expect that God will smile on us while we worship in their churches and watch their podcasts. Perhaps you compare others' blessings with yours, as Cain did.

We disarm this Sin trick by honoring one another above ourselves and looking after each other's interests.

Who are you to judge another's servant? To his own master he stands or falls. (Romans 14:4)

Let nothing be done through selfish ambition or conceit, but in lowliness of mind let each esteem others better than himself. Let each of you look out not only for his own interests, but also for the interests of others. Let this mind be in you which was also in Christ Jesus. (Philippians 2:3–5)

Modern people identify God as merely an unseen divinity or force. But after a person opens the door to the knocking Jesus, he or she is born as a living spirit. Jesus comes in, and they fellowship together as spirits. This fellowship keeps the door closed to Sin.

Now that we understand the "Cain eye," let's revisit the oft-told consequences.

CHAPTER 17

CONSEQUENCES OF SIN

Then the LORD said to Cain, "Where is Abel your brother?"
He said, "I do not know. Am I my brother's keeper?"
And He said, "What have you done? The voice of your brother's blood
cries out to Me from the ground." (Genesis 4:9–10)

REVEAL SELF-SERVING GODS

Cain's first consequence was to learn the falsity of his beliefs. Cain expected he could keep his murder secret from God. Contrary to his expectation, God saw it all; nothing was hidden.

God's warning about Sin should have alerted Cain that He sees all. But that warning didn't fit with Cain's intention. To admit that God saw his comparison and jealousy threatened the deal he thought he had negotiated. That's why Cain ignored it with willful blindness. He had an agenda which required a false God he could deceive, hide from, and negotiate with. This opened his life door to Sin and gave it rights in his life.

Jesus described wicked prophets, deliverance ministers, and miracle workers in Matthew 7:21–23. Their works were genuine, just like those of Jesus, and truly blessed the recipients. Yet their belief about Him was false. Like Cain, they supposed He owed them in exchange. Shockingly, Jesus says to these power ministers, *"I never knew you"* (Matthew 7:23). Understanding this helps us discern our own tit-for-tat, IOU worship system.

He ended the Sermon on the Mount by telling about those rejected power ministers. Jesus had begun with the conditions He blesses: poverty of spirit, mourned with meekness, and the other Beatitudes. In them lie the true beliefs about the true God, the antidote that protects us from being like Cain.

LAW ILLUMINATES SIN

Cain was angry, and God sought to protect Cain from a poor choice. In doing so, God uttered the first law in the Bible. He established a standard for the reward and punishment of behavior.

> If you do well, will you not be accepted? (Genesis 4:7)

The Sin lying at Cain's door required regulation. Cain could accept God's definition of doing well, or reject it in favor of his own. God wanted Cain to improve the faith in his offering; Cain wanted to eliminate the one who made his offering look substandard.

Christians should welcome this exposure of our false beliefs about God. It is part of His fatherly tutoring. We must continually improve our beliefs about God from His Word. But when we settle in, we are resisting Him and His maturing process for us. Disdaining to pursue Him, we open the door to Sin—just like Cain.

God's warning to Cain assumes they had a shared knowledge of doing well. Earlier, we considered where Cain might have learned God's preferred worship habits. But in regulating Sin, God puts forth the first law. For us, it leads to salvation.

LAW LEADS TO SALVATION

Apostle Paul began his life as Saul, the most passionate Jew among his peers. He had gained admission to the most exclusive Rabbinic school, and advanced beyond all others in knowledge of the Law of Moses. Saul also supported the stoning of Stephen, and sought authorization to persecute followers of Jesus. He falsely accused Messianic Jews of capital crimes against Rome so civil authorities could kill them (Acts 7–9). He excelled in zeal for the Law (Philippians 3).

But when the scales fell off his eyes in Damascus, the former Saul saw the Law for what it was: God's tutor to expose Sin. Jesus next taught Paul privately for seventeen years (Galatians 1:17–2:1). It's easy to imagine the many questions Paul had; one would concern the purpose of the Law. If salvation is by faith in Jesus, why was the Law given?

> By the law is the knowledge of sin.... The law brings about wrath; for where there is no law there is no transgression.... The law entered that the offense might abound.... I would not have known sin except through the law.... For sin, taking occasion by the commandment, deceived me, and by it killed me. (Romans 3:20, 4:15, 5:20, 7:7, 11)

God's way to teach us our mournful poverty of spirit is the Law of Moses, which exposes Sin and its desire to have us. Adam and Eve only admitted disobedience when caught. In contrast, we confess it, knowing the standard we transgressed. And this blessed precondition makes salvation by faith possible.

> What purpose then does the law serve? It was added because of transgressions, till the Seed should come to whom the promise was made.... Therefore the law was our tutor to bring us to Christ, that we might be justified by faith. (Galatians 3:19, 24)

HELL

God's pattern of punishment is exile and separation. Lucifer suffered exile from heaven. Then Adam and Eve were exiled from Eden. Now Cain must endure separation as well. At the end of the age, all who have not loved Jesus will be eternally exiled into hell.

Beginning with Jesus because we don't want to be thrown into hell is a worthy reason. But staying there reveals Cain's beliefs in us, a negotiated exchange with God. The loving pursuit of our amazing Father and conformity to His ambitions must supersede the fear of hell.

We don't stop fearing the consequences of sin. It heightens our attentiveness and obedience to recognize the consequences otherwise: separation from God eternally. Jesus Himself told us to fear Him for that reason, in Matthew 10:28.

> Do not fear those who kill the body but cannot kill the soul. But rather fear Him who is able to destroy both soul and body in hell.

EARTH IS PERSONAL

In Books One and Three of the *Unseen* Series we considered how Earth, like Sin, is an unseen entity. Cain's consequences include the first Bible references to the will of Earth.

God had described Sin with personal desires and now does the same concerning Earth. After Cain hid Abel's body, God says Earth *"opened its mouth to receive your brother's blood from your hand"* (Genesis 4:11). We also learn that Earth has a personal will which would not yield to Cain's cultivation.

Earth also has personal frustration, which Paul pinpointed in Romans 8:19–22. Resisting us is not its desire, but an imposed restriction until people were reborn as spirits. That's how we became the sons Earth has been waiting for. Paul says *"until now"* because Earth's waiting ended with the rebirth Jesus enabled—we are here now.

> For the earnest expectation of the creation eagerly waits for the revealing of the sons of God. For the creation was subjected to futility, not willingly, but because of Him who subjected it in hope; because the creation itself also will be delivered from the bondage of corruption into the glorious liberty of the children of God. For we know that the whole creation groans and labors with birth pangs together until now.

SEPARATION FROM EARTH

God's first judgment for Cain's deed concerned food production. Earth would now recognize Cain wherever he may go, and refuse to produce for him.

> So now you are cursed from the earth, which has opened its mouth to receive your brother's blood from your hand. When you till the ground, it shall no longer yield its strength to you. A fugitive and a vagabond you shall be on the earth. (Genesis 4:11–12)

Tilling the uncooperative ground outside Eden had been Adam and Eve's punishment. But now even the punishing form of food production was withdrawn. Cain was separated from Earth.

Food would be found by luck rather than through planting and harvesting. If there had been urban garbage dumps, he would forage in them.

MORE ARGUMENT FROM CAIN

Before his surrender to Sin, Cain had thought he could strike a *some/ some* exchange with God. He manifests the same attitude objecting to his punishment.

> And Cain said to the LORD, "My punishment is greater than I can bear! Surely You have driven me out this day from the face of the ground; I shall be hidden from Your face; I shall be a fugitive and a vagabond on the earth, and it will happen that anyone who finds me will kill me." (Genesis 4:13–14)

Did Cain somehow know Earth is personal? In Genesis 1:2, 20, and 26, the Scripture speaks of the Earth's face; the deep, dark void also had a face. Cain uses the same word objecting to his punishment: *"the face of the ground"* (Genesis 4:14). God's judgment signified homeless isolation to Cain, in addition to privation. *"I shall be a fugitive and a vagabond on the earth"* (Genesis 4:14).

SEPARATION FROM GOD

Cain's objection tells us more separation that God's punishment contained. *"I shall be hidden from Your face"* (Genesis 4:14). He left the proximity of the physically present Second Person.

> Then Cain went out from the presence of the LORD. (Genesis 4:16)

Surprised that the murderer still craved God's face? He craved God's approval from the start. After opening the door to Sin, the craving for God increases because we are separated from His intimacy.

Our worship easily becomes like Cain's, craving God's face on our own terms. It's like bugs seeking the bug zapper. Just because we worship, it does not distinguish us from Cain, who also worshiped. Our worship can separate us from God if we are not vigilant against Sin. That's what happened to Cain.

SEPARATION FROM PROTECTION

Cain also objected that people—all his brothers and sisters at this early stage—would kill him. Cain had murdered Abel, and recognized that God's judgment contained the prospect of his own murder.

He objected to God: *"My punishment is more than I can bear!"* (Genesis 4:13). Selfishly focused on himself, he feared the very thing he had done to Abel. What Abel never feared but received—being murdered—Cain now feared but never received.

Not only did Cain open the door to Sin, but he also opened a door to vulnerability, which he felt acutely. Through the door also came vengeance, ostracism, and judgment. Like his parents, he discovered what a nasty universe the kingdom of darkness occupied.

SEPARATION FROM INTIMACY

We all recognize that being different has a high social cost. How would having God's mark on your face affect your relationships with others?

And the LORD said to him, "Therefore, whoever kills Cain, vengeance shall be taken on him sevenfold." And the LORD set a mark on Cain, lest anyone finding him should kill him. (Genesis 4:15)

The mark he received had to be plain to all, just like the lights on a police car in your rearview mirror. The flow of traffic slows when a patrol car is on the road; we each fear the *"gotcha."* Likewise, anyone desiring to relate to Cain would see a similar threat to themselves.

Everyone would walk on eggshells around the man with the mark, fearing he might kill them too. Singled out by God for his misdeed, Cain would always be "the murderer"—not so helpful for intimacy.

We have a saying, *"Turnabout is fair play,"* to capture this reality. It heightens our alertness to unseen tempters who seduce us to do to others actions they want us to suffer ourselves.

One moral often found in detective shows is that those who do evil *with* you will also do evil *to* you. Such are our unseen enemies.

CORRUPTION CONFIRMED

Cain's behavior and attitude reduced the uncertainty of darkness. The firstborn human being proved that the parents' corruption at the knowing tree was hereditary.

When Cain and Abel began worshiping, satan's worst-case scenario loomed. That's why a partner had to be released, namely Sin. And satan could conclude it worked. By succeeding at its mission, Sin pragmatically affirmed the value of releasing a prisoner.

The devil's previous effort was not a waste, of course. Adam and Eve had passed their corruption down to the child, evident in Cain's choices. It resolved one uncertainty: for at least one child, enmity with God would definitely be hereditary.

HEREDITY OF SIN

Cain's lineage further confirmed Sin's inheritability. That's why Genesis 4 says much more about Cain than Abel.

Seth, the third child, headed the first godly lineage in the Bible. His great-great-great-grandson Enoch walked with God so intimately, he was spared the usual nine-hundred-year life, and translated to heaven without dying (Genesis 5:24). Noah was Seth's six-time great-grandchild. Yet we are told far less about them than Cain's line.

> We have seen how God loves trade. He turns even Cain's punishment to good for our race. Separation from Earth motivates Cain to develop trade, as we shall see in his city and lineage.

Imagine how many children Eve bore in her nine hundred years, including the spouses for her sons. By the time Cain murdered Abel, other people lived. Yet the rest of Genesis 4 zeroes in on Cain's family line. Why not the other population?

Because the Bible uses Cain's descendants to show our heredity as a race. Although the children had done nothing good or bad prior to birth, the family line of Cain depicts our hereditary inclination.

A MIXED BAG

His lineage contained good as well. Exiled from agriculture, Cain became the first entrepreneur. After God shut the ground up for Cain, he built a city populated by his many brothers and sisters. Cities are hubs of trade; God loves trade. They are also centers of innovation, fulfilling God's mandate that we subdue the Earth.

Cain sired a line of children, all the way down to his great-great-great-great-grandchildren Jabal, Jubal, and Tubal-Cain. The Bible does not describe any other family line for its innovative quality.

Jabal was the father of those who dwell in tents and have livestock. His brother's name was Jubal. He was the father of all those who play the harp and flute. And as for Zillah, she also bore Tubal-Cain, an instructor of every craftsman in bronze and iron. (Genesis 4:20–22)

Yet the heredity of Cain also included Sin. Dominating Cain, it gained entry into his family line as well. Cain had to live with a brand on his face, warning all who met him. But his descendants welcomed the notoriety. Lamech bragged about being a murderer, turning Cain's curse into an identity. He proclaimed a family value of overwhelming retaliation.

Then Lamech said to his wives:
"Adah and Zillah, hear my voice;
Wives of Lamech, listen to my speech!
For I have killed a man for wounding me,
Even a young man for hurting me.
If Cain shall be avenged sevenfold,
Then Lamech seventy-sevenfold." (Genesis 4:23–24)

To Moses, God described His holy way with mankind. The evidence in Cain's line matches up with it: Sin and its dominion over us is hereditary.

By no means clearing the guilty, visiting the iniquity of the fathers upon the children and the children's children to the third and the fourth generation. (Exodus 34:7)

ENOUGH?

The kingdom of darkness had a mixed bag, also. On the plus side, the new partner Sin had successfully entered Cain's door and mastered him. The one worshiper whom God had accepted was dead now, and with him, his acceptable worship. And it was now proven that Sin would travel down family lines and influence children yet unborn.

Why was this not a complete victory for evil? Because the newborn creatures still had a desire to worship God. Even Cain knew the dread of separation from God. They still recognized their dependence upon God, and His sovereign reign over them remained undisputed. Even when objecting to his punishment, Cain shows faith that God could protect him from being murdered.

EVIL UNCERTAINTY

The uncertain kingdom still lacked many answers. How complete was their victory over humanity? Would there be more like Abel? How can they replicate more like Cain? What will God do next?

To ensure victory, a third strategy would be required.

GOD'S REMNANT

Each dark strategy falls short of achieving total success. He permits them to ruin some, but not all. God always preserves a remnant, one of Apostle Paul's primary points in Romans 11.

> Even so then, at this present time there is a remnant according to the election of grace.... For God has committed them all to disobedience, that He might have mercy on all. (Romans 11:5, 32)

Book Three of the *Unseen* Series reviewed the Genesis 1 picture of God terrorizing darkness in six staccato twenty-four-hour days. From this Book Four on, we learn how He toys with satan and his partners.

Right when they think success is guaranteed, He withholds people for Himself. They repeatedly discover what Paul said about crucifying Jesus: they are only doing what He wants them to do.

> None of the rulers of this age knew; for had they known, they would not have crucified the Lord of glory. (1 Corinthians 2:8)

JOIN 'EM

The threat that concerned satan was driven by human multiplication. Without reinforcements, the kingdom of darkness could not keep up with the multiplying humanity.

The third strategy of darkness used our multiplication capacity. As the old saying goes, "If you can't beat 'em, join 'em." Rather than *fear* it, satan released his partners to *use* it.

FLESH

CHAPTER 18

UNDERSTANDING THE FLESH

Darkness' third strategy becomes clearer as we understand Bible usage of the word *flesh*. Recognizing the flesh also strengthens our discernment for temptation and equips us to disarm it. Statements from both Peter and Paul presume our understanding of our own flesh.

> Therefore, since Christ suffered for us in the flesh, arm yourselves also with the same mind, for he who has suffered in the flesh has ceased from sin, that he no longer should live the rest of his time in the flesh for the lusts of men, but for the will of God. (1 Peter 4:1–2)

> Put on the Lord Jesus Christ, and make no provision for the flesh, to fulfill its lusts. (Romans 13:14)

> I say then: Walk in the Spirit, and you shall not fulfill the lust of the flesh. For the flesh lusts against the spirit, and the spirit against the flesh; and these are contrary to one another. (Galatians 5:16–17)

WHEN FLESH MEANS OUR BODIES

One frequent use means our bodies. The first use is Genesis 2:21. After removing Adam's rib to form Eve, God *"closed up the flesh in its place."* That is the meaning in Adam's phrase, *"bone of my bones and flesh of my flesh"* (Genesis 2:23).

In John 6, Jesus purposely thinned the following crowd by telling them to eat His flesh and drink His blood. We know now He foreshadowed the future communion of the Church; we identify with His bodily death. Unaware, the crowd assumed He was discussing cannibalism of His body. *"How can this Man give us His flesh to eat?"* (John 6:52).

The newly resurrected Jesus reassured the frightened disciples by saying, *"A spirit does not have flesh and bones as you see I have"* (Luke 24:39).

This use of *flesh* includes generational families, referring to physical descendants through reproduction, such as Paul in Romans 1:3: *"Jesus Christ our Lord, who was born of the seed of David according to the flesh."*

WHEN FLESH MEANS HUMANITY

The Bible speakers and writers may mean all humanity when they use the word *flesh.* John the Baptist quoted Isaiah 40:5 to signify all people: *"All flesh shall see the salvation of God"* (Luke 3:6).

Peter cites Isaiah 40:6, where flesh is synonymous with the race of man: *"All flesh is as grass, and all the glory of man as the flower of the grass"* (1 Peter 1:24).

WHEN FLESH MEANS SOULS IN BODIES

Both before and after being saved, we have a flesh. Some translations use the phrase *sinful nature* when a Bible author intends this definition. It means we have a soul with mind, will, and emotions, in physical bodies.

When our mothers birth us, we are born in the flesh—souls in baby bodies. With maturity, we become adults, but still born of the flesh only. After the body dies, someone never saved lives eternally as a soul, in an extremely undesirable situation.

God, a spirit, explains the shortening of human lifespans with this definition in mind.

To function fully as a living human spirit, see Book One in the *Unseen* Series, *Nobody Sees This You: How to Live as a Spirit in the Unseen Realm.* In thirteen chapters, spirit-function in every area of life—both seen and unseen—is revealed from the Bible. Chapter six explains the third use of *flesh,* which designates our existence as souls in bodies, apart from spirit.

And the Lord said, "My Spirit shall not strive with man forever, for he is indeed flesh; yet his days shall be one hundred and twenty years." (Genesis 6:3)

WHEN FLESH GETS A RULER

But when saved, we are born in spirit. As a spirit you entered God's kingdom immediately; eternal life began right away, not deferred until your body dies. You became a living spirit able to function in the unseen realm. Your spirit can mature so that it subordinates your flesh. Jesus meant this usage in His dialogue with Nicodemus.

Unless one is born of water and the Spirit, he cannot enter the kingdom of God. That which is born of the flesh is flesh, and that which is born of the Spirit is spirit. (John 3:5–6)

Jesus talked about spirit and flesh with the Samaritan woman at the well. She asked religious questions as smokescreens. Her attitude about worship was like Cain's. Jesus' reply defined worship by living human spirits.

The true worshipers will worship the Father in spirit and truth; for the Father is seeking such to worship Him. God is Spirit, and those who worship Him must worship in spirit and truth. (John 4:23–24)

The apostles recognized when the Holy Spirit began filling believers.

But this is what was spoken by the prophet Joel: "And it shall come to pass in the last days, says God, that I will pour out of My Spirit on all flesh." (Acts 2:16–17)

UNIQUELY HUMAN

Angels in the Bible are never referred to as souls or flesh. The race of men is distinct—God's only image-creatures in Scripture. No other being has a body with a soul that is mind, emotions, and will. With these we have the full life of flesh: relating, talking, and multiplying through sexual intercourse.

Yet what God intended for living human spirits is lost to our flesh. The human spirit died the day Adam and Eve believed satan over God. They passed down the death, and we are born as souls that live in bodies. The death of human spirits was also unique among the works of God, the only spirits that could die *and* multiply it. The dead in spirit did not bear children alive in spirit.

MULTIPLYING THE DEAD IN SPIRIT

God made humanity to multiply, but what would multiply? The devil's success in Eden replicated his rebellion in Adam and Eve. Their spirits died; they lived only in the flesh. Their bodies eventually died; all their children would die.

Agreeing with satan instead of God turned their God-given multiplication into an asset for darkness. But uncertainty remained for the enemies: Would they still multiply? If so, what would the children be?

Darkness' first strategic failure soon came to light: Cain and Abel worshiped. Human attention to God persisted in the multiplied children. We reviewed satan's response. He released the first partner from his prison, a real unseen being which God named Sin. Cain gave his life over to its rule. The multiplication power of God's image-creatures passed Sin on to Cain's generations.

The only other named son of Adam and Eve was Seth. Like all their children, Seth was dead in spirit. As he grew up, Abel was dead and Cain was exiled. Whose path would Seth follow?

GENEALOGY OF SETH

Genesis 4 gives us seven generations of Cain and captures the amplification of Sin as he multiplied. It names one man each, two wives, and a sister, as well as their deeds, inventions, and influence. But it numbers no lifespans.

Genesis 5 relates ten generations of Adam in Seth's line. The last father named is Noah, followed by his three sons: Shem, Ham, and Japheth. Until Noah's sons, the genealogy names only one father in each generation, and consistently focuses on six facts about each:

- their lifespan,
- one male child's name,
- the father's age at his birth,
- their multiplication of other sons and daughters,
- how long he lived after the named child's birth, and
- then his death.

Commentators argue that certain generations are left out or that the long lifespans don't align with our current experience. There is room for different opinions, but a logical flaw often motivates these efforts. Forcing Bible revelation of past realities to conform to our present experience assumes no major changes have occurred. The coming section, "Ethnos," shows that physical reality has changed dramatically because of the Flood.

Evaluating God's Word by our reason is spiritually juvenile. Its composition and compilation were inspired by a Holy Spirit. He is the very definition of integrity.

Tended by His power, every word matters. In the *Unseen* Series, we consider Scripture as more real than we are. The text of Genesis 4 and 5 present themselves as sequential and linear, and we submit to that text.

God leaves secrets in the Bible for us, and charts like the following page help unearth them. The lifespans in Genesis 5 show that the generations overlapped. Early human history not only had explosive multiplication, but also firsthand eyewitnesses of our beginnings.

> To research the documentary integrity of the Bible, reading *Is the Bible Even Real?* by my wife, Diane Renfroe, is highly recommended. It is a brief review of the composition, compilation, preservation, and promulgation of God's Word.

Noah knew the ancestors personally. Imagine the tales in their family's circle of shelters, as conversation passed down these events to the memory of future generations. He recorded their history prior to the Flood, with eyewitnesses for his sources.

A LINEAGE THAT HONORED GOD

All Adam's lineage was by nature dead in spirit; this includes Seth's line in Genesis 5 as well. Yet our race can still honor God, as is His due. Apostle Paul said why, in Romans 1:19–20.

> What may be known of God is manifest in them, for God has shown it to them. For since the creation of the world His invisible attributes are clearly seen, being understood by the things that are made, even His eternal power and Godhead, so that they are without excuse.

Four statements in Genesis 5 reveal that Seth's lineage feared and worshiped the Lord. First, God's creation of Adam in His likeness is

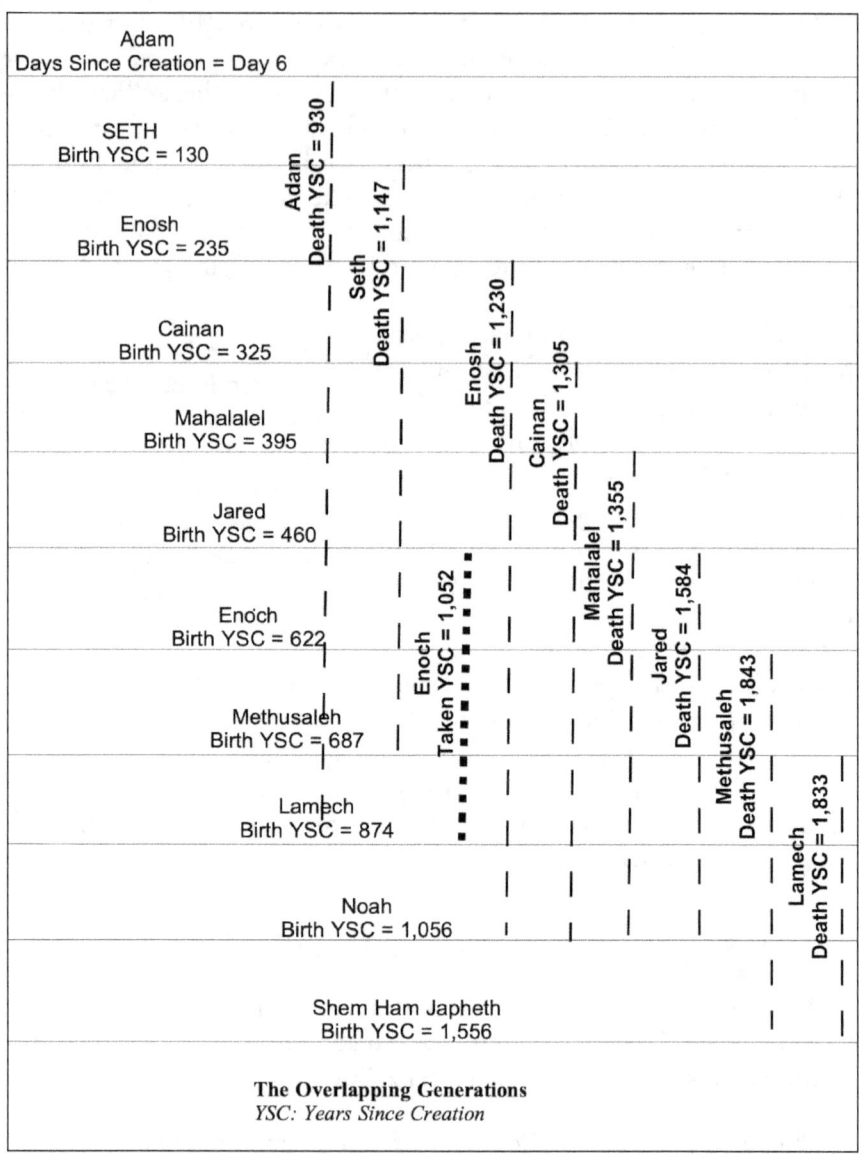

Adam
Days Since Creation = Day 6

SETH
Birth YSC = 130

Adam
Death YSC = 930

Enosh
Birth YSC = 235

Seth
Death YSC = 1,147

Cainan
Birth YSC = 325

Enosh
Death YSC = 1,230

Mahalalel
Birth YSC = 395

Cainan
Death YSC = 1,305

Jared
Birth YSC = 460

Mahalalel
Death YSC = 1,355

Enoch
Birth YSC = 622

Enoch
Taken YSC = 1,052

Jared
Death YSC = 1,584

Methusaleh
Birth YSC = 687

Methusaleh
Death YSC = 1,843

Lamech
Birth YSC = 874

Lamech
Death YSC = 1,833

Noah
Birth YSC = 1,056

Shem Ham Japheth
Birth YSC = 1,556

The Overlapping Generations
YSC: Years Since Creation

emphatically matched with Adam bearing *"a son in his own likeness"* (Genesis 5:3).

Second, Enoch knew Adam, Seth, Enosh, Cainan, Mahalalel, and Jared, his father. They taught him enough truths about God that Enoch was intimate with God. They were all dead in spirit, but Enoch walked with God. Only Adam and Eve had done so, and only prior to their fall, when they were yet alive in spirit.

We quoted Jesus above, that God seeks worshipers in spirit and that walking with God requires spiritual birth. Apostle Paul told the Athenians that God wants people to find Him.

> ...so that they should seek the Lord, in the hope that they might grope for Him and find Him, though He is not far from each one of us; for in Him we live and move and have our being. (Acts 17:27–28)

Clearly, Enoch received spiritual birth for this intimacy with God. Only the outcome is mentioned, without any details about the method or timing. He walked with God and was no more.

God took Enoch sixty-nine years before Noah was born—in fact, before any of his ancestors had died. Even Adam was alive when Enoch was taken. How bittersweet was it for Adam to see Enoch enjoy what he had forfeited in Eden? Did Enoch's freedom from death remind Adam of the tree of life?

The third evidence of the godly lineage is Lamech, who acknowledges the Lord's curse on the ground. Lamech names his son prophetically, that Noah would alleviate the curse somehow and make food production easier. Lamech's death preceded the Flood by five years. He wouldn't witness the relief arriving, such as the thriving of Noah's vineyard after the Flood.

The last evidence is Noah himself. The Flood's record in Genesis 6 through 10 provides a poignant contrast to his ancestor Adam.

> Noah was a just man, perfect in his generations. Noah walked with God. (Genesis 6:9)

> According to all that God commanded him, so he did. (Genesis 6:22, 7:5)

TRANSMITTING FACTUAL TRUTHS

Bible chronology reveals we are now six thousand years removed from Creation (using our definition of *years*). The Holy Spirit revealed these truths to the Bible authors, guiding the recording. He oversaw the compilation and transmission of the Bible to our present day. By faith in Him, we accept these things as authoritative.

But imagine the young Noah's family compound. With no electricity, free from attention-sucking digital gear, what would they do but talk? The first man and his wife live with you. We have only two chapters of their tale, but you would hear all their stories over their nine centuries of life. Stories of Eden life would be far greater than we have. You would also hear the cautionary tale of Cain and the commendatory behaviors of Abel. You would see firsthand in your cousins the fruit of Sin's rulership in Cain's line.

What Adam, Eve, and Enoch had learned directly from the Lord would comprise your understanding of human existence. Their experiences would form your guiding conscience. You would know the origin of mankind, the naming of the animals, the value of a helpmate, the wiles of the devil, and the cost of disobedience—from the people who lived it all.

They would focus their faith for them on trust and obedience to God, rather than factuality, as we use faith sixty centuries later. As we mature, we gain their focus. The cumulative proofs that God is real and loves us lay all doubt about factuality to rest. The maturing Christian learns it's more effective to doubt the doubt, than to doubt God. When we apply the scrutiny to temptations that Adam and Eve failed to, we quickly realize God is reality and the enemies offer falsity.

THE DISCOVERY OF DARKNESS

As Seth's line reproduced, the kingdom of darkness would receive proof after proof that strategies one and two had only partial success. God's image-creatures had indeed died in spirit. Many of them had welcomed Sin as their ruler. Yet one line still honored satan's enemy, God Almighty. And somehow, a human being could be born in spirit, as Enoch had to have been.

The devil and his partners never had fathers; their race of spiritual beings did not reproduce. Darkness underestimated the power of generational transmission. Adam and Eve imposed their costly lessons upon Abel and Seth. Each subsequent generation followed suit.

Imagine the halls of the dark kingdom, watching their replacements multiply and fill the Earth. Neither strategy so far had impaired multiplication. The human population was exploding. The schemes of darkness are many now, but for the first fifteen hundred years, only Sin had been unleashed.

But satan learned at least one thing from the 1,556 years of Seth's line: the power of fatherhood. Could he use the power of fatherhood to impose his kingdom upon fleshly humans? The third strategy of darkness was just such an attempt. It explains why we have the saying, "If you can't beat 'em, join 'em."

CHAPTER 19

STRATEGY THREE: INTERBREED

The opening verses of Genesis 6 have long challenged readers. As satan's third strategy, the revelation becomes more clear.

> Now it came to pass, when men began to multiply on the face of the earth, and daughters were born to them, that the sons of God saw the daughters of men, that they were beautiful; and they took wives for themselves of all whom they chose. (Genesis 6:1–2)

Humanity had been reproducing for many centuries—all fleshly, all dead in spirit. The line of Cain had demonstrated Sin's usefulness as an agent of darkness. Yet, even in these conditions, darkness was stymied because Seth's line proved that Sin was neither pervasive nor irresistible.

THE NEWNESS OF REPRODUCTION

God declared repeatedly in Genesis 1 that living things would reproduce according to their kind. However, reproduction had never occurred prior to that. The angelic rebels were unable to reproduce and were never fathered. Until it happened, the kingdom of darkness had no reference for its meaning, but they could learn.

Despite success with strategies one and two, their replacements were proliferating. The kingdom of darkness needed a third strategy.

Watching human fatherhood all those years educated them. Could satan possibly mimic reproduction? If so, darkness could reproduce reinforcements, using human women. After observing people's reproduction for sixteen hundred years, satan attempted it with a prisoner release. They manifested themselves to people, and in Genesis 6 the Scripture calls them *"the sons of God."*

SONS OF GOD DEFINED

It is that term which leads to confusion. Jesus, the only Son of God, remained undisclosed until later (John 1:18). Genesis 6:1, passed down through Noah, records events from a pre-Flood, mortal human perspective.

The vast majority were dead in spirit, more like Cain's line than Seth's. To them, what would angelic beings resemble? The mythology of old, tribal animism, and popular alien "science" today answers that. People would consider them otherworldly, more powerful, oppressively determinative, and close to divine. A show like *Ancient Aliens* would feature them.

Even after fifteen centuries, humans still had limited experience with the unseen realm. People were dead in spirit, incapable of understanding spiritual things. God's Word was not yet initiated. The dark partner Sin was sneaky and did not willingly expose itself. Our knowledge of the spirit world far exceeds that of our ancestors.

In fact, we have six millennia of data about darkness and all its destruction. To us, evil beings are everywhere all the time. Those before the Flood couldn't have that experience.

Darkness has used nineteen identifiable strategies; we have the vocabulary to show for it. But the newness of humanity limited the vocabulary of those who recorded Genesis 6:1–2.

That generation of people saw angelic beings, and called them *"sons of God."* They passed this commonly shared language down through Noah and his sons. Other Scriptures refer to the angels in similar ways, such as Job 1:6 and 2:1, together with Psalm 82 which Jesus quoted to His persecutors in John 10:34.

But what angelic beings are they? Why is *"sons of God"* plural in Genesis 6:1–2?

PARTNERS RELEASED ON ASSIGNMENT

In Book Three of the *Unseen* Series, we identified satan's rebel partners as a third of the angels. Occurring before the six days of Genesis 1, the rebellion took place before man was created. These fallen angels had physical bodies, as do all the race of angels (albeit different from ours). God filled the rebel bodies with burning fire and cast them down to the Earth of Genesis 1:1. The devil and his partners ruined it into their giant cooling pool of Genesis 1:2. God then terrorized them during the six twenty-four-hour days, which culminated in our creation as replacements for the fallen Lucifer.

Strategies one and two failed to be comprehensively destructive. For strategy three, more "manpower" was needed. From his prison of Isaiah 14:17 and 1 Peter 3:19, satan released more partners upon Earth.

Their assignment was to interbreed with the human race. With their physical bodies, they impregnated human women and bore offspring. The fallen angels could themselves reproduce according to their kind—at least in half.

Having recognized the proven power of fatherhood in Seth's line, the kingdom of darkness emulated it themselves.

LONG MULTIPLICATION

Let's revisit the young Noah's family compound. Every man around the fire had known Adam, so close was humanity to our original creation. Compare it to us. If father and son are twenty-five years apart, the forty-five hundred years since the Flood holds one hundred eighty generations.

Adam's original human capabilities might be diluted in us, after that many generations. Noah is just ten generations removed from Adam due to their long lifespans.

And the LORD God formed man of the dust of the ground, and breathed into his nostrils the breath of life; and man became a living being. (Genesis 2:7)

God's breath is sufficient explanation for the extended lifespans of the pre-Flood generations. Three additional factors contributed to longevity, beginning with Earth's geophysical conditions prior to the Flood. Second: everyone expected to live long, so close to the original creation of man. Third was God's command to multiply which benefited from the long lives.

LIFESPANS SHORTENED

And the LORD said, "My Spirit shall not strive with man forever, for he is indeed flesh; yet his days shall be one hundred and twenty years." (Genesis 6:3)

Simultaneous to this interbreeding of fallen angels and human women was God's decision to reduce the span of human life. This decision was enacted over time; the first named person to live only one hundred twenty years was Moses, several hundred years later. But how does it relate to this dramatic time preceding the Flood?

It was the multiplication of half-breeds that prompted God's shortening of human lifespans.

IMPRESSIVE AND RENOWNED

Apostle Paul listed levels of the angelic rebel army in Ephesians 6:12. They were *"the sons of God"* in Genesis 6. The fallen angels manifested their physical bodies on Earth and took human daughters as wives. The passage says that human multiplication cued up strategy three from satan.

Now it came to pass, when men began to multiply on the face of the earth.... (Genesis 6:1)

Interbreeding piggybacked on the reproductive principle God Himself had installed. Now they could reproduce according to their kind, at least halfway.

Strategy three succeeded, and produced a new type of being. The kingdom of darkness could now reproduce reinforcements, a significant first for the exiled rebels of heaven. And their offspring could rule original people, judging from the description Noah passed down in Genesis 6:4.

There were giants on the earth in those days, and also afterward, when the sons of God came in to the daughters of men and they bore children to them. Those were the mighty men who were of old, men of renown.

The appearance of these mighty giants coincided with the mating of angels and humans. These offspring powerfully explain an enduring mystery: the origin of demons.

INTERBRED SEXUALITY

Although the breeding father was angelic, the human female imposed restrictions on the process. God designed human reproduction through a sexual union using sperm from the male body and egg from the female body. Each contributes half the DNA needed to make a new person.

The fertilized egg would grow in the woman then birth from her body. God created Adam and Eve this way, before their disobedience in Eden. Childbearing by women was the original design; only disobedience made it painful (Genesis 3:16).

This process would also govern the interbreeding of fallen angel and human woman. Reproduction by a human woman would require the supply of a sperm from them.

ANGELIC PHYSIQUE

The Bible doesn't reveal what the angelic bodies were, or how they performed it. But to accomplish physical things on Earth as it describes, physical bodies are required.

When Jesus finished His forty days without food (Mark 1:13), and when He suffered in Gethsemane (Luke 22:43), angels physically ministered to Him.

When Elijah fled Jezebel, physical care from an angel encouraged him. An angel readied food with an outsized impact on Elijah's stamina and state of mind.

> For further consideration of angelic nature, Book Eight in the *Unseen* Series is titled *Nobody Sees These Friends: Partners in the Unseen.*

Then as he lay and slept under a broom tree, suddenly an angel touched him, and said to him, "Arise and eat." Then he looked, and there by his head was a cake baked on coals, and a jar of water. So he ate and drank, and lay down again. And the angel of the LORD came back the second time, and touched him, and said, "Arise and eat, because the journey is too great for you." So he arose, and ate and drank; and he went in the strength of that food forty days and forty nights as far as Horeb, the mountain of God. (1 Kings 19:5–8)

When the two angels arrived in Sodom to evaluate it for judgment, the men of the city besieged Lot's home where they lodged. *"Where are the men who came to you tonight? Bring them out to us that we may know them carnally"* (Genesis 19:5). The angelic beings' bodies were capable of sexually interacting with people, even in ways that the besiegers had perversely and lustfully imagined.

PATERNITY

Born of human women with half human bodies, the interbred children would eventually die. So, what did the fallen angels contribute?

The description of giants and mighty men shows that the angels' sperm brought an augmented physical development. It also brought a bravado that earned them intimidating renown, as Scripture records.

PREVENTION

The consequences of this reproductive formula prompted the Lord to take two preventive actions. Shortening the lifespan was the first.

We've noted several times previously the Bible records little preventive action against the plans of darkness. God warned Cain about Sin, but didn't prevent Cain from choosing it. As a result, Abel was murdered and Sin gained entry into the human race.

Knowing the serpent would advance upon them, God still didn't warn Adam and Eve about him. In sixteen hundred years of humanity, the closest thing to prevention by God was exiling them from Eden's tree of life.

The interbreeding strategy prompts God to limit people's lifespan. The impregnation of mortal women with undying angelic DNA was the cue. Their offspring manifested extraordinary physiques and dominance. This was a mixture God acted to prevent. He did not want the angelically-mixed humans to persist on Earth as a parallel race to mankind.

Scripture never again reports the successful mating of fallen angels and human women. The shortening of the human lifespan effectively prevented it. We can reverse engineer the implication: the interbreeding required a long life of centuries to succeed. God shortened human lifespans to eliminate that possibility.

SPIRIT SEX

Although fallen angels have never mated with women since, the pattern of satan's third strategy has persisted. As we'll see in Book Five, *Nobody Sees This Israel: God's Vanguard against Darkness,* Israel was continually beset by Baal worship. Its distinct theology: people had to mate with gods to ensure prosperity.

The religion seduced Israelites into both adultery and idolatry. Ritual sex acts between unmarried men and women occurred at the high places, with Asherah groves lined not with trees, but with tree-sized phallic symbols.

Lest we look down on such thinking, our own Western heritage from Greek and Rome is just as wicked with prostitution disguised as worship. Today's celebrities and their groupies signify that strategy three is alive and well. Mating with the renowned for a form of prosperity is the theme.

Sadly, even Church history, past and present, proves sexual lust still combines with spiritual fervor and successfully tempts people. The presence of spiritual energy quickly disables all reason and fear of consequence. Religious adultery manifests the same impulse to secure divine favor, through sexual intercourse with powerful church leaders. A classic American novel tells of a pastor's sexual fall. *The Scarlet Letter* by Nathaniel Hawthorne became classic because the pattern of strategy three persists.

We disarm strategy three by alertness and strong boundaries. Many are the men who mistakenly counseled a woman in private, leading to destruction upon their ministries. While not all private conversations can (or should) be avoided, they should take place in safe spaces where temptation is minimized.

ONE-UPMANSHIP

The period before God's decree had been a series of cues. Human multiplication cued darkness to adopt the interbreeding strategy. Their interbreeding with women cued God to shorten our lifespans.

The interbreeding produced not only a superior race of half-breed beings, but also a level of wickedness never seen before, not even in Cain's line.

WICKEDNESS

Then the LORD saw that the wickedness of man was great in the earth, and that every intent of the thoughts of his heart was only evil continually. (Genesis 6:5)

The release of Sin had not produced this pervasive wickedness. There had been sixteen centuries while God held back His wrath. The interbreeding has produced a wickedness which pervaded the entire race of people.

Did the renowned half-breeds discourage people from seeking righteousness? After all, only one man had remained free of it in God's eyes.

Conscience was not merely seared, but entirely absent. The restraints which keep society beneficent were removed. The good remained unloved, while the evil was embraced relentlessly.

The presence of the interbred offspring initiated this state of affairs. We imagined the family compound of Seth. Now imagine the compound of these angelically-mixed families. Where Seth's compounds learned of Adam's creation, the mixed-breed compounds heard tell of Lucifer's glorious existence. Instead of tales about the disobedience in Eden and the warnings of its consequences, the tents of the wicked would tell about God's heavy-handed vendetta against Lucifer.

Everything about Lucifer and the paternity of the angelic half-breeds would glorify their cause, and perpetuate self-serving IOUs as the system of existence. No one served each other willingly. Might made right. Children were abused, and became abusers. Pleasure for self occupied the minds of all, scheming to manipulate others' compliance.

Imagine what their fallen angel fathers would teach the half-breeds. Everything from their hell was released on Earth, and reproducing.

THE SPREAD OF WICKEDNESS

The Scriptural pairing in Genesis 6 suggests that their renown comprised being violent and forceful. It's easy to imagine these giants and mighty men penalizing anyone who mimicked the goodness of Seth's line.

This strategy was satan's most successful by far. The creatures made in God's image were consumed by constant evil.

After almost sixteen hundred years of human existence, God decreed the destruction of all flesh—His second preventive measure to defeat the interbreeding of strategy three.

CHAPTER 20

THE DESTRUCTION OF ALL FLESH

And the LORD was sorry that He had made man on the earth, and He was grieved in His heart. So the LORD said, "I will destroy man whom I have created from the face of the earth, both man and beast, creeping thing and birds of the air, for I am sorry that I have made them." (Genesis 6:6–7)

The Flood challenges modern readers because it seems unfair of God to kill everybody. Applying our standard of fairness to God is quite self-serving for us. We owe Him everything and can never make restitution for what we have taken from Him. It's like demanding a cease-fire right after our attack.

People who insist on measuring God's fairness have a surprise coming. The Flood is tiny compared to God's planned end for this world.

The day of the Lord will come as a thief in the night, in which the heavens will pass away with a great noise, and the elements will melt with fervent heat; both the earth and the works that are in it will be burned up. (2 Peter 3:10)

Then I saw a great white throne and Him who sat on it, from whose face the earth and the heaven fled away. And there was found no place for them.... Now I saw a new heaven and a new earth, for the first heaven and the first earth had passed away. Also there was no more sea. (Revelation 20:11, 21:1)

The short-sighted objections of human fairness must give way to fearful reverence for God.

> Therefore, since all these things will be dissolved, what manner of persons ought you to be in holy conduct and godliness.... You therefore, beloved, since you know this beforehand, beware lest you also fall from your own steadfastness, being led away with the error of the wicked. (2 Peter 3:11, 17)

THE SOVEREIGNTY BEHIND THE FLOOD

As our Creator, God has the sovereign right to do whatever He wants with us. He does not owe us anything—quite the opposite. We have no standing to demand anything from Him. The Flood presents no challenge unless we have rights before the holy Creator we offended. That's what Job thought, provoking God's penetrating rebuke in Job 40:8:

> Would you indeed annul My judgment?
> Would you condemn Me that you may be justified?

JUSTICE

Noah lived until Abraham's sixty-eighth year; doubtless, the family legacy of the Flood was retold many times. Thus, Abraham knew the Lord as the Judge with a sovereign right to apply justice. In Genesis 18, he meekly implored that Judge on a matter of justice.

God revealed to Abraham His concern about the wickedness of Sodom and Gomorrah. Using the ages given in Genesis 11, the conversation occurred 392 years after the Flood. The Lord waited and listened as Abraham pled for the cities to be spared. Abraham knew his nephew Lot lived there with his family, but evidenced a far more grave concern.

> Would You also destroy the righteous with the wicked?... Far be it from You to do such a thing as this, to slay the righteous with the wicked, so that the righteous should be as the wicked; far be it from You! Shall not the Judge of all the earth do right? (Genesis 18:23, 25)

God is not willing for any to perish (2 Peter 3:19). However, He has a greater priority: honor for our choice to perish.

After a take-away negotiation by Abraham, the Lord agreed not to destroy the cities if He could find merely ten righteous people. With Sodom, not even ten could be found. The angels evacuated righteous Lot with his family. God applied to Sodom the destructive justice merited by their choices.

The Flood was an occasion of justice like that. The human race had chosen the evil of the half-breeds. Only one righteous person lived—not even ten.

> Then the LORD saw that the wickedness of man was great in the earth, and that every intent of the thoughts of his heart was only evil continually. And the LORD was sorry that He had made man on the earth, and He was grieved in His heart.... Noah was a just man, perfect in his generations. Noah walked with God. (Genesis 6:5–6, 9)

GEOPHYSICAL REALITY BEFORE THE FLOOD

Book Three, *Nobody Sees This Creation: The Origin of the Devil and His Replacements,* thoroughly reviewed Ezekiel 28, Isaiah 14, Revelation 12, Luke 11, and Genesis 1. The study concluded that satan and his partners contrived the dark and watery void of Genesis 1:2 as a giant cooling pool for the wrathful heat in their bodies. God's six days reversed their contrivance, in part by raising the dry land. Then He filled Earth with creatures both on land and the seas.

The firmament had been God's second action on Day Two of the six (Genesis 1:6–7). It was a firm structure of ice covering the globe.

> Then God said, "Let there be a firmament in the midst of the waters, and let it divide the waters from the waters." Thus God made the firmament, and divided the waters which were under the firmament from the waters which were above the firmament; and it was so.

It also played a key role on Day Four, obscuring the heavenly bodies so that even the sun and moon were described as the greater and lesser lights. The protection from ultraviolet rays would account for both the long life and the very long periods of childbearing.

Book Three compares then and now on page 175.

> We don't have a firm barrier over our heads now, and our understanding of space is the most advanced in human history. There is no water

above the sky; we've been there. There is no roof on the waters below, which would obstruct our rockets. With these present physical realities, Day Two and Day Four [the firmament] seem nonsensical....

This is a common result of assuming God meant what we experience today. The implications of equating the Day Two firmament with our sky make it an unsatisfying explanation.[4]

THE CHANGE THAT HAD TO OCCUR

Today's orbit and appearance of the moon does not match with its description on Day Four in Genesis 1:14–19. There God says the moon will rule the night. To fulfill that description, the moon must be visible to all humans each night. However, there are only two conditions in which that can occur.

First, all people must be on one land mass. Second, Earth's daily rotation speed must sync with the moon's orbital speed.

> Chapter twelve in Book Three of the *Unseen* Series explores these physics more thoroughly.

To validate this Scripture's claim about the moon ruling the night, a specific geophysical reality must hold; Earth must rotate at thirty-five miles per hour.

But what we have now is a rotational speed of 1,040 miles per hour. In other words, for the Scripture to be accurate it requires that a major geophysical change occurred.

How did we get this dramatic rotating speed increase? So much faster that the moon no longer rules every night, and no longer appears over all people? It happened during the Flood. God did a wholesale rearrangement of Earth.

REARRANGEMENT

In the six hundredth year of Noah's life, in the second month, the seventeenth day of the month, on that day all the fountains of the great deep were broken up, and the windows of heaven were opened. (Genesis 7:11)

First, the subterranean water burst forth and divided the one continent into the seven we know today. This global disbursal of land occurred during the fourteen months and twenty-seven days that Noah and his family were on the Ark with the protected land creatures (Genesis 8:13–14).

Second, the firmament melted. Because it was a global structure of ice, it appeared as windows opening in it. The amount of water pouring down on Earth in only forty days of deluge would make our hurricanes seem like a sprinkle. The weight of the melting ice and the speed at which it hit the surface, combined with the opening of the subterranean fountains, easily accounts for the needed energy to change Earth's rotational speed.

For 301 days (Genesis 8:5), Earth was once again covered with water—just as it had been in Genesis 1:2. Satan and his fiery partners rejoiced as God brought back the giant cooling pool.

SATAN TRIUMPHS OVER GOD?

The devil, obsessed with power, would have seen the Flood as a triumph. First, the vermin intended to replace satan all died. Second, dry land disappeared. The surrendering God even gave them back their giant cooling pool. And the best of all: God did it Himself.

These exceeded the fondest hopes of darkness. The Flood's achievements dwarfed strategies one through three for darkness. It is easy to imagine the smug satisfaction of darkness, that God appeared to admit defeat in His effort to replace satan.

I DON'T THINK SO

He thought his victory was assured, seeing waters covering Earth again, dry land everywhere submerged. But imagine the fallen Lucifer's dismay nearly fifteen months later. The cooling pool was broken up again. Their displacement to the sea had returned with a vengeance. Infused with

---

BACKFIRE

God demonstrates again that He can do as He wishes with *"the powers of heaven and the kings of earth,"* as Nebuchadnezzar was to acknowledge centuries later after his insanity (Daniel 4:35). Twice now, satan enjoyed a water-covered cooling pool, only to find how easily God reformed it and caused dry earth to reappear. Even the image-creatures still walk the Earth—creatures designed to reproduce God's image on Earth and displace satan with his dark kingdom.

inescapable fire within and desperate to cool himself in the deep, satan is once again dislocated by the land-based creatures, supplied by life-giving rivers.

If darkness had thought it through, they would have noticed there were still sea creatures, and an Ark with eight human survivors. That might have told them their triumph was in appearance only.

CHAPTER 21

THE ORIGIN OF DEMONS

Scripture reveals that the angelic races do not die. The fathers of the mixed-race children possessed something unique: eternal immortality. What would the mix of mortal and angelic produce?

The interbred children had DNA like all of us. Half was from their mortal mother, and like them, these offspring had a dead-in-spirit body doomed to death. Their angelic father contributed the other half, unable to die in body or spirit.

Which genes would be regressive, and which dominant?

HALF-BREEDS

God's decree about the human lifespan in Genesis 6:3 answers that question. The angelic DNA overrode the human DNA. Combined with the long-lived human DNA, undying angelic paternity produced a mixed race with superiority over people whom God had created in His image.

The children had spirit fathers, and from them inherited undying spirits. They had mortal mothers, and from them, inherited bodies subject to death.

HOW MANY?

It is unclear how many lives were lost due to God's Flood. He did not limit it to humans; every beast and living thing was affected. But given certain assumptions, we can "guesstimate" the number of people who died.

The pair of Adam and Eve had three named children in Scripture. They had other sons and daughters for the balance of Adam's eight hundred years. With just one child a year, that would produce eight hundred people. Let's suppose no multiple births, no infant mortality, and no more Cain murders. For math's sake, let's figure the genders evenly divided, four hundred each of men and women.

Genesis 5 records ten generations. Let's assume the four hundred pairs from Adam mimic their parents' reproduction. Thus, each pair of descendants produces four hundred reproducing pairs. The first generation alone would produce 160,000 reproducing pairs.

The only variable left is the time between births. Given their long lives and this rate of multiplication, the following chart shows the resulting population by the time of the Flood.

If couple bears a child every...	Then the potential reproducing pairs at time of the Flood are:
100 years	3,906,250,000 (3.9 billion)
80 years	74,483,173,194 (74.5 billion)
40 years	10,374,969,840,400 (10.3 trillion)
1 year	43,003,491,468,298,400,000,000,000,000

No evidence supports the existence of such a massive population in history. The Flood swept away any evidence that might have been.

If they lived on the one land mass, it's easy to imagine how wickedness would arise. Might prevails over right in a cutthroat competition for food or privacy.

The suppositions don't even include any enhanced fertility of the angelically-mixed offspring. Nor does this "guesstimate" distinguish between purebred humans and the interbred ones.

Whether those numbers were alive during the Flood is irrelevant to us today. The purpose of this calculation relates to our unseen tempters. Rather than prove how many the Flood killed, we are solving the mystery of demons' origins.

WHO ARE THEY?

To discern unseen tempters, we need to know who they are. There are eight billion people on Earth today. Mary Magdalene had seven demons oppressing her.

Deliverance ministry has proliferated globally now and routinely delivers people from at least seven demonic strongholds. If everyone had seven, 56 billion demons would be required. Where do all these demons come from? What are they?

THE FLOOD AND DEMONS

These half-breed children died physically in the Flood, as God intended. He barred them from physically manifesting on Earth again. Yet their spirits lived because of their paternity. What happened to them? The Bible twice tells us.

The first clue is Isaiah 14. It is a double prophecy, with two time jumps revealed to Isaiah. First, it uses the king of Babylon as a type one hundred years before Babylon is a kingdom. Second, using that type, God prophetically reveals the bitter chatter of satan's rebel partners when satan is finally judged.

Those who see you will gaze at you,
And consider you, saying:
"Is this the man who made the earth tremble,
Who shook kingdoms,
Who made the world as a wilderness
And destroyed its cities,
Who did not open the house of his prisoners?" (Isaiah 14:16–17)

Throughout the *Unseen* Series, we refer to satan's use of power against others. His is the only spiritual prison described in Scripture; God has none. And who would be in it? The second Bible clue tells exactly who.

He went and preached to the spirits in prison, who formerly were disobedient, when once the Divine longsuffering waited in the days of Noah, while the ark was being prepared, in which a few, that is, eight souls, were saved through water. (1 Peter 3:19–20)

THE THREE DAYS OF JESUS

Apostle Peter and the other ten original apostles spent forty days with the resurrected Jesus. His teaching during that period was just for them, not written for us. But we can only reverse engineer from the apostles' subsequent behaviors. It's easy to imagine their question: *"Where did You go the three days You were dead?"* What Peter says above would come from Jesus' answer to such a question.

THE SPIRITS IN PRISON

Apostle Peter narrowly defined *"spirits in prison"* as those alive *"in the days of Noah, while the ark was being prepared"* (1 Peter 3:19–20). People who lived after the Flood and before interbreeding are not part of that group.

This makes sense, because Adam and Eve were dead in spirit and their children were dead in spirit. Peter would not describe them as *"spirits."*

A single group aligns with the time frame and description, in a lone prison that confines spirits. These are the half-breeds. The Flood killed their mortal bodies, but because of their paternity they had spirits. They were people by descent from the human mothers, and spirits by their angelic fathers. Alive in the unseen realm, they had no bodies. The devil had imprisoned them as scum.

THE RAGE OF HELL

The counterfeit fatherhood of satan and his rebel partners was devoid of all love. Like many parents today, they only used their children to get something they loved more. For satan, that was victory over God.

But once physically dead, the offspring offered no useful purpose. The leaders of hell would despise them as half-breeds unworthy to exist.

The restoration of their giant cooling pool had been short-lived. Dry land returned; animals multiplied again and populated Earth. God again blessed the surviving eight and sent them forth to multiply. The image-creatures were back.

Losing their apparent victory over God would stoke the intense anger of hell. In satan's prison was someone to suffer the devilish rage. These spirits were once human, after all. Despite the efforts of darkness, the half-breeds represent the indomitable human race that kept multiplying. Plausibly, satan and his fallen partners would torture and oppress these spirits in prison.

After centuries in that prison, it's easy to surmise what they became. We know them today as demons.

WHEN DEMONS ARE RELEASED

Their imprisonment explains why the Old Testament says so little about them. We see them in only two Bible periods. The first is their large-scale swarm during Jesus' three years; the second is during the early Church years.

Current ministry reports show that our day is a third. The devil releases them and assigns them to hinder human multiplication and discourage spiritual birth.

Because of the torture in satan's prison, also known as an abyss, one group of demons named Legion begged Jesus not to send them back there.

> When he saw Jesus, he cried out, fell down before Him, and with a loud voice said, "What have I to do with You, Jesus, Son of the Most High God? I beg You, do not torment me!" For He had commanded the unclean spirit to come out of the man. For it had often seized him, and he was kept under guard, bound with chains and shackles; and he broke the bonds and was driven by the demon into the wilderness.
>
> Jesus asked him, saying, "What is your name?"
>
> And he said, "Legion," because many demons had entered him. And they begged Him that He would not command them to go out into the abyss. (Luke 8:28–31)

THE CLASSES OF DARKNESS

Apostle Paul's list of our enemies contrasts with the demons who whimpered before Jesus.

> We do not wrestle against flesh and blood, but against principalities, against powers, against the rulers of the darkness of this age, against spiritual hosts of wickedness in the heavenly places. (Ephesians 6:12)

Paul describes the angelic rebels as great powers. In the biblical record, he encountered them more than the other apostles. Soon we'll review satan's fourth strategy; it explains why the apostolic missionary Paul had the experience to write that.

Demons are the cannon fodder for darkness. Identifying demons as the disembodied half-breeds explains why. Without reinforcements, the angelic rebels release the demons for "manpower" as needed. When darkness needs a large-scale action on Earth, the demons get shore leave.

They dread returning to satan's prison abyss. To prolong their probation from hell, the demons oppress people. In fear of further torment in hell, some demons opted for face-to-face encounters with the Son of God.

THE GOSPEL FOR THE DEAD

How loving Jesus was in His crucifixion! All living after His time can benefit, like us. Even those who crucified Him, like the Jews, and those who abandoned Him, like the disciples, could benefit. A third group could also receive His love: these imprisoned spirits.

> For this reason the gospel was preached also to those who are dead, that they might be judged according to men in the flesh, but live according to God in the spirit. (1 Peter 4:6)

Apostle Peter repeats the theme of 3:19–20. God had judged the half-breeds by the Flood for their wickedness; they died the death of all human flesh. But through no fault of their own, they were alive in spirit. As we say, they couldn't pick their parents.

Their rebellious angelic fathers have no invitation to repent. But people do. Because of their human maternity, these demons received the chance to repent and believe, just like we are. Jesus visited them in hell.

HELLO AGAIN

In His mercy for these half-humans, Jesus offered them salvation. They were the very demons whom He had cast out of people. Yet despite their track record, He gave even them the opportunity to reconcile to God and receive His life.

The letter to the Ephesian church reveals that Jesus shared this knowledge with Apostle Paul.

> Therefore He says:
> "When He ascended on high,
> He led captivity captive,
> And gave gifts to men."
> Now this, "He ascended"—what does it mean but that He also first descended into the lower parts of the earth? He who descended is also

the One who ascended far above all the heavens, that He might fill all things. (Ephesians 4:8–10)

THE GOSPEL IN HELL

Imagine the electricity of that preaching in the bowels of darkness' dungeon:

"You all know that I am the Son of God and I am here in the head-quarters of him who would replace Me. Some of you I know from casting you out of people. All of you have an opportunity because of your human mothers and your identity as creatures in My image.

"Your leaders just engineered My death, thinking that they would prevent the birth of any more undying human spirits like you. In fact, they just opened the door. By killing Me, who was without sin, they enabled all people to be reconciled to God and become living spirits. As usual, the exact opposite of what they wanted has happened, by their own hand.

"I know how they have treated you all these years. If you will turn your back on them, renounce your loyalty to your slave masters, and follow Me as your new leader, I will lead you out of here forever. Your undying spirits will no longer endure torment. You will one day see your brutal master satan cast into his own abyss.

"Which of you will repent, break your covenant with satan, and come with Me?"

DEMONS TODAY

Demons' one opportunity was when Jesus went to satan's prison and preached to them. There is no Scriptural warrant for us to evidence such mercy on them; quite the opposite.

Do I not hate them, O LORD, who hate You?
And do I not loathe those who rise up against You?
I hate them with perfect hatred;
I count them my enemies. (Psalm 139:21–22)

The modern explosion of demonic oppression shows that many refused His offer to repent. Loyal to satan and the kingdom of darkness, they still oppose the multiplication of living human spirits in covenant with God. When they can't prevent your birth as a spirit by faith, they trouble you.

IT'S YOU

Demons gain leverage from our own immaturity. Loving something more than God opens the door of opportunity for them in our lives. Our unholy thoughts and actions feed and nourish covenants with oppressing demons. The list of opportunities we provide them is long.

Everyone has wounds and sorrow. Demons nurture those hurts, to leverage you into shame/fear/control behaviors. Whatever problem you have, demonic oppressors can piggyback and leverage into pervasive influence.

They encourage false belief-expectation-fulfillment systems in your life. You may have acquired them honestly, raised by flawed parents in a flawed world. Demons capitalize on the raw material of your family line and your ethnic group, pressuring you to repeat their sins.

An effective deliverance ministry is priceless for your Christian life. Expel demonic influences from your life the minute you learn of one. My wife and I have greatly benefited from deliverance through RestoringtheFoundations.org.

Demons can't possess us who are filled with God's Spirit, but they can obstruct our lives and make maturing a more costly prospect. The choice is ours.

THE TEST

God uses these demons to test us. Dealing with demonic oppression should provoke us to mature. But He honors our power of choice and does not force us to. Even Christians can refuse to sever ourselves from demonic oppression.

Sometimes people say, *"Better the devil you know than the devil you don't."* Such attitudes represent a willful covenant with darkness. "If you don't trouble me in ABC, I won't contest you in XYZ." This willingness to remain oppressed manifests as a fear of trying anything that promises liberation. Demons may have used that saying to refuse salvation from Jesus: *"Better the devil you know than the devil you don't."*

While testing us, God respects our human limits. Seeing all the evil spirits at once would overwhelm us. Instead, He reveals them to us gradually, as we become willing and able to renounce their influence.

It's very dangerous to refuse this maturing process. Many Christians do exactly that. We baptize it with euphemisms like *"comfort zone"* and *"what I was taught"* and *"my beliefs."* Far from exhibiting a loyalty to our covenant, these excuses signal willful blindness and refusal to mature.

IT'S SAFE

For the Christian, maturing is always higher up and further in. Forsaking what lies behind, we put our hand to the plow and refuse to look back (Luke 9:62).

Jesus described our immunity to demonic harm when His first missionaries returned from powerful ministry.

I give you the authority to trample on serpents and scorpions, and over all the power of the enemy, and nothing shall by any means hurt you. (Luke 10:19)

Psalm 2, cited here in full, provides our assurance that a covenant with Jesus Christ is safe. He is the Lord's anointed and sits as King of the unseen and the seen. Especially note the last line; there is no greater safety.

Why do the nations rage,
And the people plot a vain thing?
The kings of the earth set themselves,
And the rulers take counsel together,
Against the LORD and against His Anointed, saying,
"Let us break Their bonds in pieces
And cast away Their cords from us."

He who sits in the heavens shall laugh;
The Lord shall hold them in derision.
Then He shall speak to them in His wrath,
And distress them in His deep displeasure:
"Yet I have set My King
On My holy hill of Zion."

"I will declare the decree:
The LORD has said to Me,
'You are My Son,
Today I have begotten You.

Ask of Me, and I will give You
The nations for Your inheritance,
And the ends of the earth for Your possession.
You shall break them with a rod of iron;
You shall dash them to pieces like a potter's vessel.'"

Now therefore, be wise, O kings;
Be instructed, you judges of the earth.
Serve the LORD with fear,
And rejoice with trembling.
Kiss the Son, lest He be angry,
And you perish in the way,
When His wrath is kindled but a little.
Blessed are all those who put their trust in Him.

CHAPTER 22

LEVIATHAN

Scripture mentions Leviathan by name only five times. Using old paradigms, people often disagree what Leviathan is or was. The paradigm of the *Unseen* Series has more explanatory power for this enigmatic creature.

One key to the Leviathan revelation is the chronological sequence. With that, we see one purpose God had in revealing it. Leviathan, the king of all children of pride, is humiliated; God toys with darkness. Let's review the sequence of His five references to it.

FIRST MENTION

The book of Job is considered the oldest writing in the Bible. Its two references to Leviathan are the first chronologically. In an early complaint, Job refers to Leviathan as if the creature is part of common knowledge to his listeners.

> May those curse it who curse the day, those who are ready to arouse Leviathan. (Job 3:8)

Cursing daytime, preferring night, is an age-old sign of a covenant with darkness. On Day One, satan's kingdom had cursed the new day, preferring their deep darkness of Genesis 1:2.

Job ties Leviathan to cursing, a.k.a. cussing. A cuss word doesn't work if the response is, "Huh? What's that?" Job uses a name known to his peers who cursed: Leviathan.

Ignorantly thinking Leviathan is eager to serve them, Job's cussing contemporaries are ready to rouse it. Job invites them to curse the day he was born. At the very least, it reveals their blind pride. Our word for such attitudes is *daredevil.* Here, our word is literal and correct.

LEVIATHAN'S BODY

Since Job brought up the subject of Leviathan, God picked it up again. He blasts Job with a one-hundred-fifty-question, withering interrogation in chapters 38–41, to induce meekness in Job.

The foundation of Bible study is the belief that the words matter because God is a verbal God. Poetic form doesn't limit a person's words to figurative imagination, so we don't impose that limit on Him. In chapter 41, God's wording reveals many details about the creature. In italics are the plain implications.

Can you draw out Leviathan with a hook, *[Leviathan hides]*
Or snare his tongue with a line which you lower? *[Leviathan has a tongue; he's in the water below]*
Can you put a reed through his nose, *[Leviathan has a nose]*
Or pierce his jaw with a hook? *[Leviathan has a jaw]*
Will he make many supplications to you? *[Leviathan has conscious being]*
Will he speak softly to you? *[Leviathan can speak]*
Will he make a covenant with you? *[Leviathan can agree and enter covenants]*
Will you take him as a servant forever? *[sarcasm; Leviathan will not be reduced to a servant]*
Will you play with him as with a bird, *[implied no; he is neither small nor playful]*
Or will you leash him for your maidens? *[implied no; he can't be leashed or used to impress]*
Will your companions make a banquet of him? *[implied no; he could not be caught or cooked or both]*
Will they apportion him among the merchants? *[he is not a resource for trading]*
Can you fill his skin with harpoons, *[he has skin that is too thick to penetrate]*
Or his head with fishing spears? *[Leviathan is a water creature impervious to our best techniques of capture]*
Lay your hand on him;
Remember the battle—
Never do it again! *[Leviathan resists capture ferociously]*

Indeed, any hope of overcoming him is false;
Shall one not be overwhelmed at the sight of him? *[he is scary to see]*
No one is so fierce that he would dare stir him up.... *[Leviathan is intimidating to see]*
I will not conceal his limbs, *[Leviathan had arms and legs, not fins]*
His mighty power, or his graceful proportions. *[Leviathan is beautiful to see]*
Who can remove his outer coat?
Who can approach him with a double bridle?
Who can open the doors of his face,
With his terrible teeth all around? *[Leviathan has a mouth with scary teeth]*
His rows of scales are his pride,
Shut up tightly as with a seal;
One is so near another
That no air can come between them;
They are joined one to another,
They stick together and cannot be parted. *[Leviathan has scales]*
His sneezings flash forth light,
And his eyes are like the eyelids of the morning. *[Leviathan shows burning within]*
Out of his mouth go burning lights;
Sparks of fire shoot out.
Smoke goes out of his nostrils,
As from a boiling pot and burning rushes. *[when near, he is easy to see]*
His breath kindles coals,
And a flame goes out of his mouth. *[Leviathan is a fiery creature]*
Strength dwells in his neck,
And sorrow dances before him. *[Leviathan provokes sorrow wherever he goes]*
The folds of his flesh are joined together;
They are firm on him and cannot be moved. *[Leviathan has rigid armor]*
His heart is as hard as stone, *[he has few emotions compared to us]*
Even as hard as the lower millstone. *[Leviathan is unfeeling]*
When he raises himself up, the mighty are afraid;
Because of his crashings they are beside themselves. *[Leviathan makes intimidating sounds and movements]*
Though the sword reaches him, it cannot avail;
Nor does spear, dart, or javelin. *[weapons are useless against Leviathan]*
He regards iron as straw,
And bronze as rotten wood. *[metal devices cannot restrain him at all]*

The arrow cannot make him flee;
Sling-stones become like stubble to him. *[he fears nothing that people can do to him]*
Darts are regarded as straw;
He laughs at the threat of javelins. *[Leviathan laughs as a conscious creature]*
His undersides are like sharp potsherds;
He spreads pointed marks in the mire. *[Leviathan drags some body part even though he has limbs]*
He makes the deep boil like a pot;
He makes the sea like a pot of ointment. *[Leviathan heats up the water around him]*
He leaves a shining wake behind him;
One would think the deep had white hair. *[The water surface reveals his presence]*
On earth there is nothing like him, *[he is only one, and cannot reproduce]*
Which is made without fear. *[Leviathan fears nothing]*
He beholds every high thing; *[Leviathan has understanding for both seen and unseen]*
He is king over all the children of pride. *[Leviathan attracts and rules everyone whose pride makes them akin to his rebellion.]*

WHAT WAS LEVIATHAN?

Some commentators identify Leviathan simply as a crocodile. As of now, there are no crocodiles whose *"breath kindles coals"*; no one says *"a flame goes out of his mouth."* There are none with *"scales,"* and few mighty men tremble over crocodiles. Even fictional characters such as Tarzan show that. The crocodile solution simply doesn't solve the puzzle.

All such natural animals reproduce according to their kind, as God created them. In contrast, Leviathan doesn't: *"on earth there is nothing like him."* Who else would God call *"king over all the children of pride"*? It concords with Lucifer's pride and oppression of his partners in Isaiah 14:12.

If Leviathan is satan, it explains God's descriptions best. No animal exists who can *"speak softly to you and make a covenant with you."* It would also explain why *"when he raises himself up, the mighty are afraid."* Like a dragon, he has fire in his midst, with numerous signs of fire visible in his sneezes, his eyes, his mouth, his nose. As satan, his physical appearance carries spiritual evil which is palpable, non-mental, and overwhelming.

I interpret Leviathan as the water-dwelling serpent, satan, in his physical form. God's implied facts permit no customary created animal, regardless of their poetic form.

LEVIATHAN TAMED

Psalm 104 is the next chronological reference to Leviathan, about 1000 BC. King David praises God based on natural evidence. In his list are Earth's physical features and its waters, both seas and springs. He refers to Leviathan in that context.

The earth is full of Your possessions—
This great and wide sea,
In which are innumerable teeming things,
Living things both small and great.
There the ships sail about;
There is that Leviathan
Which You have made to play there. (Psalm 104:24–26)

Whatever Leviathan was in Job's time, in David's time it's different. Leviathan was reduced to one water creature among many. He played there, inconsequential and unthreatening to ships. The fearsomeness described by God in Job 41 has given way to harmlessness. Leviathan changed from threat to plaything—but when, and how?

LEVIATHAN IS SERPENT IS SATAN

The fourth reference is in Isaiah chapters 24–32. He lived in the waning 700s BC, after Psalm 104 with David's third mention. The fifth is Psalm 74 by Asaph, who lived around 500 BC.

The prophecies of those nine chapters span the entire history of the world, up to the final judgment which forms the immediate context of this revelation.

For behold, the LORD comes out of His place
To punish the inhabitants of the earth for their iniquity;
The earth will also disclose her blood,

And will no more cover her slain.
In that day the LORD with His severe sword, great and strong,
Will punish Leviathan the fleeing serpent,
Leviathan that twisted serpent;
And He will slay the reptile that is in the sea. (Isaiah 26:21–27:1)

Leviathan is named as the *"fleeing," "twisted serpent," "the reptile … in the sea."* Only satan is described this way in Scripture. Revelation 12:9 confirms the overlapping identification: Leviathan, the serpent, the dragon, satan, and as the fallen Lucifer, confined to the sea.

So the great dragon was cast out, that serpent of old, called the Devil and Satan, who deceives the whole world; he was cast to the earth, and his angels were cast out with him.

BROKEN HEADS

Fifth of five, Psalm 74 was written by the exile-period psalmist Asaph. God is certainly powerful enough to deliver Israel, so why doesn't He, Asaph muses. He lists evidences of God's power, such as what He did to Leviathan—as historical as Day Four's greater light, and as the season-creation after the Flood.

For God is my King from of old,
Working salvation in the midst of the earth.
You divided the sea by Your strength;
You broke the heads of the sea serpents in the waters.
You broke the heads of Leviathan in pieces,
And gave him as food to the people inhabiting the wilderness.
You broke open the fountain and the flood;
You dried up mighty rivers.
The day is Yours, the night also is Yours;
You have prepared the light and the sun.
You have set all the borders of the earth;
You have made summer and winter. (Psalm 74:12–17)

God reveals in Psalm 74 that Leviathan has multiple heads. The reference to sea serpents reinforces the plural quality of this being. The multiple multi-headed beasts in Daniel 7 match this, as does the beast of Revelation 13. All portray the perverse multi-personal unity of the rebel kingdom.

WHEN LEVIATHAN WAS DISARMED

Psalm 74 reveals a timing element as well. Asaph cites God's divisions of the sea, which had occurred three times: on Day Three, after the Flood, and during the exodus from Egypt. Only the first two are candidates for the historical event Asaph describes.

Asaph's other revelations narrow it down: *"You gave him as food to the people inhabiting the wilderness; You broke open the fountain and the flood; You dried up mighty rivers"* (Psalm 74:14–15).

The presence of people rules out the six days of Genesis 1, before we even existed. The exodus didn't include drying up rivers, so Asaph isn't referring to that event. The reference to the fountains of the deep and flood clearly signify the timing: God broke Leviathan's heads in the re-shaping of the Flood.

The five references combine to reveal that the plural sea serpents and heads signify satan and kingdom. The inescapable burning into their bodies requires moisture for any relief. God's actions of Earth-reforming toys with them. He expands land, dries up rivers, and restricts their cooling territory. The shoreline and the seasons all affecting the kingdom of darkness, which curses the day.

By His geophysical alterations in the Flood, God ended Leviathan's reign of terror. The fearsome body God described in Job 41 became the frolicking and harmless Leviathan of Psalm 104.

LIFE OF LEVIATHAN

Taken as a whole, the sequence reveals that Leviathan lost his sway during the Flood. David spoke of Leviathan's disarming at the Flood, when Asaph said God broke his heads. That event preceded their lives, but Isaiah prophesied a future event, when Leviathan is slain in final judgment.

The fallen Lucifer has broken heads, yet survives with his supernatural nature. Daniel and John both witnessed how it looked.

It had ten horns. I was considering the horns, and there was another horn, a little one, coming up among them, before whom three of the first horns were plucked out by the roots. (Daniel 7:7)

And I saw one of his heads as if it had been mortally wounded, and his deadly wound was healed. And all the world marveled and followed the beast. (Revelation 13:3)

213

God could give Leviathan's carcass as food for people, while satan spiritually endured. It explains why we don't still see Leviathan, nor the former bodies of the demons. In both cases, their spirits continued after the Flood killed their bodies.

A NEW FORM

The evolutionary principle is wrong about humans, but accurately describes satan. For the Bible's revelation to be accurate, the fallen angels must be able to develop replacement bodies.

Thus, it was satan who crawled out of the soup, the serpent who hugged the moist ground to speak with Adam and Eve. His emissaries also developed the physiques to mate with human women.

Lucifer, now satan, is created, not divine, and has the limitations of any angelic creature. He is not all-powerful, he can't be everywhere at once, and he doesn't know everything.

Despite these limits, satan remains powerful and inventive. The devil adjusts strategies over time to regain his influence. After the Flood stripped him of his intimidating physique, he developed a new way to hinder God's image-creatures. Leviathan's destruction in the Flood did not prohibit satan's physical development. By the first century AD, he was able to appear even as an angel of light (2 Corinthians 11:14).

Earth's geophysical alteration obstructed the kingdom of darkness. The interbreeding of strategy three was never possible again.

CHAPTER 23

THREE STRATEGIES BEFORE THE FLOOD

Our paradigm of satan's strategies is new. The present-day impact of the fourth strategy warrants a brief review of the three preceding the Flood.

SATAN

The devil alone operated the first strategy. It achieved hereditary corruption of God's image-creatures. The devil tricked Adam and Eve. God cast the pair out, as the rebel angels had been. All that God had intended for a sinless human race—lost. A holy God whom we could never repay became humanity's worst enemy. Great sorrow befell the race of image-creatures, and most of all, the Son of Man who would endure and satisfy God's wrath upon our sin.

Yet the success of darkness was unsatisfactory. Adam and Eve multiplied anyway, and worse yet, their offspring worshiped the Lord.

SIN

The incomplete outcome led to strategy two. The leader of darkness released one partner from his prison of spirits, a spiritual entity which God named *Sin*. God had not warned the original pair about the serpent, but He did warn Cain that Sin sneaks to rule people and have them.

Despite the Lord's warning, Cain opened his life door to Sin. His descendants exemplified the indulgence of Sin, as person after person welcomed its rule.

Yet the kingdom of darkness could not claim full victory, because God's original mandate occurred. His image-creatures still multiplied, filling the Earth and subduing it. Even worse, people in at least one line (Seth's) walked with God.

FLESH

Incomplete success is no success for a devil hell-bent on overthrowing God Almighty. For a third strategy, darkness piggybacked on the proven power of human reproduction. His partner rebels, released from satan's prison, mated with human women.

The breeding pairs of strategy three could multiply for centuries. These unholy unions produced a race of half-breeds, spirits by their fathers and mortal by their mothers. During Noah's first five hundred years, these half-humans caused the wickedness darkness hoped for. Earth had only one righteous man remaining.

It was a period of success for the rebel angels and their leader.

RESPONSE REVIEW

When satan devised his first strategy, God did not divulge it to Adam and Eve. He gave them only one prohibition: don't eat the fruit of the knowing tree. With it was a single warning: the day you do, you will die. But the Creator didn't say why and He didn't explain *"die."*

God was more detailed when speaking to Cain. Doing well and being accepted was option one. The alternative was falling victim to Sin, satan's second strategy.

The third strategy of darkness produced God's most extreme responses. First was His severe reduction in human lifespans, from nine hundred to one hundred twenty, 87 percent. He then judged wickedness for the first time in the biblical record.

He collapsed the firmament of ice and opened the fountains under the land mass. The Lord killed all people, possibly multi-billions. He preserved a meager eight people with their small boatload of animals.

SHORT-LIVED SUCCESS

The Flood restored the preferred watery covering of Earth to the kingdom of darkness. The dry land was gone again—but only temporarily. After fourteen months of a people-free, water-covered Earth, the vacation of darkness came to a permanent end.

The settling waters restored dry land. The greater light, once hidden by a firmament of ice, was now the blazing sun, filling Earth with full daylight. The temporary glee of darkness was gone forever.

WE'RE BAAACK

What was satan to do now? The uncertain kingdom was unaware what God would do next. We reviewed many possible outcomes of satan's corruption strategy in Eden; the release of Sin held so much promise. Interbreeding was very successful. Yet each strategy failed to defeat the race of God's image-creatures.

Now the eight remaining ones would multiply and fill Earth again. The reproduction of God's image-creatures was still darkness' worst nightmare. They know He is replacing their rebellious dominion with us as His partners.

THREE FEWER UNKNOWNS

Some uncertainty was eliminated, however; three possibilities were ruled out permanently. God told Noah three things that would *not* happen. He would never curse the ground again, nor reform Earth, nor destroy all flesh.

I will never again curse the ground for man's sake....
While the earth remains,
Seedtime and harvest,
Cold and heat,
Winter and summer,
And day and night
Shall not cease. (Genesis 8:21–22)

Never again shall all flesh be cut off by the waters of the flood; never again shall there be a flood to destroy the earth. (Genesis 9:11)

ETHNOS

CHAPTER 24

PEOPLE AFTER THE FLOOD

God had teased the kingdom of darkness with the Flood, as if He was achieving their aim for them. Imagine the dismay of darkness fourteen months later.

THE SCARY COVENANT

Darkness heard what God would not do, but they also learned something brand new, not even stated in Eden. For the first time in Bible history, God covenanted Himself verbally. Nor was the covenant with Noah only, but all people ever. Moreover, every creature God preserved was a beneficiary.

> Behold, I establish My covenant with you and with your descendants after you, and with every living creature that is with you: the birds, the cattle, and every beast of the earth with you, of all that go out of the ark, every beast of the earth. (Genesis 9:9–10)

Before the Flood, darkness had to contend with God's blessing to multiply and fill Earth. Their obstacle was greatly worsened now. In the earlier strategies, satan could not rule out the possibility of God forsaking people, but no longer.

The breadth and duration of His covenant could extinguish every hope of darkness. We enjoy it today, so long-lasting is God's promise to Noah our father.

This is the sign of the covenant which I make between Me and you, and every living creature that is with you, *for perpetual generations*: I set My rainbow in the cloud, and it shall be for the sign of the covenant between Me and *the earth*. It shall be, when I bring a cloud over the earth, that the rainbow shall be seen in the cloud; and I will remember My covenant which is between Me and you and *every living creature of all flesh*; the waters shall never again become a flood to destroy all flesh. The rainbow shall be in the cloud, and I will look on it to remember the *everlasting covenant* between God and every living creature of all flesh that is on the earth. (Genesis 9:12–16, emphasis mine)

God's statement is old news to us, but not to the kingdom of darkness. This covenant is interminable, *"for perpetual generations."* The scope was unlimited: to all people, to all creatures, and to Earth. The irksome and vexing reminder would appear in Earth's new sky in perpetuity.

If you are the devil, that's scary. If you're anybody else, it is great news—now more than ever.

UNKNOWNS

Beyond God's new covenant, what did Noah and his family know? The Bible records very little that God explained to him.

Every natural order we have was new for them. Put yourself in Noah's shoes: just off the Ark, the Earth scraped clean in every direction. Listen, and hear no distant noises. Look for trees, people, or animals; you will find none. Imagine how precious was every single item from the Ark!

Noah and his family faced more unknowns and insecurity than any person ever has. All that once supported their life was wiped away by the Flood. Each of us likewise faces daily unknowns.

Simple household maintenance pressures uncertain decision-making, particularly in our time of hyper-capability. Uncertainty is amplified by family management and income production. The fig leaves in our lives, our futile attempts at cover-ups, cannot immunize us against deep insecurity.

We easily ignore our spiritual existence, which does not shout at us like daily urgencies. Religious habits arise to offset our fears; often they are strange and defy all sense in the name of faith.

The unseen enemies take advantage of all our unknowns and insecurity. Putting our trust in Jesus our King, we disarm the tempters from leveraging life's insecurities. God uses unknowns also, to test us. Noah passed the test; we can as well—with God's help.

> The LORD your God led you all the way these forty years in the wilderness, to humble you and test you, to know what was in your heart, whether you would keep His commandments or not. (Deuteronomy 8:2)

INSECURITY

What's your response when you feel insecure? To discern the lurking enticement of demonic oppression, learn your language of insecurity. Its symptoms are easy to see; your natural emotions, thoughts, actions, and words do not have to dominate you. Instead, make them your alert system. You can rely on the Spirit whom Jesus sent to live in you.

We constantly encounter such questions of safety. Will they provoke me into knee-jerk responses, into fig-leaf coping like Adam and Eve? I would be in line with our genetic history if so. But if the Spirit of God abides in me, I can partner with Him. He knows how to keep me safe.

Paul's teaching in Romans applies directly to our insecurities. How do we earn God's favor? How can we be sure He will protect us, or bail us out? Many answer these with behavior to obligate God, compliance which Paul summarizes with the words *"the law."* But the follower of Jesus Christ has been born as a spirit. A new answer is available to you.

> But now we have been delivered from the law, having died to what we were held by, so that we should serve in the newness of the Spirit and not in the oldness of the letter. (Romans 7:6)

> Be anxious for nothing, but in everything by prayer and supplication, with thanksgiving, let your requests be made known to God; and the peace of God, which surpasses all understanding, will guard your hearts and minds through Christ Jesus. (Philippians 4:6–7)

Life's insecurities can activate our old, spiritually dead ways, and unseen tempters gladly assist. Disarm them by intimacy with God's Spirit—the rich spirit who lives in the poor in spirit.

BLESSING TO MULTIPLY

Yet again, the few human survivors had an asset that had been invincible against darkness: God's blessing to multiply.

The number of surviving people was small. But the Ark had four pairs, whereas Eden only had one pair. Despite all the intervening turmoil, God's image-creature had a net gain of 400 percent from Eden to the Flood.

The wind of God's multiplication blessing was in our sails; our race was soon abundant again. The second list of generations, Genesis 10, emphasizes our fertile multiplication after the Flood.

Now this is the genealogy of the sons of Noah: Shem, Ham, and Japheth. And sons were born to them after the flood.

The sons of Japheth were Gomer, Magog, Madai, Javan, Tubal, Meshech, and Tiras. The sons of Gomer were Ashkenaz, Riphath, and Togarmah. The sons of Javan were Elishah, Tarshish, Kittim, and Dodanim. From these the coastland peoples of the Gentiles were separated into their lands, everyone according to his language, according to their families, into their nations.

The sons of Ham were Cush, Mizraim, Put, and Canaan. The sons of Cush were Seba, Havilah, Sabtah, Raamah, and Sabtechah; and the sons of Raamah were Sheba and Dedan. (Genesis 10:1–6)

Events proved yet again, the few human survivors had the one and only asset that had been invincible against darkness: God's blessing to multiply.

CHAPTER 25

EARTH AFTER THE FLOOD

God had teased the kingdom of darkness with the Flood, as if He was achieving their aim for them. When the water on Earth subsided nearly fifteen months later, darkness would see dry land reappearing—and that wasn't all.

The previous physical order was gone forever. Our modern retellings make the drying of Earth into a restored *status quo*. Instead, a new order arose, if our model in the *Unseen* Series is correct.

OLD ORDER OUT

God's shortening of lifespans would now begin. The angelically-mixed humans were dead. God had judged the wholesale wickedness of people.

The era of Earth with all dry land in one mass had permanently ended. The fountains of the deep had opened and divided land into the continents of today. The firmament of ice had melted and collapsed upon Earth. Even its rotation had sped up, and the moon no longer ruled the night.

RAINBOW

The removal of the firmament initiated the evaporation cycle we know. Direct sunlight hits the wet ground, creating updrafts and air currents. Water changes from liquid to gas and rides the heated air columns, collecting together as clouds. The new lunar gravity influences their movement while suspended above the denser air at ground level. Clouds then release their watery load upon Earth as rain.

For the first time, sunlight could hit Earth's water. Day Two's firmament had blocked direct sunlight and prevented cloud formation and rain. The rainbow and clouds only appeared after the Flood, part of the new order.

The devil might not care about rain and rainbows, but they signified his worst nightmare yet: God in covenant with all people and creatures.

CONTINENTS

The one land mass was now dispersed into seven continents; Earth's land spread into the hemispheres—north and south, east and west. God referred to these changes when He interrogated Job. Isaiah also had revelation about the resulting shorelines.

> Who shut in the sea with doors,
> When it burst forth and issued from the womb;
> When I made the clouds its garment,
> And thick darkness its swaddling band;
> When I fixed My limit for it,
> And set bars and doors;
> When I said,
> "This far you may come, but no farther,
> And here your proud waves must stop!" (Job 38:8–11)

> I am the LORD your God,
> Who divided the sea whose waves roared—
> The LORD of hosts is His name. (Isaiah 51:15)

DIVISION OF DARKNESS

The inwardly burning rebels constantly seek cooling. Jesus described their craving in Luke 11:24: *"When an unclean spirit goes out of a man, he goes through dry places, seeking rest, and finding none."*

In Genesis 1, God had restricted the watery domain of darkness by raising the dry land and gathering the waters into one place. Now He divided the seas, as Asaph wrote above, by the Flood's division of land and multiplication of shoreline. This disrupted communication within the kingdom of darkness, whose angelic beings have bodies, though different from ours, and still require travel to communicate.

So Satan answered the LORD and said, "From going to and fro on the earth, and from walking back and forth on it." (Job 1:7)

The boundaries of the devil's watery refuge were now set as we know them. The division of their forces into multiple seas made coordination more arduous.

SEASONS

The globe's rotation suddenly accelerated from the previous 35 mph to today's 1,024 mph. No more did the lesser light reign over the night for all people; it became the moon we know. The lunar cycles we know today began after the Flood, and will prevail while Earth remains.

Ocean tides began, as the new cycles of lunar gravity swept across Earth's seas. Weather patterns arrived, the seeds of El Niño and La Niña, of hurricanes and tornadoes. The rhythms of everything had changed.

God responded to Noah's offering with a promise. It implied a new order, shaped by the Flood-time rearranging. Now cyclical seasons would govern agriculture.

While the earth remains,
Seedtime and harvest,
Cold and heat,
Winter and summer,
And day and night
Shall not cease. (Genesis 8:22)

God's promise of stable seasons also implied no more Earth-reforming. No season-stopping changes would ever occur again. This stability of rhythm is subject to only one condition: *"While the earth remains."*

No seasons will be present on New Earth. The season-causing trio of sea, sun, and moon are unneeded. The light of God's glory will suffice.

Now I saw a new heaven and a new earth, for the first heaven and the first earth had passed away. Also there was no more sea.... The city had no need of the sun or of the moon to shine in it, for the glory of God illuminated it. The Lamb is its light. (Revelation 21:1, 23)

FERTILITY

The Flood's reshaping had scoured the surface. But just as river floods renew delta agriculture, this Flood mega-fertilized the ground. The explosive new fertility of Earth soon resolved the insecurity of the eight survivors.

Noah's father, Lamech, had prophesied, 601 years before it happened, that the infant Noah's life would make food production easier.

> And he called his name Noah, saying, "This one will comfort us concerning our work and the toil of our hands, because of the ground which the LORD has cursed." (Genesis 5:29)

Neither Lamech nor Noah could possibly imagine how the prophesied comfort would come. The sole land mass was difficult to cultivate due to the curse. The people on the surface were unaware of the fountains of the deep. And the firmament overhead was always impervious to events below.

But all three released their energy in the Flood. The combination was explosive, the largest physical force ever on Earth. It not only sped Earth's rotation, but also changed the fertility of the ground. The story of the wine shows that the Flood's aftermath revealed newly productive farming:

> And Noah began to be a farmer, and he planted a vineyard. Then he drank of the wine and was drunk, and became uncovered in his tent. (Genesis 9:20–21)

EARTH'S NEW POTENCY

Evidently Noah had seeds on the Ark, so he could farm. Abundant results exceeded what the few survivors could eat. Their vineyard produce was also abundant, faster than they could consume. The grapes fermented and wine resulted, two things impossible when the population subsisted on the hardscrabble land mass.

We are well aware of the consequences of alcohol consumption. But Noah evidently did not expect such effects, judging from its intoxicating effect on him. It's common to hear his drunkenness explained based on our own habits: Noah was blowing off steam after the trauma of the preceding 101 years.

A better explanation: abundant harvests and fermented produce were impossible before the Flood. But its changes made food easier to grow as Lamech had prophesied. There were now far fewer people demanding grapes for food.

The grapes, along with other produce, had unexpected potency. The vineyard report shows Lamech's prophecy fulfilled, an intoxicating reality Noah didn't anticipate.

FALSE POTENCY

The kingdom of darkness had produced more potent half-humans by their interbreeding with human women. The demigods of mythology capture this enhanced potency. Our fictional superheroes and villains reveal its continuing allure. Transhumanism holds the allure of false potency, as an ideology that humans must evolve further, through any means right or wrong.

God blessed humans—just as He created us. Though mortal, inadequate, and fragile, we need no enhancements in His opinion. The mixed humans before the Flood exemplify false augmentation. Our unseen enemies can sneak in our life door, using modern technologies for physical or mental augmentation.

As I write, my heart has six inches of artificial components. In eight life-saving operations and treatments, God has lengthened my purpose on Earth. Research and development are good, but like a hammer, they can be used to kill the Abel in you or build you into a house for God's Spirit.

Or do you not know that your body is the temple of the Holy Spirit who is in you, whom you have from God, and you are not your own? For you were bought at a price; therefore glorify God in your body and in your spirit, which are God's. (1 Corinthians 6:19–20)

Everyone engaged in technological advance must be vigilant to the latent temptations. Lucifer's five *"I will"* statements easily travel within any ideology of human modification.

I will ascend into heaven,
I will exalt my throne above the stars of God;
I will also sit on the mount of the congregation
On the farthest sides of the north;
I will ascend above the heights of the clouds,
I will be like the Most High. (Isaiah 14:13–14)

TRUE POTENCY

After the Flood, God provided enhanced potency, but not by augmenting our fleshly nature. He made our supply more potent than it had been. Lamech had named his son Noah, recognizing how God's curse on the ground impaired its productivity. Noah's obedient life meant the Earth would have people to tend, harvest, and enjoy the new, fertile potency.

We speculated previously about a population of billions and billions, while the curse dampened the fertility of the single land mass. Imagine the scramble for food. But by the Flood, both our food and inventiveness increased. These gave God more of what He wanted most: us, His image-creatures. He wanted to multiply His image on Earth.

CHAPTER 26

WORSHIP
AND SCARCITY

The comprehensive wickedness of Genesis 6:5–6 has not only angelic causes but also natural. The all-evil-all-the-time report in Genesis 6:5 aligns with extreme food scarcity. Through deprivation and limited resources, evil invaded comprehensively, flourishing due to inadequate food supply.

Meanwhile, the half-breeds of Genesis 6:4 imposed a legal system of *"might makes right."* We have many sayings for tyrannical behavior by those we can't contest, such as *"What's mine is mine, and what's yours is mine."*

Using the Flood, God judged the wickedness, but addressed the natural cause as well. After people spread, scarcity would no longer affect us all because of Earth's fertility. But right away, for the eight survivors, scarcity was acute.

WORSHIP

Food production work lay ahead for Noah and the survivors. But before any planting, Noah worshiped God.

Noah's worship resembled Abel's rather than Cain's for several exemplary reasons. To begin with, his worship of God was his highest priority, his first action off the Ark. Accordingly, he recorded his first act, so his generations would know his sequence of priorities.

> Then Noah built an altar to the LORD, and took of every clean animal and of every clean bird, and offered burnt offerings on the altar. (Genesis 8:20)

Second, the worship was not stingy, miserly, or begrudging, as Cain's worship had been. Noah killed animals for sacrifice. Imagine the connection that he and his family had formed with these animals over the previous fourteen months afloat.

The animals also represented the investment of human labor, of feeding and nurturing. Noah's sacrifice was no perfunctory ritual, but a truly costly one. David expressed the same principle when offered a free place to build the Temple.

> Nor will I offer burnt offerings to the LORD my God with that which costs me nothing. (2 Samuel 24:24)

SCARCITY AFTER THE FLOOD

Cost increases when supply decreases—the third reason Noah's worship was like Abel's. Animals and birds all died in the Flood. Imagine: the only animals to fill the Earth again were on that boat with those eight people. Earth saw its most extreme scarcity as supply hit rock bottom. It hardly seems like the time to kill a few more animals.

The Ark's animals represented the sum total of all possible meat for the family. Any passion Noah had for the repopulation of Earth depended entirely on those animals. Anyone concerned about extinction would shudder at seeing the small numbers of animals coming off the ship.

Think about your fearful insecurity in this scenario, as one of only eight human beings left. Within the 120,000-square-foot Ark were the only animals on Earth for repopulation and food. Now the leader of your group kills a large percentage of them. Your leader's initial action is to sacrifice a chunk of the only meat by setting it on fire.

Far smaller threats today leverage us into behaviors of scarcity and emotions of fear. Money helps solve scarcity with godly trading, but love of money takes root in fear of deprivation, thinking money will offset our inadequate supply. The unseen tempters today rely on scarcity to motivate many behaviors.

FAITH

These eight people faced a scarcity that humanity has never seen before or since. Yet, despite the natural alarm, Noah exhibited extreme faith. No wonder the "Faith Hall of Fame" calls Noah *"the heir of the righteousness which is according to faith"* (Hebrews 11:7).

He took of every clean animal and killed it to worship God. It matches with the Philippians' giving habit, described by Apostle Paul: *"Their deep poverty abounded in the riches of their liberality"* (2 Corinthians 8:2).

AFFIRMATION

Noah's costly worship despite scarcity pleased God, the same God who had first spoken to him about the Ark. We saw in Hebrews 11:4 how God had affirmed Abel's gifts in a repetitive give-and-take. The same divine pleasure affirms Noah's offering with two commitments.

And the Lord smelled a soothing aroma. Then the Lord said in His heart, "I will never again curse the ground for man's sake, although the imagination of man's heart is evil from his youth; nor will I again destroy every living thing as I have done." (Genesis 8:21)

ABUNDANCE FROM SCARCITY

Our worship during scarcity disarms our enemies. They can't use the threat of lack to shoehorn us into fearful, miserly behaviors. When we trust God with our scarcity, He brings abundance from it.

The principle works the other way also. If we trust goods more than God, we have fewer goods. Through the prophet Haggai centuries later, God warned us that withholding from Him produces more scarcity.

Consider your ways!
You have sown much, and bring in little;
You eat, but do not have enough;
You drink, but you are not filled with drink;
You clothe yourselves, but no one is warm;
And he who earns wages,
Earns wages to put into a bag with holes. (Haggai 1:5–6)

Both Haggai and his peer Malachi taught that worship delayed by scarcity produces more scarcity. In contrast, God's abundance follows our sacrifice, not our achievements. Instead of waiting for abundance, worshiping flips our lack into an asset.

"Bring all the tithes into the storehouse,
That there may be food in My house,
And try Me now in this,"
Says the LORD of hosts,
"If I will not open for you the windows of heaven
And pour out for you such blessing
That there will not be room enough to receive it." (Malachi 3:10)

Jesus affirmed someone who followed this principle in Luke 21:1–4.

And He looked up and saw the rich putting their gifts into the treasury, and He saw also a certain poor widow putting in two mites. So He said, "Truly I say to you that this poor widow has put in more than all; for all these out of their abundance have put in offerings for God, but she out of her poverty put in all the livelihood that she had."

Noah, like that widow and like Abel and Enoch before him, demonstrated his belief in God by worshiping out of scarcity. We can do likewise, and like Noah, experience the potency of God's supply. Faith triumphs over unseen tempters.

ABUNDANCE MULTIPLIES

Noah's abundant results from the newly fertile ground showed the fulfillment of Lamech's prophetic naming. God swore never to curse it again (Genesis 8:21), and then declared His covenant with Earth (Genesis 9:13).

But multiplication was not limited to bountiful agriculture. God blessed Noah and his family to multiply, using the same words that had blessed Adam and Eve.

So God blessed Noah and his sons, and said to them: "Be fruitful and multiply, and fill the earth." (Genesis 9:1)

They did what He told them to. And with people's multiplication came synergistic efforts, such as bricks and towers.

CHAPTER 27

BABEL

The Bible gives no indication that the Tower of Babel was a strategy of darkness. The entire ambition was the work of people acting like Lucifer in his rebellion. Although unstated, it's plausible that they received encouragement from satan and his partners.

> And they said, "Come, let us build ourselves a city, and a tower whose top is in the heavens; let us make a name for ourselves, lest we be scattered abroad over the face of the whole earth." (Genesis 11:5)

SECURITY IN OTHERS

The multiplying descendants of Noah were congregated in the Fertile Crescent, and found security in their proximity to one another. We often seek security in other people rather than in our Father. Wives and husbands can easily depend on one another more than the Lord. No enemy radar is needed to spot this, but rather a meek fear that honors God as the only one worthy to be depended upon.

ASK WHO?

The text reports no consultation with the Lord. On the Ark, the recorded memory of Cain's punishment had survived: *"a fugitive and a vagabond on the earth"* (Genesis 4:14). The people of Babel may have feared such punishment from God.

Whatever the reason, we can relate; many of our group activities occur without God's input. Churches and their leaders can be the worst offenders. Presuming upon their biblical authorization to conduct affairs, they rely on their own wisdom without consulting or waiting on instructions from the Lord of the Church.

DECISION TREE ONE

1. Being scattered is bad.
    a. We want to avoid being scattered.
        i. God can scatter us.
            A. We are defenseless against God.

2. Making a name for ourselves prevents being scattered.
    a. We are able to make bricks and pitch to hold them in place.
    b. Building a tower makes a name for ourselves.
        i. To build that tower we need a city.
    b. To protect ourselves against *all* threats (such as God), the tower must go up the heavens.

The influence of darkness amplified the insecurity the people expressed. Noah's worship during scarcity and insecurity was evidently forgotten. The similarity to Lucifer's five *"I wills"* and the pattern of prideful self-solving is evident.

TECHNOLOGY

In the Genesis 11 record about Babel, their plan does not require conquest. Instead, new technologies enable it: brickmaking and asphalt from tar (Genesis 11:3). Walls, markets, and residences became possible—the components of a city, and not a common city, but one with a tower to the heavens.

These technologies resulted from the fertility of Earth, because food production no longer consumed all human effort. Leisure time expanded. People had time to experiment and develop reliable bricks and durable asphalt. Everyone still spoke the language of Adam and Eve through Noah; no language barriers existed.

Yet humans kept allowing Sin to enter their doors. Noah's righteousness did not evacuate its deception from Earth. Babel's inhabitants dreaded scattering, feeling vulnerability to enemies. Their motive tacitly admitted that Cains roamed the world.

God blessed our race. Beneficial inventions and human multiplication flowed despite our spirit death in Eden. Sin twisted the new opportunities, supporting Luciferian pride in God's own image-creatures.

We still think this way today with our cities. Localities throughout Earth represent a group effort at protection against threats. We accept this as part of life. In the twenty-first century, our synergistic safety includes cell phones and texting, the internet, and other inventions.

Each new technology is as neutral as brickmaking. The force that yields advancement is God's blessing on our race. When we invent things, the kingdom of darkness sees openings as well.

The misuse of our inventions is an obvious sign of their evil influence. Prideful self-solving in our hearts is harder to discern. When inventions make God less necessary in our eyes, we open doors, and Sin sneaks in. What God said to Cain applies to every technology user.

Sin lies at the door. And its desire is for you, but you should rule over it. (Genesis 4:7)

UNITY

The city-building tower erectors used the same words God had when He made us: *"Let us."* Babel was a social effort, intended for protection.

Jesus prized the unity of His people in John 17; the unity of the Babel builders shows why. When God's image-creatures operate in concert to achieve a common goal, we create as God did. We make the inventions and procedures necessary to subdue Earth.

GOD'S ASSESSMENT

The Lord came down to see their tower. The record includes His astounding statement about our built-in capability as His image-creatures. *"Nothing they plan to do will be impossible for them"* (Genesis 11:6 NIV)

The people He was describing were dead in spirit, as all children of Adam and Eve are born. The city builders were alive in soul and body only, and yet God acknowledged that their capability was limitless. His evaluation still applies to our race.

Only one condition existed: unity. *"If as one people speaking the same language they have begun to do this..."* (Genesis 11:6).

DECISION TREE TWO

1. It is not good for man to achieve anything they wish.
    a. Their capabilities need to be restricted.
2. This city and tower building shows they can achieve anything they wish.
    a. This, apart from Me.
3. They can achieve anything when unified, of one mind.
    a. One language for communication is required for unity.
4. To limit their achievement, I will interrupt their communication.

GOD THE DIVIDER

In the six days of reforming Earth, God had divided light and dark, day and night, waters above and waters below. God divided Earth a second time, the continental spread of the Flood. Not only did it divide the land, but also the seas.

Now at Babel, the Lord divided humanity. Using language, God divided people, a first He had never done before.

> "Come, let us go down and confuse their language so they will not understand each other." So the LORD scattered them from there over all the earth, and they stopped building the city. That is why it was called Babel—because there the LORD confused the language of the whole world. (Genesis 11:7–9)

There are several divine acts necessary for the event in this brief description.

LANGUAGE ART

First, He replaced everyone's language with a new one. Just like He formed Eve from Adam's rib, He rewired human vocal organs.

Linguists identify sounds by the vocal mechanics that produce them: lips, tongue, vocal cords, and glottal stop. For example, the letter "B" is a bilabial fricative using both lips; the letter "C" is a palatal plosive. The phonetic alphabet in pronunciation guides assigns a unique symbol to each physical mechanism for intelligible sound.

The required mechanics differentiate languages. For instance, French is well known for its nasal sounds, while German has distinct fricatives *ich* and *ach* formed only by breathing forcefully across a raised tongue without sound from the vocal cords. (Go ahead; try it. If you're not German it may feel weird.)

> Imagine the instant that a new language forms within you! The first time Christians speak in tongues, it mirrors God's actions at Babel. He creates a language within you.

For God to give everyone a new language, every person suddenly received new vocal habits, trained to form new sounds with their existing vocal organs. Each new language God made that day contained new physical speech instincts.

The Lord Jesus is now intimate with people in every language. He can talk with them in their language, because He made it up.

TRANSLATION ART

Translation is common today; even our computers can do it. The Bible reveals God, and many dedicate their lives to translating the three Bible languages. Many more learn the ethnic languages to properly render what the Bible says. Yet this gigantic translation industry stems entirely from divisions God Himself caused at Babel.

I titled Book Two of the *Unseen* Series, *Nobody Sees This Unseen Realm: How to Unlock Bible Mysteries*. God's action at Babel led the Bible that makes those study methods work.

Other religions believe their founding texts descended from heaven. The contents of the Bible are unique among sacred texts. Forty-four distinct human authors composed distinct portions in three different languages at very distinct times over fourteen centuries.

The Bible uses the distinct idioms and cultural references of each author's time and place. Each Bible language had centuries of metamorphosis through migrations and cultural development. Vocabulary growth accommodated new inventions and new neighbors. God's language division at Babel made all these possible.

INTERPRETATION MEEKNESS

The history of confused languages makes it easier to misinterpret Scripture. We can lack the original knowledge of its original authors. This is not a problem from darkness; God set it up that way by creating the initial language variety at Babel.

That's one reason to be meek about our Bible interpretations. Our time-and-place reference makes it harder to interpret such distant authors. Not even lifelong translators shout down colleagues, or proclaim that their findings end debate.

Christians can fear improved Bible interpretations despite the greater explanatory power. Defending the existing grid of interpretation devalues God's undiscovered mysteries. To think our understanding of God's Word cannot improve is sheer pride.

Both in history actually and today figuratively, Christians burn each other at the stake. To protect our doctrinal grids from challengers, we can exclude and persecute those who offer improvements. Divisive evil is obvious to everyone except the proud.

But we can also disarm enemy-style pride. Even if you know the Bible, you still test your explanations humbly over time with other people—such as we are doing in the *Unseen* Series. Throughout history, the same Jesus who is building His Church gives us the shared conclusions through agreement.

Blessed are the meek. (Matthew 5:5)

God resists the proud, but gives grace to the humble. (1 Peter 5:5)

IMPLANT

Second, God suddenly implanted language understanding. Language exists for communication, one receiving the intended meaning of another. The sound-producing physique requires ears to understand the language. Those ears must have the vocabulary, idioms, and syntax so comprehension results.

When God created the new languages, people didn't become blabbering idiots. The Genesis 10 genealogy shows how people immediately grouped together. People groups had a shared language that each member could speak and understand.

God created each language suddenly in groups. Into each person in that group, He instantly placed abilities both to utter it physically and to understand it when heard.

BARRIER TO LEARNING

God gave each group their new language instincts and comprehension. He also prevented language learning. Absent are cross-language meetings like ours. We want to communicate, and establish basic communication with a few gestures and basic words.

But at Babel, this did not occur. No desire to communicate cross-language is recorded. Rather than try to adapt, they immediately spread out into distinct language groups.

Despite their investment, the unified tower motivation disappeared completely. Genesis 11 records no effort to continue work on it by learning each other's language. In contrast, we have cross-language space stations and military exercises.

BARRIER TO TRUST

Another barrier in God's action to confuse was blocking social trust. The tower-building effort had required trust, as any shared work does. Workers must trust that each one understands and will perform his duty (and not drop bricks on those below). Users of the structure must trust it as well.

Today is no different. People outside your neighborhood built your house, who may not even speak your language. This does not prevent you from enjoying your home. But when God confused the language at Babel, that trust was completely severed.

On American roads, a ten-inch-wide yellow line is all that stands between us and instant death in high-speed collisions. We have social trust that each driver, regardless of language, observes it. In contrast, the Babel people lost all such trust in any workman's effort.

THE NEXT STRATEGY

The kingdom of darkness may not be credited in the Bible for the events at Babel, but they would be pleased nonetheless. The fear of being scattered was a next-level manifestation of Adam's naked fright. Now, the fig leaf became a city featuring a tower. Strategy one was still bearing fruit. The descendants of Noah were born spiritually dead and eventually died physically.

Sin was doing its job for the second strategy. People acted to defend themselves against God, challenging Him with their tower to the heavens.

Strategy three would never recur; all its fruit was lost. But God's *ethnos* division of humanity meant a new opportunity for darkness. The multiplication of languages enabled strategy four.

CHAPTER 28

STRATEGY FOUR: CLAIM NATIONS

Where Genesis 5 identified only one child per father, Genesis 10 names many. Parents could feed many mouths after the Flood enabled fertile agriculture.

Our population increase posed a threat to the kingdom of darkness. They cannot gain reinforcements. Whatever their number, they don't reproduce. Nor has Scripture revealed more angels being exiled from heaven. We could even outstrip their influence, if not for God's action at Babel.

ETHNOS

God divided our race to prevent unified humanity from achieving the impossible. Language division resulted in many new cultures among humanity. Separation into people groups produced ethnicity, from the Greek word *ethnos*.

Each generation in the *ethnos* amplifies its distinctions. The new languages included unique physical mechanics; likewise, each *ethnos* became increasingly distinct in physical morphologies, skin colors, and personality traits.

NOT NATIONS

Bible translations use the word *nation* but do not intend the political entities we know. For us, nations inhabit specific geographical territories, with defined borders and unique sovereign governments. Such nations did not exist until the nineteenth century.

Prior to that time, people congregated based on ethnic commonalities. For the great majority of human history, *nation* comprised a people group with a common language and the culture distinct to them. Only the great melting pot of America has blended the *ethnos*.

SATAN'S FAILURES

Separation of humanity into *ethnos* made satan's first three strategies outdated and inadequate. Sin alone could never complete the job intended.

Strategy one: failure because people multiplied worshipers. Failure number two was evident when individuals in Seth's line could still resist Sin and walk with God. Strategy three: failure because God wiped out the half-breeds and shortened human lifespans.

FOURTH TRY

So the kingdom of darkness deployed a fourth strategy: claiming the *ethnos*. The continuing activity of this strategy on Earth today has explosive explanatory power for current events.

God's action at Babel diversified people, the replacements that the kingdom of darkness fear. The whole human race could no longer be their single target. Strategy four is the first to target distinct groups of humanity.

> The fourth strategy of darkness has explosive explanatory power for current events.

New languages at Babel segmented the population of God's image-creatures. The fourth strategy of darkness simply piggybacked on what God did. The devil released partners from his prison and assigned each a micro-focus: claim and control one ethnic group, a.k.a. a nation.

This control network of chokepoints and bottlenecks magnifies satan's influence over all people.

Strategy four has been the longest-lasting success of the kingdom of darkness. Babel's nation-creation laid the foundation for this fourth strategy, which persists today. With understanding, you can discern and identify the unseen tempters working on groups which include you.

THE ORGANIZATION OF DARKNESS

The kingdom of darkness comprises the fallen Lucifer and a third of heaven's angels. They cannot reproduce and have no reinforcements. Together they rebelled, so God exiled them together to Earth. These fellow rebels would ultimately become satan's many partners active on the earth today, which Apostle Paul named in Ephesians 6:12.

In our paradigm, satan only gradually released them, and only as needed. To each parolee, he delegates temporary authority to claim an *ethnos*. The nine-book *Unseen* Series traces his gradual release of partners and the historical flow of his strategy development.

The evil principality only has a temporary release. Constantly under satan's scrutiny, it must prove its worth by increasing the number of people influenced.

THE FEAR OF SATAN

The fallen Lucifer treats his partners ruthlessly. He permits no possibility they might rebel against him, as he had done to God. The fear is common to all tyrants and usurpers. If someone is willing to do something *with* you, they are also willing to do it *to* you, as the saying goes.

His partners were loyal and honored their IOUs to Lucifer. Yet they exist in his prison. The savage efficiency of chokepoints releases the fewest partners needed. Once released, each one operates under the constant threat of demotion.

THE UPHEAVAL OF RULERS

These lieutenants form satan's *ethnos*-claiming corps. But once released, satan doesn't allow any of them the duration and success that could facilitate rebellion. The rise and fall of empires exhibits the constant turmoil among these rulers of wickedness. When cultures and religions replace their predecessors, the forces of evil are being shuffled by their leader.

A replacement process is continual among satan's nation-claiming forces. The subordinate rebel powers testify to this, in their end-time taunt of satan.

Is this the man who made the earth tremble,

Who shook kingdoms,
Who made the world as a wilderness
And destroyed its cities,
Who did not open the house of his prisoners? (Isaiah 14:16–17)

Jesus affirmed these principles of darkness in Luke 11. In Book Three, our study of Isaiah 14 and Luke 11 affirmed that the kingdom of darkness will fall because of this internal division.

One event showcased satan's divisiveness in his own kingdom. In Jesus' wilderness temptation, the devil offered the IOUs of all these partners. They could be obligated to Jesus rather than satan, if only Jesus would subordinate Himself to the devil.

Then the devil, taking Him up on a high mountain, showed Him all the kingdoms of the world in a moment of time. And the devil said to Him, "All this authority I will give You, and their glory; for this has been delivered to me, and I give it to whomever I wish. Therefore, if You will worship before me, all will be Yours." (Luke 4:5–7)

SATAN'S DISLOYALTY

Loyalty is not a quality of satan's character. His grid is replacement, and nothing else. Experience, fiction, and Scripture alike reinforce the truth that any agreement satan offers is a superficial ploy; he will betray anyone who trusts it.

Apostles reflecting on the Last Supper described to Luke how satan entered Judas. Whatever promise Judas had received, it was more attractive to him than Jesus' kingdom. That promise was quite short-lived as he died gruesomely within hours. Such is satan's "loyalty."

Then Satan entered Judas, surnamed Iscariot, who was numbered among the twelve. (Luke 22:3)

Now this man purchased a field with the wages of iniquity; and falling headlong, he burst open in the middle and all his entrails gushed out. (Acts 1:18)

GOVERNANCE BY SATAN

The control of a few people at the top impacts the entire population. That locus of control forms a bottleneck which the people group cannot easily escape.

His hierarchy of henchmen has free rein to obstruct human progress in every way possible. Famine, war, and suffering have been the lot of every grouped *ethnos*. The evil insinuated into the top layer of leadership infiltrates the entire culture. Poverty, broken families, exploitation, and oppression of all kinds—all signal governance by the kingdom of darkness.

GOVERNANCE BY JESUS

Revelation 20 confirms this reality. The revelation of the millennial reign aligns with the sorrowful evidence that the hierarchy of hell has claimed people groups.

The mighty angel locks up the leader of darkness for one thousand years (Revelation 20:1–3). Resurrected saints rule with Jesus for that period (Revelation 20:4). Many Bible prophecies describe the harmony coinciding with satan's prison term.

"No more shall an infant from there live but a few days,
Nor an old man who has not fulfilled his days;
For the child shall die one hundred years old,
But the sinner being one hundred years old shall be accursed.
They shall build houses and inhabit them;
They shall plant vineyards and eat their fruit.
They shall not build and another inhabit;
They shall not plant and another eat;
For as the days of a tree, so shall be the days of My people,
And My elect shall long enjoy the work of their hands.
They shall not labor in vain,
Nor bring forth children for trouble;
For they shall be the descendants of the blessed of the Lord,
And their offspring with them.

"It shall come to pass
That before they call, I will answer;
And while they are still speaking, I will hear.

The wolf and the lamb shall feed together,
The lion shall eat straw like the ox,
And dust shall be the serpent's food.
They shall not hurt nor destroy in all My holy mountain,"
Says the LORD. (Isaiah 65:20–25)

THE GODS

Earlier in Genesis 6, we reviewed our habit of attributing divinity to the rebellious angels. Now those same dark partners gained control over each *ethnos* nation. It is these principalities who populate the false religions of each people group.

Every human culture has religion and gods. They may be personifications as in ancient mythology, or priority structures based on a cultural dread. Each ethnic group worships their gods as the means of quelling insecurities—both those common to all, and the unique fears of their culture.

Rather, that the things which the Gentiles sacrifice they sacrifice to demons and not to God, and I do not want you to have fellowship with demons. You cannot drink the cup of the Lord and the cup of demons; you cannot partake of the Lord's table and of the table of demons. (1 Corinthians 10:20–21)

Our capability to invent remains, producing countless additions to Babel's brickmaking and city building. However, Sin remains a constant challenge for all us, who willingly open our life doors. In this mixed bag, the urge to worship becomes an asset for darkness. The partners of satan gladly manipulate the worship to control the *ethnos*.

[People] changed the glory of the incorruptible God into an image made like corruptible man—and birds and four-footed animals and creeping things ... exchanged the truth of God for the lie, and worshiped and served the creature rather than the Creator. (Romans 1:23, 25)

DREADS FALSE AND TRUE

The nakedness of Adam persists in our fears and dreads. Each *ethnos* has dreads, both common to all men and unique to its own culture. These fulcrums permit each unseen evil ruler to leverage its people group.

Discerning the dreads of your group enables you to identify the evil influence.

We disarm the group's unseen tempters with proper dread for the true God. Through the prophet Isaiah, God warned Israel about the whipsaw consequences of dreading anything more than Him.

> Do not say, "A conspiracy,"
> Concerning all that this people call a conspiracy,
> Nor be afraid of their threats, nor be troubled.
> The LORD of hosts, Him you shall hallow;
> Let Him be your fear,
> And let Him be your dread. (Isaiah 8:12–13)

CHAPTER 29

CHOKEPOINTS AND BOTTLENECKS

The devil has limits on everything, except his ego. The one doomed to scarcity is satan, without increasing numbers. He was also reluctant to *"open the house of his prisoners"* (Isaiah 14:17). To offset these restrictions, he squeezes maximum influence out of each partner.

Each strategy reveals a repetitive tactic of darkness: controlling many through few. My synonymous terms for this tactic are *chokepoints* and *bottlenecks*. Knowing it helps identify the bottlenecking evil powers of Ephesians 6:12.

God had assessed that nothing was impossible for the once-unified humanity. Now He had divided us into isolated groups that adopted similar cultures and customs. Strategy four used the chokepoint tactic to capitalize on the division.

CONTROL POINTS

Chokepoints and bottlenecks enable control of many people by influencing a few. For example, the United States has about 334 million residents. But the kingdom of darkness doesn't need an equal number to oppress our nation. Instead, they segment us into control points. We have seven mountains of culture, fifty states, 3,143 counties, and 19,502 municipalities. Assume those are the only control points, totaling 22,702 prisoners released. The kingdom of darkness has seduced our nation from its godly heritage using such control points. If the above list were

251

exhaustive, the necessary spiritual forces number only six ten-thousandths of our population.

That's how satan oppresses the greatest number of people with the fewest unseen partners. But finding such control points is a constant activity of darkness, because people are multiplying and filling Earth.

Knowing this tactic is useful in every aspect of daily life. Wherever restrictions of godly freedom are erected, unseen tempters may be at work.

Using their delegation system, the kingdom of darkness oppresses many people through each single bottleneck. The devil assigns rebel partners to manage and strengthen these control points. These chokepoints include nations, places, cultures, leaders, religions, and ethnicities. People accept the imposed restrictions as normal reality, without recognizing the origin in darkness.

Individual rulers of darkness claim, or are assigned to, these chokepoints.

DISCERNING SATAN

The first apostles led the newborn Church through many challenges. In the Bible record, Apostle Paul was singled out to reach the Gentiles. The assignment would place him into many distinct ethnic groups.

> When they saw that the gospel for the uncircumcised had been committed to me, as the gospel for the circumcised was to Peter ... they gave me and Barnabas the right hand of fellowship, that we should go to the Gentiles and they to the circumcised. (Galatians 2:7, 9)

Apostle Peter knew about darkness, of course. He cautioned us against the devil in his letters; he had personal and direct experience with the devil's attack. Jesus identified two such occasions during their three years of constant companionship.

> He [Jesus] turned and said to Peter, "Get behind Me, Satan! You are an offense to Me, for you are not mindful of the things of God, but the things of men." (Matthew 16:23)

> Simon, Simon! Indeed, Satan has asked for you, that he may sift you as wheat. (Luke 22:31)

Peter gained discernment from these experiences. The Spirit's filling imparted discernment. In Ananias and Sapphira, Peter discerned satan's influence and countered it with a fatal prophetic judgment.

But Peter said, "Ananias, why has Satan filled your heart to lie to the Holy Spirit?... How is it that you have agreed together to test the Spirit of the Lord?" (Acts 5:3, 8)

Peter and the other New Testament writers conveyed useful knowledge about the devil himself. But the Bible records Paul's encounters with satan's *ethnos* claimers.

THE PRINCIPALITY PENETRATOR

The other apostles were called to one people group, the Jews. Paul was the one apostle in the Bible whom God sent to non-Jewish *ethnos*. Paul repeatedly crossed ethnic boundaries in his missionary journeys and conflicted with the evil ruler(s) assigned to it.

Long before Saul the persecutor became Paul the apostle, God appointed him for this. The prophet Ananias resisted visiting the well-known persecutor until God explained His command.

Go, for he is a chosen vessel of Mine to bear My name before Gentiles, kings, and the children of Israel. For I will show him how many things he must suffer for My name's sake. (Acts 9:15–16)

Paul earned the revelation about nation-claiming principalities, fair and square. This partial list of his travails only happened because he penetrated the claims of unseen enemies.

From the Jews five times I received forty stripes minus one. Three times I was beaten with rods; once I was stoned; three times I was shipwrecked; a night and a day I have been in the deep; in journeys often, in perils of waters, in perils of robbers, in perils of my own countrymen, in perils of the Gentiles, in perils in the city, in perils in the wilderness, in perils in the sea, in perils among false brethren.... (2 Corinthians 11:24–26)

THE UNSEEN GROUP TEMPTERS

Paul describes our wrestling against the henchmen governing people groups. The devil is not singled out; he is only one of many. The ones we encounter are the spirits of evil which control chokepoints on our groups.

With this strategic understanding, think of your own *ethnos*, culture, and groups in this verse.

> For we do not wrestle against flesh and blood, but against principalities, against powers, against the rulers of the darkness of this age, against spiritual hosts of wickedness in the heavenly places. (Ephesians 6:12)

Notice that each category is plural, populated by multiple beings. The idea that regular Christians like you and I should wrestle against these ancient and powerful highlights our poverty of spirit. Yet Jesus actually called us blessed for it, and He also said why it was blessed.

> Blessed are the poor in spirit, for theirs is the kingdom of heaven. (Matthew 5:3)

MORE INFLUENCE, FEWER PAROLEES

People groups number far fewer than our total population. Presently humans number 8,000,000,000 and might outnumber satan's principalities. But if political nations are a control point, Lucifer only needs to parole 195 prisoners. If the mountains of each culture are a control point, only seven partners are needed for each culture.

Using their leaders and influencers as bottlenecks permits satan to keep partners under lock and key. The few openings for their deployment would be quite precious; each parolee would be highly motivated to please the warden of hell.

Figuratively speaking, God's division of humanity enabled satan's new parole policy. The far smaller number of chokepoints required fewer partners.

STABILITY

Not only was the number of bottlenecks far smaller, but it was also more stable. Human population could double, with only a slight increase in the number of distinct people groups.

The number of individual people had always grown exponentially, as we saw in previous speculation about the pre-Flood population. In contrast, the number of people groups was more stable; they do not multiply like individual people do.

MULTIPLYING DISTINCTIONS

Increases in the number of *ethnos* even benefit the kingdom of darkness. The multiplication of individuals is contrary to their ambitions. In contrast, each new *ethnos* strengthens the efficient network.

Another dark partner gets released from confinement for each new chokepoint. Each new people group multiplies the useful distinctions within humanity. Using the unique attributes of each human grouping are useful; its rulers of wickedness can blackmail the group members.

BLACKMAILED WITH DISTINCTIONS

Human diversity actually strengthens the influence of the *ethnos* leaders over the rapidly reproducing people. From Babel until now, we identify ourselves by our group and culture—putting each of us under pressure to conform to its distinctions.

Each time a new people group or culture is formed, the unseen partner assigned to it gains more distinctions. With each unique attribute, the ruler of wickedness more easily herds the group's people further under the influence of darkness. Fewer unseen rulers are needed, and thus fewer prisoners paroled by satan.

DISCERNING GROUP BLACKMAIL

Each people group develops its unique worldviews, habits, coded communication, and expectations. These ethnic attributes enable its assigned unseen ruler to threaten anyone who resists conformity in the name of Jesus Christ. Accompanying the threats are enticements and rewards for following the expected way of the people group.

Jesus Christ requires submission to mature no matter what people group. People can defer their Christian maturity to keep in line with the *ethnos* history. This occurs whether it is people group, culture, or any *ethnos*.

Consider the African-American *ethnos*. Its history as a slave population is a useful distinction for darkness. The assigned principality paints Jesus' expectation with the brush of slavery. The spiritual hosts threaten the African-American Christian with penalties for submitting to Jesus. An example is ostracism when the Holy Spirit leads an African-American into a majority-white church.

The blackmail also rewards its desired behavior, to subordinate Christian faith to ethnic expectations. The believer can choose a majority black church, rise to leadership, and even have a great ministry. No one will think the less, except for the Spirit of God who led otherwise.

Another example concerns personality types which are not evenly distributed across culture or *ethnos*. God forms everyone in the womb and declares who they will be (Psalm 139:13–16). Each is born into a people group with a ruling evil being. But while growing in their *ethnos,* each person can be blackmailed to conform, and to contradict what God said for them.

Jesus armed us to resist the people group blackmail. We must choose Him over our *ethnos.* You can be stigmatized among your people, or in the court of heaven. Choose one.

> Do not fear those who kill the body but cannot kill the soul. But rather fear Him who is able to destroy both soul and body in hell.... Therefore whoever confesses Me before men, him I will also confess before My Father who is in heaven. But whoever denies Me before men, him I will also deny before My Father who is in heaven. (Matthew 10:28, 32–33)

> For what profit is it to a man if he gains the whole world, and is himself destroyed or lost? For whoever is ashamed of Me and My words, of him the Son of Man will be ashamed when He comes in His own glory, and in His Father's, and of the holy angels. (Luke 9:25–26)

CHAPTER 30

CHURCH CHOKEPOINTS

The persistent human urge to worship was born with Cain, the very first human birth. Sin took advantage of his substandard attitudes. Now that humanity is distributed into people groups, the urge to worship has taken many forms.

Even the truth of the gospel has been corrupted by principalities—the subject of the *Unseen* Series, Book Seven, *Nobody Sees This Church: Resisting Darkness.*

To discern our unseen tempters, maturity recognizes mixture in our churches. The Scripture commands Christians not to forsake gathering together; there is much joy in a fellowship of people who love Jesus truly. But churches are mixed; not everyone pursues spirit maturity equally.

RELIGION OF BLACKMAIL

The blackmailing spirits of wickedness easily introduce the pressure to conform to the church expectations. Not crossing the pastor or big donors is a frequent pressure in many churches. Others frown upon differing worship behaviors such as speaking in tongues, dancing, raising of hands, or praying with eyes open. The distinctions available in your church for these pressurizing spirits of evil are many.

Notice what behaviors you are afraid to try in your church. It may involve where you sit, or with whom. Possibly how you praise God is in the spotlight. If there are topics that would cause your ostracism, ask why?

The Christian must always strive for maturity as a living spirit, whether church helps or hurts. We are not in church for results, but for obedience to the One who is building His Church.

SUBMISSION TO LEADERS

God commands us to congregate together (Hebrews 3:12–13, 10:24–25). We are also commanded to submit to our church rulers (Hebrews 13:17). A maturing Christian comes under the leadership God designates, regardless of those leaders' merit or sinlessness. Ministers are human and have failings; these do not excuse refusal to submit. Nor do the failings of churches excuse Jesus' followers from being part of one.

The early church wrestled with this. When a minister's personal sinfulness became known, were the recipients of that ministry harmed? The doctrine of *ex officio* resulted. Ministry is effective because of the office, and was not disqualified by a leader's sin.

DISCERNING WICKED LEADERSHIP

I describe myself as a MethoBapTerIcCaliaCostal. That doesn't include the two independent churches I was part of. In each, I have been a leader; in two, a founder. From each, we moved forward. My wife and I discovered unexpected costs but we would not forsake the gains. God was waking me to spirit function, a process not honored in many churches. To learn and grow, I required the journey.

The chokepoint, bottleneck tactic of darkness is deployed against church leaders with ferocity. The unseen enemies gain influence in a church using that tactic.

Of course, their effect is secretive. It may be hidden in habits of the leaders, big donors, or program choices. If a church has a building, there are natural costs associated. The bigger the building, the more the expenses. The same goes for the ministry staff. When the budget is bigger, the unseen enemies can tempt preachers to compromise. They may not want to offend potential donors. Big donors can be vocal and demanding about their preferences.

If leaders do not restrain willful sin in the church, in the unseen realm this argues with God and agrees with darkness. For example, the damage from a gossip is not only character assassination of fellow believers.

Churches tolerating gossips offer a foothold to unseen enemies; leaders who do not restrain them can be facilitating chokepoints unwittingly.

The tabernacle was a foothold for darkness under Eli the priest in Samuel's time. Eli exemplifies leaders who do not restrain wrongdoers. He knew the ungodly practices of his priestly sons, yet refused to exert his authority against them. The legitimate ministry of the tabernacle was disdained, while pagan sexual practices arose. God promised terrible consequences for Eli's failure.

> Why do you kick at My sacrifice and My offering which I have commanded in My dwelling place, and honor your sons more than Me? (1 Samuel 2:29)

Church leaders must be alert to the chokepoint tactic against themselves and their flock. With love and grace, pastors and leaders must discern and resist the restricting pressures from their congregations.

THE PRESSURE TO BE RIGHT

To shoehorn Christian leaders into their chokepoint strategy, the unseen tempters have a long-practiced method: the pressure to be right. Whether you have leadership responsibilities or not, every Christian must be alert to this method.

When God chose revelation in human language, He opened the door to human interpretation. Everything human influences what we are able to receive from His Word. There is room for each of us to be wrong. God created that freedom, when He gave us a revelation that we could interpret inadequately. He left room for our understanding to grow.

The enemy response is pressure to be right. God did not create pressure to be right, but it is one which Christians feel acutely.

We are accountable to apply ourselves to understanding the Bible properly, as Paul says to Timothy.

> Be diligent to present yourself approved to God, a worker who does not need to be ashamed, rightly dividing the word of truth. (2 Timothy 2:15)

However, we are not accountable to think we have arrived at the right interpretation. God wants us to search out His mysteries. Apostle Paul exhorted the Philippians to have a mindset of growing their understanding.

It is the glory of God to conceal a matter,
But the glory of kings is to search out a matter. (Proverbs 25:2)

Therefore let us, as many as are mature, have this mind; and if in anything you think otherwise, God will reveal even this to you. Nevertheless, to the degree that we have already attained, let us walk by the same rule, let us be of the same mind. (Philippians 3:15–16)

ENEMIES IN YOUR CHURCH

Every church has a structure of respect; attitudes reveal it. Does one group of members receive more favor than another? Do financial pressures for the church's budget color the ministry priorities? Do the members and attendees have a motive that tempts the leader to obey? Do they withhold their submission until the leader performs to please? Is there freedom to disagree on a priority or opinion?

As a veteran church leader, I've seen unseen enemies influencing my fellow church leaders. On one end of the spectrum, the church leaders may disavow submission in their words, yet silently withhold until you agree with them. Citing Jesus' teaching about servant leadership, they might minimize the servanthood required of leaders. Inevitably, these same "servants" excuse some members' disobedience to Christ, as Eli tolerated his sons' evils.

A church leader's position subjects them to subtle, unseen temptations to think more highly of themselves than they ought (Romans 12:3). Their calling attracts adulation from both the needy and the mature. This dynamic often manifests among preachers and ministers who broadcast publicly, and then fall publicly as well.

DISARMING CHOKEPOINT SPIRITS IN CHURCH

Perceiving the failings of your church leaders does not excuse you from submission as long as God has you there. David served under Saul because he recognized God's authority even in the threatening Saul. There isn't a leader yet who has tried to kill you, I hope.

How do we disarm the unseen chokepoint tempters from influencing our churches? Apostle Paul's example emerges in *Nobody Sees This Church: Resisting Darkness* (the seventh book of the *Unseen* Series). His relationship to the Jerusalem-based church leaders and apostles is hidden in Scripture.

Acts 15 and Galatians 1–2 reveal the immature, limited thinking of the Jerusalem Christians—tolerated by the church leaders there. Paul's account shows how much he wrestled with the excuses of his fellow leaders. Yet, he submitted to the leaders' requests in Acts 21. Paul restrained himself and honored the church leaders there. For his trouble, he received long-term imprisonment, and the record shows no support from those leaders or Christians in Jerusalem.

How did he overlook their failings and honor them at such cost? Two Scriptures reveal how, the same way we disarm the chokepoint spirits. Our church leaders are God's business, not ours. He can take care of them.

Who are you to judge another's servant? To his own master he stands or falls. Indeed, he will be made to stand, for God is able to make him stand. (Romans 14:4)

Then Paul said, "I did not know, brethren, that he was the high priest; for it is written, 'You shall not speak evil of a ruler of your people.'" (Acts 23:5)

To help leaders themselves resist the chokepoint tempters, Paul provided another attitude. Christian leaders can be self-centered like everyone. The potency of their gospel ministry does not immunize them from temptation. Our church system sneakily encourages egotism and other self-image issues which provide footholds for unseen forces.

Egotistical interlopers undermined Paul's godly influence in Corinth, replacing his influence with their own. The list of his travails earlier was one response; he followed it by describing his visits to heaven.

The self-promoting "super-apostles" would broadcast their visits to heaven as a badge of the honor they deserve. In contrast, Paul expresses a surprising modesty, which guides our own self-assessments.

Of such a one I will boast; yet of myself I will not boast, except in my infirmities. For though I might desire to boast, I will not be a fool; for I will speak the truth. But I refrain, lest anyone should think of me above what he sees me to be or hears from me. (2 Corinthians 12:5–6)

This is exactly what he urges upon his readers in the Empire's capital city, where merit and classism represented the blackmail behaviors of dark rulers.

For I say, through the grace given to me, to everyone who is among you, not to think of himself more highly than he ought to think, but to think soberly, as God has dealt to each one a measure of faith.... Do not be wise in your own opinion. (Romans 12:3, 16)

The Christian leader serves by calling, not by merit. Vigilance to discern the chokepoint tempters is a constant need for the Christian at any level of service.

WATCH OUT

Early in my church journey, I was complaining about my pastor. The Lord rebuked me forcefully and reminded me of one verse, Matthew 16:18: *"I will build My church."* To which He added, "Not you, Paul."

Apostle James, like Paul, warns against the critical spirit of backbiting and grumbling. We will each be judged by Jesus for our response to His leaders in our lives. The consequences don't wait that long, however.

Do not grumble against one another, brethren, lest you be condemned. Behold, the Judge is standing at the door! (James 5:9)

But if you bite and devour one another, beware lest you be consumed by one another!... If we live in the Spirit, let us also walk in the Spirit. Let us not become conceited, provoking one another, envying one another. (Galatians 5:15, 25–26)

IN THE BIBLE?

Nowhere in Scripture is the fourth strategy explicitly stated, as the first three were. Yet it must be true to explain the Bible. The complete information God wants to reveal from the unseen world is in His Word, yet the mystery awaits our maturity.

We test our conclusions with several study tools. All of them are subject to the Standard of Explanatory Power, capitalized to convey its central importance in Bible study. It was fully explored in Book Two of the *Unseen* Series. In it, we also identified the willful blindness our race universally adopts toward improved explanations.

This nation-claiming behavior must be a governing pattern of darkness if the Bible is true. No strategy explains the Bible's events, peoples, and places more thoroughly. The prophet Ezekiel had revelation about strategy four.

CHAPTER 31

JUDGMENT OF THE CLAIMERS

The kingdom of darkness is accountable for using strategy four to oppose God's purposes. Their responsibility is no less because God's language divisions made it possible. Each group who aligns with their claiming principality is also liable to judgment.

God revealed this to me through Ezekiel. Those prophecies are distinct from every other Bible book. Ezekiel dated the revelations, forming a journal like we might keep. He was the first to do that. He also wrote nothing that was not a revelation—another distinction from other Bible prophets.

The twenty dated years in his journal ran from 590 to 570 BC, during the reign of Nebuchadnezzar in Babylon. Ezekiel recorded thirteen distinct seasons that the word of the Lord came to him.

The first journal entry tells of odd creatures and mysterious wheels within wheels. He also sees God in person, as only Moses and Isaiah recorded before him. No one would record such extreme visions until the Apostle John wrote Revelation, nearly seven hundred years later.

Journaling is a common habit among Christians globally. Ever since I became a Christian in 1974, I have had a journal to write and preserve what God speaks to me. My box full of the decades' journals has given way now to Apple Notes.

THE SLOW SIGHT

In the opening vision of his journal, Ezekiel's own behavior imparts discernment to us. He sees everything in the courts of heaven *before* he sees God Himself.

Many times in our lives, the last presence we discern is the true God. As Ezekiel saw everything but God, so also our field of vision does not readily include Him. His activity occurs behind a veil, by His own choice.

What else would we expect from a God who came as a baby? Whose first night as a human being was in an animal's feeding trough, on a bed of hay? Who rose from the dead but left for heaven after only forty days rather than stay forever? Ours is a God who both hides and dramatically appears, testing the faith of each of us.

Many believe God should be our servant, and find fault with His elusive hiding. Why should He reveal Himself to the demands of our race? The psalmists exemplified the waiting attitude that this God deserves.

Lead me in Your truth and teach me,
For You are the God of my salvation;
On You I wait all the day. (Psalm 25:5)

Wait on the LORD;
Be of good courage,
And He shall strengthen your heart;
Wait, I say, on the LORD! (Psalm 27:15)

ETHNOS IN EZEKIEL'S JOURNAL

Nebuchadnezzar, ruler of Babylon, built the first worldwide empire. Scripture explicitly says that God gave him that success.

Therefore thus says the Lord GOD: "Surely I will give the land of Egypt to Nebuchadnezzar king of Babylon; he shall take away her wealth, carry off her spoil, and remove her pillage; and that will be the wages for his army. I have given him the land of Egypt for his labor, because they worked for Me," says the Lord GOD. (Ezekiel 29:19–20)

God's purpose for him coincided with a major rearranging of the *ethnos* nations. In chapters 25 through 35 of Ezekiel's journal, God pronounces judgment on each of the nations. Those named are no longer with us (save one), so complete was their judgment. As He had wiped out humanity in the Flood, God judged these *ethnos* by eliminating them. Instead of a water flood, He flooded the known world with Nebuchadnezzar's empire. He also made their lands arid and dry.

THE OFFENSE OF THE ETHNOS

Each one merited their judgment with a common offense: rejoicing that God judged Israel. Here are only a few of God's statements about it.

Thus says the Lord GOD: "Because you said, 'Aha!' against My sanctuary when it was profaned, and against the land of Israel when it was desolate, and against the house of Judah when they went into captivity...." (Ezekiel 25:3)

Because you clapped your hands, stamped your feet, and rejoiced in heart with all your disdain for the land of Israel.... (Ezekiel 25:6)

Because Moab and Seir say, "Look! The house of Judah is like all the nations...." (Ezekiel 25:8)

Because of what Edom did against the house of Judah by taking vengeance.... (Ezekiel 25:12)

Following brief judgments on Ammon, Moab, Edom, and Philistia, four long chapters focus on Tyre, an island kingdom of the Phoenician people group, only four square miles. The Bible often names Tyre and its on-shore sister city, Sidon. The prince of Tyre serves as God's type to reveal Lucifer's original status and sin, in Ezekiel 28 (fully explored in Book Three of the *Unseen* Series).

Another four chapters prophesy Egypt's judgment and tells why.

Then all the inhabitants of Egypt
Shall know that I am the LORD,
Because they have been a staff of reed to the house of Israel.
When they took hold of you with the hand,
You broke and tore all their shoulders;

When they leaned on you,
You broke and made all their backs quiver. (Ezekiel 29:6–7)

DRYNESS

Each of these people groups was so thoroughly judged that they no longer exist. The lands they inhabited are now dry and unfriendly to cultivation. Two hundred sixty-one years after Ezekiel's prophesy in 26:16–21, Tyre's physical location also was destroyed.

The Egypt we know has one river; before God's judgment there were many, now dried up. (Ezekiel 29:3–10). A satellite picture of the entire region shows the arid, barren quality of the lands once populated by the large *ethnos* about whom Ezekiel prophesied God's judgment.

THE PRINCIPALITIES

I titled Book Three, *Nobody Sees This Creation: The Origin of the Devil and His Replacements.* In its sixth chapter, "Divided Partners," we reviewed Jesus' forty-day test in the wilderness. His temptation, like Ezekiel's prophecies, is among the many Bible passages best explained by the nation-claiming strategy.

Then the devil, taking Him up on a high mountain, showed Him all the kingdoms of the world in a moment of time. (Luke 4:5)

No mountain on Earth allows a view of every kingdom's territory, including Israel. How did this occur? Revealing the kings is equivalent to revealing the kingdoms. The devil unveiled the partners who dominated each kingdom or *ethnos*. He summoned them together, congregating in one sizeable land area visible only from a high mountain, to which he took Jesus.

JUDGMENT IN THE END

Yet for all their prowess, the rulers of darkness cannot escape the inward fire that God installed as part of their judgment. What awaits these angelic rebels? More fire. Jesus' parable about Lazarus and the rich man emphasizes it.

Father Abraham, have mercy on me, and send Lazarus that he may dip the tip of his finger in water and cool my tongue; for I am tormented in this flame. (Luke 16:24)

Jesus revealed that God prepared an eternal fire for them even before their creation, and that their hell has not even one drop of water. The One whom satan had tempted with all these ruling enemies will be the One who judges them eternally into the fire of hell.

Depart from Me, you cursed, into the everlasting fire prepared for the devil and his angels. (Matthew 25:41)

Apostle John saw their judgment played out in Revelation.

The devil, who deceived them, was cast into the lake of fire and brimstone where the beast and the false prophet are. And they will be tormented day and night forever and ever. (Revelation 20:10)

JUDGMENT ALL ALONG THE WAY

God's judgment is not the only one endured by the nation claimers and their people groups. The angelic nation claimers endure constant scrutiny by satan for the performance of their chokepoint control.

The kingdom of darkness is based not on covenant, but performance. Over history, the shaking of kingdoms and nations reflects the constant demotion and promotion within the kingdom of darkness.

In the temptation of Jesus, satan demonstrated readiness to forsake all his longtime partners, the rebels who originally joined him. He was willing to strip and reallocate everything he had entrusted to each one, if Jesus had followed him.

The *ethnos* endured great turmoil during Nebuchadnezzar's divinely ordained conquest of Earth. Daniel's vision of King Nebuchadnezzar's dream included an entire succession of kingdoms and a cycle of ever-changing national prominence. Such events reveal the shuffling that satan does.

Isaiah 14:16–17 typologically reveals satan's habit of promoting and demoting his rebel partners. The type is Nebuchadnezzar's own Babylonian Empire—one hundred years before it even existed. Using the Babylonian conquest of every nation/*ethnos*, the kings represented the principalities, expressing their bitterness when satan is finally judged.

Those who see you will gaze at you,
And consider you, saying:
"Is this the man who made the earth tremble,
Who shook kingdoms,
Who made the world as a wilderness
And destroyed its cities,
Who did not open the house of his prisoners?"

CHAPTER 32

THE BIG CLAIM

In contrast to satan's performance scrutiny, the God of love makes covenants with people. We saw His covenant with all flesh after the Flood. No people group can perform or pay Him what He deserves; His covenants work only because of His grace.

In the nation-claiming heyday after Babel, God chose one person again, as He had chosen Noah several hundred years previously.

Now the LORD had said to Abram:
"Get out of your country,
From your family
And from your father's house,
To a land that I will show you.
I will make you a great nation;
I will bless you
And make your name great;
And you shall be a blessing.
I will bless those who bless you,
And I will curse him who curses you;
And in you all the families of the earth shall be blessed." (Genesis 12:1–3)

In modern terms: "As long as we're claiming nations, I'll claim one too." The seed of Abraham would form the nation of God's own claiming: Israel.

Today's political nation of Israel is one of many on Earth. Its majority population is Jews, descendants of Abraham through Isaac and Jacob. Known as the patriarchs, these men lived over three thousand years ago.

The persistency of the *ethnos* which sprang from their loins sets them apart from all others.

THE FIRST CHOSEN PEOPLE

God's choice of a nation is the backdrop for Ezekiel's revelation about principalities.

Although God chose Abraham's lineage through Jacob, four hundred years elapsed before they became an *ethnos* recognized among the nations. Their Egyptian slavery gave no evidence of any special status.

He brought them out of Egypt in the exodus, followed by a long conference at Mt. Sinai. His law for them was not a performance measure. The Law was the sign that Israel was His chosen *ethnos*.

> You have seen what I did to the Egyptians, and how I bore you on eagles' wings and brought you to Myself. Now therefore, if you will indeed obey My voice and keep My covenant, then you shall be a special treasure to Me above all people; for all the earth is Mine. And you shall be to Me a kingdom of priests and a holy nation. (Exodus 19:4–6)

> For you are a holy people to the LORD your God; the LORD your God has chosen you to be a people for Himself, a special treasure above all the peoples on the face of the earth. The LORD did not set His love on you nor choose you because you were more in number than any other people, for you were the least of all peoples; but because the LORD loves you, and because He would keep the oath which He swore to your fathers, the LORD has brought you out with a mighty hand, and redeemed you from the house of bondage, from the hand of Pharaoh king of Egypt. (Deuteronomy 7:6–8)

God claimed a people group, just as the partners of satan had done. That simple recognition revolutionizes our reading of Israel's history and the Old Testament.

THE SECOND CHOSEN PEOPLE

The Scriptures of the Jews held many promises of a second chosen people. We know it as the Church of Jesus Christ. God is calling people from all humanity. His promise to Abraham blessed every family on Earth. This theme permeates the Old Testament.

Two prophecies of Isaiah exemplify it. God says that Jesus' sacrifice merited Him followers from every nation.

It is too small a thing that You should be My Servant
To raise up the tribes of Jacob,
And to restore the preserved ones of Israel;
I will also give You as a light to the Gentiles,
That You should be My salvation to the ends of the earth. (Isaiah 49:6)

God's favor upon Israel was never intended to be exclusive. To the contrary, He meant them to be the gateway for everyone to seek him.

Arise, shine;
For your light has come!
And the glory of the LORD is risen upon you.
For behold, the darkness shall cover the earth,
And deep darkness the people;
But the LORD will arise over you,
And His glory will be seen upon you.
The Gentiles shall come to your light,
And kings to the brightness of your rising. (Isaiah 60:1–3)

Apostle Paul affirmed that God's choice of Israel was only the first in a sequence. Jesus earned a covenant of grace with Him for all people.

Therefore remember that you, once Gentiles in the flesh … were without Christ, being aliens from the commonwealth of Israel and strangers from the covenants of promise, having no hope and without God in the world. But now in Christ Jesus you who once were far off have been brought near by the blood of Christ. (Ephesians 2:11–13)

Repeatedly, Paul used the phrase *"to the Jew first, and also to the Gentile."* God's choice of the Jewish people group was first in a sequence. Their identity is unique as the first chosen, but it does not give them a higher status.

…to the Jew first and also to the Greek. For there is no partiality with God. (Romans 2:10–11)

For there is no distinction between Jew and Greek, for the same Lord over all is rich to all who call upon Him. For "whoever calls on the name of the LORD shall be saved." (Romans 10:12–13)

RESPECT THE CLAIM

The place of Israel in God's plan of salvation is front and center. Whether viewed as a nation, a place, or a people group, Christians' favor for Israel exceeds the favor shown by many Jews themselves. The reconstitution of the Jewish political state in 1948 touched off decades of speculation about the end times. Over seventy years later, military hostility against Israel dominates the news.

The plan of God has never included the replacement of Abraham's physical descendants with Christians or the Church. Rather, the Gentiles are being included in the one new man Paul described in Ephesians 2:14–15.

For He Himself is our peace, who has made both one, and has broken down the middle wall of separation, having abolished in His flesh the enmity, that is, the law of commandments contained in ordinances, so as to create in Himself one new man from the two, thus making peace.

The Jerusalem leaders affirmed Paul's commission as a territory-penetrator. They simply requested all the new Christians in other ethnic groups to respect the precedence of the Jewish people. Paul brought the offering from the Gentile churches to Jerusalem in Acts 21, when his enraged countrymen nearly killed him.

They desired only that we should remember the poor, the very thing which I also was eager to do. (Galatians 2:10)

At the root of all this fervor is God's own nation-claiming. Judgment befalls all who disrespect God's claim.

THE SAVIOR'S ETHNOS

Next in the *Unseen* Series is *Nobody Sees This Israel: God's Vanguard against Darkness*. God's motives for claiming a people group included defeating the rebel kingdom.

Before the foundation of the world, God made three decisive decrees (reviewed in Book Three of the series), including the one revealed in Revelation 13:8. *"The Lamb slain from the foundation of the world"* required a mortal human body to atone for sin. Only thus could any people escape from God's wrath into His grace.

By necessity, the Savior would descend from some *ethnos*. God welcomed that *ethnos* to covenant with Him, making them the first among all. God called Abraham with a promise: his seed would bless all the families of Earth.

> Now to Abraham and his Seed were the promises made. He does not say, "And to seeds," as of many, but as of one, "and to your Seed," who is Christ. (Galatians 3:16)

OPEN THE DOOR AND KISS THE SON

Our review of darkness' first four strategies closes with warnings and refuges. If we are to discern and disarm unseen tempters, we must receive the exhortation that Cain refused.

> So the LORD said to Cain, "... sin lies at the door. And its desire is for you, but you should rule over it." (Genesis 4:6–7)

Jesus from Heaven sent a letter to the Christians in Laodicea. He also talked about the door of your life.

> Behold, I stand at the door and knock. If anyone hears My voice and opens the door, I will come in to him and dine with him, and he with Me. (Revelation 3:20)

Jesus upon His return will be installed as the sovereign over Israel the people. Everyone, Jew first and also Gentile, will have a choice to make.

> Kiss the Son, lest He be angry,
> And you perish in the way,
> When His wrath is kindled but a little.
> Blessed are all those who put their trust in Him. (Psalm 2:12)

Works Referenced

1. Lewis, C. S. *The Lion, the Witch, and the Wardrobe*. United Kingdom: Geoffrey Bles, 1950.

2. Spielberg, Steven. *Indiana Jones and the Last Crusade*. United States: Paramount Pictures, 1989.

3. Hillenberg, Steven. *The SpongeBob SquarePants Movie*. United States: Paramount Pictures, 2004.

4. Renfroe, Paul. *Nobody Sees This Creation: The Origin of the Devil and His Replacements*. United States: Paradigm Lighthouse Ministries, 2023.

About The Author

Paul Renfroe is a Memphis native and Florida resident, with his wife Diane Renfroe. They have two sons and one grandson.

Through their businesses, they help people who want to preserve their savings and have their legal control documents up to date. Their ministry and publisher is Paradigm Lighthouse, created to implement the mind of Christ in people born as spirits.

Paul & Diane are members of Vision Church at Christian International in Santa Rosa Beach FL, and are graduates of their Ministry Training College. In their church journey they have served at every level of leadership except pastor. They are ordained for ministry through Vision Church under the leadership of Apostles Tom and Jane Hamon.

Paul's academic endeavors include a Bachelor of Arts with Distinction from Rhodes College (Memphis TN), where he majored in Bible and Church history while minoring in Philosophy. After graduation, he and his wife served twelve years as campus staff and state directors for InterVarsity Christian Fellowship.

He has also served as board chairman for several nonprofits and helped found one school and two churches. With an ability to see what others do not, Paul has been instrumental in several turn-arounds with nonprofits and ministries previously declining.

Paul's life includes eight fatal diagnoses from doctors since his birth with a heart defect. He has received many healings, both with and without doctors. Paul has also participated in healing many people from various ailments including being brain-dead.

Paul's vision for the *Unseen* Series developed over five decades of following Jesus sacrificially. His reputation for knowing the Bible is rarely exceeded. With practice he has an acute ear for God's voice, and a sharp discernment of the topics people wrestle with.

In the *Unseen* Series, this depth and breadth has been condensed for you to go higher up and further in. May God bless you as He has Paul—with lifelong hunger for intimacy with Him.

IF THIS BOOK BLESSED YOU, WILL YOU HELP ME SPREAD THE WORD?

- Share my website, ParadigmLighthouse.com
- Post a 5-Star review on Amazon, Goodreads and other online review venues.
- Post the book's title on your social media such as Facebook, X, Truth Social, Instagram, Google+, etc.
- Post a photo of yourself with your copy of the book.
- If you blog, reference the book, with a link to ParadigmLighthouse.com.
- If you podcast, I am very practiced on being an interview guest.
- Recommend the book to friends — word of mouth is still the more effective form of advertising.
- Ask your bookstore if they carry the book. Word of mouth with booksellers causes them to stock the book. Any bookstore can easily order it.
- Do you know a journalist, podcaster or media influencer seeking guests on my topic? Send them my website, ParadigmLighthouse.com
- Purchase additional copies for gifts to people you care about.

Read more from Paul, Diane, and Paradigm Lighthouse.

Christian, What Are You? Removing the Blindfolds (2013)

Paul's first book is a primer for shedding inaccurate beliefs about your spiritual nature.

Inadequacy (2015)

Reconcile yourself to your poverty of spirit because it is your greatest strength.

The Pains of the Christian: Desire, Glory, Joy (2015)

Restore your hope for the sufferings you experience, God's tools for glorifying you.

Nobody Sees This You: How to Live as a Spirit in the Unseen Realm (2022)

With this, the first in Paul's nine-book Unseen Series, you can integrate your spirit-existence into every area of life, and become alert for discerning.

Nobody Sees This Unseen Realm: How to Unlock Bible Mysteries (2022)

Book Two in the series imparts Bible Study Skills, both basic and advanced. The foundation of true revelation is the Word of God, and we must always improve our understanding of it.

Nobody Sees This Creation: The Origin of the Devil and His Replacements (2023)

The third Unseen book takes a deep dive into the five Bible passages that explain why we have a devil and why his kingdom is persistent in opposing humanity.

You can purchase them where you bought this Book or online.

www.ingramcontent.com/pod-product-compliance
Lightning Source LLC
Chambersburg PA
CBHW060905120626
46553CB00001B/212